The New York Times

EASIEST CROSSWORD PUZZLES

The New York Times

EASIEST CROSSWORD PUZZLES
150 Very Easy Puzzles

Edited by Will Shortz

ST. MARTIN'S GRIFFIN 🙰 NEW YORK

ISBN 978-1-250-02519-7

First Edition: March 2013

10 9 8 7 6 5 4 3 2 1

The New York Times

EASIEST CROSSWORD PUZZLES

ACROSS

1 German cry
4 Ice-grabbing tool
9 Bid
14 Genetic stuff
15 Cutting one may bring tears to your eyes
16 Mrs. Gorbachev
17 Oct. follower
18 Had a big influence on Philip's music?
20 Bothered terribly
22 Envision
23 "Enough already!"
24 Fanatics
27 Grey who wrote about the Old West
29 Harshly criticized Danielle's novels?
34 ___ Guevara
36 Starch from a tropical palm
37 Company that created Pong
38 The "L" in S&L
40 ___ decongestant
43 Norway's capital
44 Chef's wear
46 Clickable computer image
48 Hankering
49 Scared the daylights out of Elijah in "The Lord of the Rings"?
53 Soft powder
54 Bleepers
57 ___ as it is
60 British ref. for wordsmiths
62 Deplete
63 Trounced Chris in a comedy competition?
67 NBC comedy show since '75
68 Be in harmony
69 Lacking justification
70 Rightmost number on a grandfather clock
71 Veg out
72 Keats and Shelley
73 Charge for a bang-up job?

DOWN

1 Desi of "I Love Lucy"
2 100 smackers
3 "Show some mercy!"
4 Native American drums
5 Yoko from Tokyo
6 Zero
7 "Ye ___!"
8 Eruption that might elicit a blessing
9 Web site alternative to com or edu
10 Unnaturally high voice
11 Italian carmaker
12 Canadian gas brand
13 Speak with a gravelly voice
19 Utterly exhausted
21 State between Miss. and Ga.
25 I.R.S. agent, e.g., informally
26 Company whose mascot is Sonic the Hedgehog
28 Org. protecting U.S. secrets
30 Symbolic riveter of W.W. II
31 "Careful!"
32 Mystery writer ___ Stanley Gardner
33 Leo's symbol
34 Applaud
35 Optimist's feeling
39 Watery expanse between England and Scandinavia
41 High-voltage Australian band?
42 Actor Rob of "The West Wing"
45 Vardalos of "My Big Fat Greek Wedding"
47 Peacenik's mantra
50 Floating arctic mass
51 Became a winter hazard, as a road
52 W.W. II intelligence org.
55 Quarrel
56 Bowler's challenge
57 Battle reminder
58 Goad
59 Ringlet
61 James Bond's film debut
64 Evil spell
65 Keats or Shelley work
66 Abridge

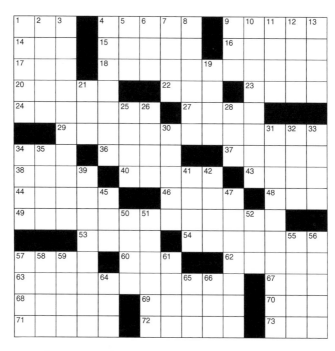

by Lynn Lempel

ACROSS

1 From Athens, say
6 Sharp product from Sharp
10 Labyrinth
14 "__ Vice"
15 Days long past
16 __ contraceptive
17 Image on an Indian pole
18 Destitute
19 Redding who sang "The Dock of the Bay"
20 Academy Award winner for playing 46-Across
23 Backbone
25 Let out, as a fishing line
26 Academy Award winner for playing 46-Across
30 "Can't Get It Out of My Head" rock grp.
31 Clear part of blood
32 Either the first or last vowel sound in "Alaska"
36 Stratford-upon-__
38 Africa's northernmost capital
40 Actress Madeline of "Blazing Saddles"
41 Lite
43 Guadalajara girls
45 Pedantic quibble
46 Academy Award-winning role for both 20- and 26-Across
49 Vie (for)
52 Eagle's home
53 Academy Award-winning film released in March 1972
57 __ Major (constellation)
58 Actress Skye of "Say Anything . . ."
59 Place for gold to be stored
63 Encounter
64 Large coffee holders
65 Follow
66 Rose of the diamond
67 Butcher's stock
68 Wild West transport

DOWN

1 World clock std.
2 __ de Janeiro
3 Consume
4 Lagasse in the kitchen
5 Japanese robes
6 Ballyhoo
7 "Let's Make a Deal" choice
8 Gait not as fast as a canter
9 W.W. I's longest battle
10 Object retrieved on an Apollo mission
11 Clarinetist Shaw
12 Congo, from 1971 to 1997
13 Spanish-language newspaper that brings "light" to its readers
21 Author Stephen Vincent __
22 Termini
23 Blast from the side of a warship
24 Homework problem in geometry
26 Brunch or dinner
27 Sacha Baron Cohen alter ego
28 Ancient kind of alphabet
29 Protein-building acid
33 Vietnam's capital
34 Complain annoyingly
35 Initial stake
37 Steer
39 Politico Palin
42 What may give pause to couch potatoes?
44 What tank tops lack
47 Ho-humness
48 Straying
49 Tree remnant
50 Number of little pigs or blind mice
51 Put back to zero, say
54 Golfer's cry
55 "__ and the King of Siam"
56 Examination
60 Anytown, __
61 Schlep
62 Links peg

by Jeremy Horwitz

ACROSS

1 Antlered animal
4 Provided with meals
7 With 58-Down, vehicle for people on the go? . . . or a hint to five strategically placed answers in this puzzle
13 Alternative to chocolate
15 Musical performance
16 Low-cost, as an airplane seat
17 1920s–'30s design style
18 Time of change
19 Intl. feminine group
20 Feminine title
21 Sir Walter Scott novel
23 Bouquet holders
25 Spy's knowledge, informally
27 Singer/actress Deanna of the 1930s–'40s
29 Pinocchio, at times
30 "__ about time!"
31 Complained loudly
35 90° angle
36 Native of Cuba's capital
38 Cry for a matador
39 Rarely
41 Charged particle
42 __ Nostra
43 Square dance maneuver
45 Senegal's capital
46 Was wide open
49 State of bliss
51 King Kong, for one
52 The second of the five W's
54 Roma is its capital
57 From one of the Baltics

59 Suffered an embarrassing defeat
60 Group artistically, as flowers
61 Desert procession
62 Smells to high heaven
63 Chicago trains
64 Brian of ambient music

DOWN

1 Not odd
2 Fabric that doesn't block much light
3 Smart aleck, say
4 Bouquet-related
5 Violinist Mischa
6 24 hours
7 Bygone Ford car, informally
8 General who became the first emperor of Rome
9 YouTube posting, for short
10 10 __ or less (supermarket checkout sign)
11 Mother-of-pearl
12 Lip __
14 Words often declared after "Well"
15 Colder and wetter, as weather
19 "Absolutely right!"
22 RCA or Samsung product
24 "Wheel of Fortune" purchase
25 Parts of a French archipelago
26 Cleopatra's river
28 Kellogg's All-__
30 Big name in pet food
32 "Don't just stand there!"

33 Lohengrin's love
34 Beloved
36 Snooker
37 Jordan's Queen __
40 J.F.K.'s predecessor
42 Where Hudson Bay is
44 Nonsensical
45 Some office stamps
46 Fancy affairs
47 Separately
48 __ dish (lab holder)
50 Life-sustaining
53 Long-haired uglies
55 Persia, now
56 Zinc's is 30: Abbr.
58 See 7-Across
59 One-spot card

by Ray Fontenot

14

ACROSS

1 In different places
6 Girls with coming-out parties
10 Bro's counterpart
13 Meddles
14 Jai __
15 Walk with a hitch
16 Relaxing spot on a veranda
18 World's fair, e.g.
19 Band of secret agents
20 Make a difference
22 Web site ID
23 Huge success at the box office
25 Braid
28 Twosome
29 Cribbage marker
30 Fluffy stuff caught in the dryer
31 Tiny hollow cylinder
33 Stick up
36 Singer Winehouse
37 Virginia site of two Civil War battles
38 Attorneys' org.
39 N.B.A.'s 7'6" __ Ming
40 Eyeing amorously
41 Person on a pedestal
42 Set down
44 Ambulance letters
45 Prepare to propose, perhaps
46 Hillside threat after a heavy rain
49 Prefix with day or night
50 Song that people stand to sing
51 Lopsided victory
55 Tennis's Nastase
56 Sheet music for Van Cliburn, say
59 Makes less bright
60 Title for Byron or Baltimore

61 A– and C+
62 Sault __ Marie
63 Laughs over some unsophisticated humor
64 German Surrealist Max

DOWN

1 Downloads for tablets
2 Stagehand's responsibility
3 Well-ventilated
4 Army enlistee
5 Jeans topper
6 Deputy __(toon)
7 Manning who has won multiple Super Bowl M.V.P. awards
8 Prohibit
9 Greek "S"

10 Traditional start of middle school
11 Architect for the Louvre pyramid
12 Athlete's pursuit
15 River through Hades
17 Irreverent weekend show, briefly
21 Colorado ski town
23 Glorious
24 Grieves for
25 With 35-Down, much-anticipated cry every April
26 Peru's capital
27 "Whenever you feel like it"
28 Made less sharp
31 Yank
32 Schlep
34 Bassoon relative
35 See 25-Down

37 2009 British singing sensation Susan
41 Big series name in auto racing
43 Smokers' residue
45 Instruction to Kate in a Cole Porter musical
46 Eight milkers in "The 12 Days of Christmas"
47 Pitch-dark
48 Suggest
49 China's Long March leader
51 Extremities
52 Showing signs of use
53 Annoys
54 It might be out on a limb
57 Acknowledgment of debt, in brief
58 State north of La.

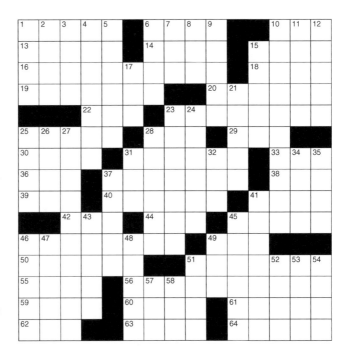

by Lynn Lempel

ACROSS

1 Wine barrel
5 Tear to pieces
10 "Porgy and __"
14 Words after "here," "there" and "everywhere" in "Old MacDonald Had a Farm"
15 "Pet" annoyance
16 For grades 1–12
17 Negative reaction to failure
19 Emergency-related
20 Snake along the Nile
21 Dublin's land
22 Former congresswoman Bella
23 Sort of words that sailors are famous for
27 Flip over
29 Synthesizer designer Robert
30 Circumvent
31 It's about six feet for a turkey vulture
35 __ de Janeiro
36 Other half of a hit 45
38 Refinery material
39 Source of the word "karma"
42 Ken and Barbie
44 Deadly 1966 hurricane with a Spanish-derived name
45 "Cats" poet
47 Feuding families, e.g.
51 Chilling, as Champagne
52 Purple spring bloomer
53 Drunk's interjection
56 Fascinated by
57 Sugar craving
60 Sewing line
61 Like names starting "Ff-"
62 Unadulterated
63 Sea eagles
64 English class assignment
65 River of Hades

DOWN

1 Spanish house
2 "Famous" cookie man
3 Chowder eater's utensil
4 Seoul's home: Abbr.
5 Perfume application
6 When repeated, a crier's cry
7 Ward off
8 Preceding night
9 __ Moines Register
10 Mattress invaders
11 "My Fair Lady" lady
12 Shoulder gesture
13 Long, drawn-out attack
18 Icy cold
22 Awestruck
24 "__ live and breathe!"
25 Surrounded by
26 All's opposite
27 Autos
28 Athletic shoe brand
31 A lively person may have a sparkling one
32 Remove, as scratches on an auto
33 Singer Guthrie
34 Egg holder
36 __ Rabbit
37 Evaluate, with "up"
40 "2 Broke Girls" and "30 Rock"
41 Place for a football pad
42 Certain believer
43 Corrida cheer
45 Mother __ of Calcutta
46 Horseshoe forger
47 Capital of Idaho
48 __ circle
49 Largest moon of Saturn
50 Quantum mechanics pioneer Bohr
54 Modest response to praise
55 Follower of Corn, Rice and Wheat in cereal names
57 Neighbor of Nor.
58 Craven of horror films
59 Photo __ (political events)

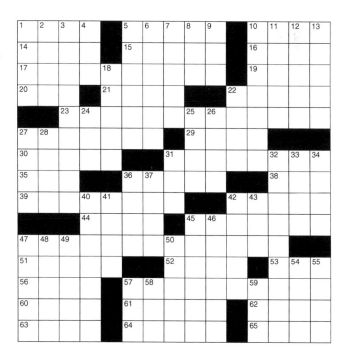

by Nancy Kavanaugh

16

ACROSS

1 Yankee's crosstown rival
4 Burro
7 Aunts' little girls
13 Lion's locks
14 ___ constrictor
15 "So fancy!"
16 Assns.
17 Sexy sort
19 Playing marble
21 Grp. that raids grow houses
22 Cry of surprise
23 Influential sort
28 Compass pointer
29 Bread eaten during Passover
33 Photocopier malfunctions
34 Israeli carrier
37 Tired
38 Cry to a matador
39 Amiable sort
41 Tree juice
42 Gandhi, e.g., religiously
44 "Gladiator" garment
45 Yearn (for)
46 Word after "force of" or "freak of"
48 Encouragement
50 Supple sort
54 Cigar residue
57 Opposite of post-
58 Rather distrustful
59 Precious sort
64 New York theater award
65 Place for pizza or ice cream
66 Put two and two together, say
67 Caterer's coffee containers
68 Feature on a skunk's back
69 Parcel of property
70 Feeling blue

DOWN

1 Reader's notes alongside the text
2 Usual wedding precursor
3 Exam takers
4 Stomach muscles, for short
5 Drunkard
6 Riyadh native
7 Polite refusal to a lady
8 Debtor's letters
9 Worker in Santa's workshop
10 Bistro
11 Nobelist Wiesel
12 Plummeted
13 Biblical kingdom east of the Dead Sea
18 Dover's state: Abbr.
20 Finish
24 Royal role for Liz Taylor
25 Serf
26 Cartoondom's Deputy ___
27 Chowed down
30 Spelling clarification that Aziz might use twice
31 Common marmalade ingredient
32 Ballyhoo
33 Adams, Tyler or Kennedy
35 Hullabaloo
36 Advantage
39 Spiritual teacher of a 42-Across
40 Teri of "Tootsie"
43 "That's obvious, stupid!"
45 Pathetic
47 Order of the British ___
49 Hairspray alternative
51 "Diamonds ___ Forever"
52 Country with Mount Everest on its border
53 Caustic cleaners
54 Venomous vipers
55 Whack, as a fly
56 Frau's spouse
60 Peyton's brother on the gridiron
61 Lid
62 Repeated words shouted after "Who wants . . . ?"
63 Summer hrs. in D.C.

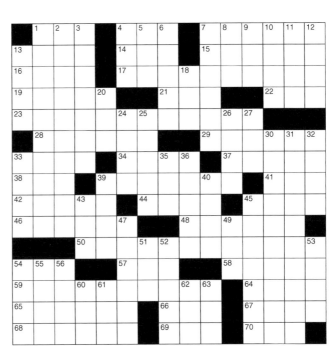

by Lynn Lempel

ACROSS

1 Late, as a library book
8 Sound of an excited heart
15 "-" marks
16 Furious
17 Surplus's opposite
18 Bring up, as a subject
19 Forget-me-__
20 Ruler on a golf course?
21 Yank
24 Floppy feature of a basset hound
26 "My country, __ of thee"
27 Morales of "NYPD Blue"
28 In favor of
30 Mushroom cloud creator, briefly
34 Scrape, as a knee
35 Songwriter Berlin
37 "__ pasa?"
38 Little bell sound
39 Electron tube
40 Be furious
41 Rock music genre
42 Heart-shaped item on a chain, say
43 Genie's home
44 Last movement of a sonata
46 Tire filler
47 Stick __ in the water
48 Atlantic food fish
50 Foreign policy grp.
52 Hawaii's state bird
53 Ruler in a vegetable garden?
56 Comic strip cry
58 Folded Mexican dish
59 Element used to make semiconductors
63 Not recognizable by

64 Raw material for a steel mill
65 Figure with 14-Down sides
66 Rainbow mnemonic

DOWN

1 Advanced deg.
2 Sailor's affirmative
3 Beach lotion letters
4 Ruler after a diet?
5 Art __ (1920s–'30s movement)
6 Join
7 Superlative suffix
8 Fine cotton
9 Like krypton
10 Ruler on a beach?
11 Easel user
12 Ache
13 Bug-eyed
14 Number of sides in a 65-Across

20 Ruler in a Utah city?
21 Court clown
22 Igloo builder
23 Spoil, as a parade
25 Zimbabwe's continent
29 Passengers
31 Consider the same
32 Order to come
33 Cone-shaped shelter
35 Bachelor's last words
36 Badminton court divider
40 Ruler with custard desserts?
42 Ruler in a W.C.?
45 Where many fed. employees live
49 "Me too"
51 Egypt's capital
53 Whine
54 Guitarist Clapton

55 Midday
57 Fill to excess
58 Rotten
59 Madam's mate
60 Corn on the __
61 ". . . __ quit!"
62 Las Vegas's home: Abbr.

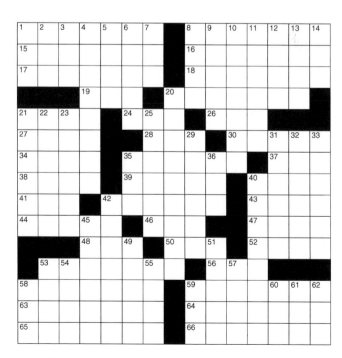

by Michael David

18

ACROSS

1 Fret
5 Singer/actress Midler
10 Heading on a list of errands
14 Memo
15 No turn may be allowed then, according to a sign
16 Lab assistant in a horror film
17 Face-to-face exam
18 Group that includes North, South, East and West
20 Actor Thornton of "Sling Blade"
22 Opposite of exits
23 Shower
24 ___ fide
25 Carlsbad feature
28 Chesapeake Bay delicacy
32 Beelike
33 Can of worms, say
34 Singer Yoko
35 Writer Ayn and others
36 Naval rank: Abbr.
37 Bare-bones
39 Frigid
40 Writing tablets
41 Dentist's directive
42 Activity a puppy loves
45 Talked back to
46 Currier and ___
47 Bit of bumper damage
48 Golden Delicious and others
51 Service provided at Meineke and Pep Boys
55 Sparring injury, perhaps
57 California wine valley
58 Bygone Italian coins
59 Artless
60 Hawaiian strings, informally
61 Ones giving or receiving alimony
62 Like some preppy jackets
63 Eat like a bird

DOWN

1 High-hatter
2 Spelling of "90210"
3 And others, for short
4 Versed in the classics, say
5 Certain spool
6 Company with a spectacular 2001 bankruptcy
7 Chicago daily, briefly, with "the"
8 Koppel or Kennedy
9 Just beat, as in a competition
10 Something always sold in mint condition?
11 Eye amorously
12 Sullen
13 Heavenly bodies
19 Feminine suffix
21 Tall tales
24 Seventh heaven
25 West Indies native
26 Rapidly
27 Old LPs and 45s
28 Quaint lodging hinted at by the outsides of 18-, 20-, 28-, 42-, 51- or 55-Across
29 Reddish/white horses
30 Biscotti flavoring
31 Like chicken breast cutlets
33 Boyfriends
37 Shenanigan
38 "Now hear this!"
40 Something brought to a birthday party
43 Easter blooms
44 Designer ___ Saint Laurent
45 Bottom of the ocean
47 The "D" of PRNDL
48 Competent
49 Grand ___ (auto race)
50 Chaste
51 Cheese popular with crackers
52 Actor Gyllenhaal
53 Crude group?
54 Take in some sun
56 Black bird

by Susan L. Stanislawski

ACROSS

1 Shaggy's nickname for his canine friend
6 Winnie-the-__
10 Did cartoons, e.g.
14 "A Fish Called __"
15 The "A" in A.D.
16 Letter before kappa
17 Less friendly
18 Mexican money
19 Hgts.
20 Rapper who came to prominence as a member of the Wu-Tang Clan
23 Karate teacher
24 Pianist's practice piece
25 Former Republican-turned-Democratic senator from Pennsylvania
30 Blouse undergarment
33 Suffix with absorb
34 Skylit rooms
35 Little 'uns
38 Mouths, slangily
40 Neither this nor that
41 104, in old Rome
42 "You betcha!"
43 Form of sparring
48 Golf legend Sam
49 Kitt who sang "Santa Baby"
53 Whiskey or vodka
57 Tulsa's home: Abbr.
58 Potpourri
59 Intends (to)
60 __ moss
61 Dispatched
62 Skip over, as a vowel
63 Roof overhang
64 Focus for an arborist
65 Screenwriter Ephron

DOWN

1 Drinks from a flask, say
2 Storage for fast Web page retrieval
3 "America's Finest News Source," with "The"
4 Ukrainian port whose staircase is a setting for "The Battleship Potemkin"
5 Trade
6 "Come to __"
7 Words below the Lincoln Memorial
8 Beginnings
9 Begin a tryst
10 Language offshoots
11 Go round and round
12 Blues singer James
13 Laundry
21 __-O-Fish (McDonald's sandwich)
22 Outputs of brainstorming
26 Nav. rank
27 Deuce topper
28 What Dubliners call their homeland
29 Speak with laryngitis, say
30 Homies
31 Hitter of 714 home runs
32 Ottoman official
36 It leans to the right
37 Rice-__
38 "Kid-tested, mother-approved" cereal
39 Brown, Dartmouth, etc.
41 Opiate often used in cough syrup
44 Lament of the defeated
45 One playing hoops
46 Snoozed
47 Cover on the front of a car
50 One might be made of bread crumbs
51 Language of India
52 Confused
53 Extraordinary, in slang
54 European-based furniture giant
55 Bulgarian or Czech
56 Focus lovingly (on)

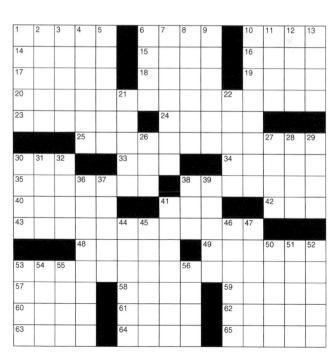

by Guy Tabachnick

ACROSS

1 Money owed
5 Lamebrain
9 Nukes
13 Good, as a driver's license
15 Addict
16 Replacement for the mark, franc and lira
17 Pilotless plane
18 "__ closed!"
19 Opera solo
20 Impatiently endure passing time
23 Hoopla
25 "Have something!"
26 Outback bird
27 Hi-__ monitor
28 Win by enough points, in sports gambling
32 Big-jawed dinosaur, for short
33 Erie Canal mule
34 No. on a business card
35 Brand of kitchen wrap
37 Rug rat
39 Hits with a fist
43 One of the Three Stooges
45 Friend
47 Grammy winner from County Donegal, Ireland
48 Perform a routine household chore
52 Dispirited
53 Post-op area
54 "__ Abner"
55 Line of Canon cameras
56 Pass through a crisis safely
60 Where the Himalayas are
61 Tied, as a score
62 Egypt's Sadat
65 Craft in which to go down a river, say

66 Part to play
67 Get ready to sing the national anthem
68 Monotonous routines
69 Concordes, for short
70 Roget offerings (abbr.) . . . or, loosely, the first and last words of 20-, 28-, 48- and 56-Across

DOWN

1 Netflix rental
2 Big part of a hare
3 Pass without effect, as a storm
4 Funny Fey
5 So
6 "Time __ a premium"
7 Fits with another, as a gear tooth
8 Forestall by acting first

9 Fervor
10 __ borealis
11 Having a store tag
12 Long baths
14 Hinder
21 Lions and tigers
22 Medical successes
23 Each of Shakespeare's plays has five
24 Nickelodeon's "__ the Explorer"
29 Tests
30 Have a nontraditional marriage, in a way
31 Talk show host DeGeneres
36 Like a perfect game in baseball
38 Some brewskis
40 In progress

41 Greek sandwich
42 Utters
44 Crystal trophy inscribers, e.g.
46 Where a lion hides
48 Onetime Wisconsin-based insurance giant
49 Directionless at sea
50 Spanish eggs
51 Radii neighbors
52 Ringo who sang "Yellow Submarine"
57 D.C. team, informally
58 Hibernian, for one
59 Tolkien's talking tree race
63 The Beach Boys' "Barbara __"
64 Hwys.

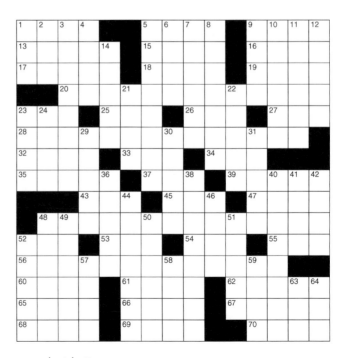

by John Dunn

ACROSS

1 Mix with a spoon
5 Not go
9 Political science subj.
13 Biblical water-to-wine locale
14 Snapshot
15 Flightless bird of South America
16 "Incidentally . . ."
18 Performs in a play
19 Response of sympathy
20 Suffix with ranch
21 Cozy dining spot
22 Lone Star State
23 Beef jerky brand
25 Egg-hatching spot
27 Filmmaker with style and total control
30 Pairs
33 ___ Hoop
36 1968 A.L. M.V.P. and Cy Young winner ___ McLain
37 Cigarette's end
38 "Holy cow!"
40 Dedicated poem
41 Striped equine
43 Suspect, in cop lingo
44 Pairs
45 Goofs
47 Carve into, as a plaque
49 Performing in a play, say
52 Following the law
56 Skating jump
58 Sony rival
59 Southwest desert that includes Death Valley
60 Sound heard in an empty hallway
61 "Never mind"
63 Secluded valley
64 Like much diet food, informally

65 1970 Kinks hit
66 Indian woman's attire
67 Found's opposite
68 Rear end

DOWN

1 Sir Walter who wrote "Ivanhoe"
2 Western lake near Squaw Valley
3 E-mail folder
4 Some stylish sunglasses
5 Pronoun for a ship
6 Locker room handout
7 Big name in arcade games
8 Chinese-American virtuoso cellist
9 Rock associated with hardness
10 "Let's be serious here . . ."
11 Presidential rejection
12 Chore
14 Deg. for a prof
17 Zap with a stun gun
23 A lumberjack might leave one behind
24 "Knocked Up" director Apatow
26 Sound heard in a movie theater
28 Loosen, as laces
29 Some whiskeys
30 Flabbergasted state
31 Consumer
32 "You've gotta be joking!"
34 Chemical in drain cleaners
35 Have a meeting of the minds
38 Rowers

39 Withdraw, with "out"
42 Packaged pasta brand
44 2011 Oscar-nominated film about African-American maids
46 Leisurely walk
48 Drain cleaner target
50 Sound heard before "Gesundheit!"
51 Large fishing hooks
53 Swamp critter
54 Walled city in Spain
55 Allow to attack
56 Pants fillers
57 The Bruins of the N.C.A.A.
59 Muscular actor with a mohawk
62 Grain in Cheerios

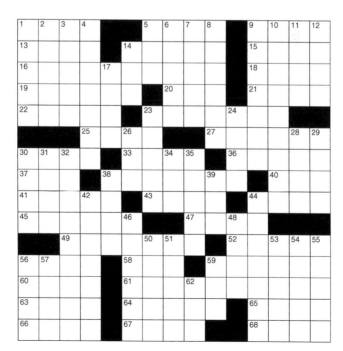

by Ian Livengood

ACROSS

1 Suffix with differ
4 Early American patriot Thomas
9 Speedy
14 Gen __ (child of a 29-Across)
15 Capital of Jordan
16 "William Tell," for one
17 Where: Lat.
18 Land that's not inland
19 Gave a speeding ticket
20 Stereotypical entree at a campaign event
23 It's transfused in a transfusion
24 Brits' thank-yous
25 __ carte
28 Powerful D.C. lobby
29 One born in the late 1940s or '50s
33 Prefix with conservative
34 __-Japanese War
35 Lerner's songwriting partner
36 Item carried by an Amish driver
39 Way underpriced
42 Ogled
43 Nothing __ the truth
46 Farmer's wish
49 10th grader: Abbr.
50 __-Caps
51 Cheerleader's cheer
52 Authored
53 The starts of 20-, 29-, 36- and 46-Across, e.g., when repeated quickly in order
58 Protein acid, for short
60 U.C.L.A. athlete
61 "If you ask me," in texts
62 Sainted ninth-century pope
63 Daily reading for a pope
64 Clean air org.
65 Orange soda brand
66 "Sailing to Byzantium" poet
67 Roll of green?

DOWN

1 Beyond the metro area
2 Interstellar clouds
3 __ Bridge (former name of New York's R.F.K. Bridge)
4 Walked back and forth
5 Love personified
6 Apple computer
7 Poet Ogden
8 Thing
9 Absolutely dependable
10 ". . . blackbirds baked in __"
11 Honeybunch or snookums
12 Rage
13 Annual June honoree
21 Jazz style
22 Taxi
26 __ Alcindor (Kareem Abdul-Jabbar, once)
27 Live and breathe
29 Gargantuan
30 Taiwanese-born director Lee
31 Charles of "Algiers," 1938
32 "Alley __!"
34 Luminous stellar explosion
36 Protestant denom.
37 Cheyenne's home: Abbr.
38 Cool, in old slang
39 "__ News Sunday Morning"
40 Attila, for one
41 Love or rage
43 Wee 'un's footwear
44 Lively, in music
45 In phrases, something to share or hit
47 Dishcloth
48 A little on the heavy side
49 12th graders: Abbr.
52 Rosés, e.g.
54 "I'm __!"
55 Great Lake between Huron and Ontario
56 Heavy instrument to march with
57 Lose freshness, as a flower
58 1936 candidate Landon
59 __ culpa

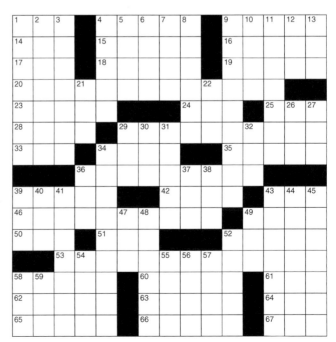

by Kurt Mueller

ACROSS

1 Stick in one's __
5 Czech capital
11 Banned organic compound, for short
14 TV's warrior princess
15 Compassionate
16 Kind of baseball or battery
17 A classic beauty who is not all there
19 Satellite-based navigation aid, in brief
20 That is, in Latin
21 Plains tribe
22 Wrap worn in India
23 Broadcast
25 Mini-hospital
27 Booster of the Apollo space program
33 Frigid
34 Younger brother of Cain and Abel
35 Lowest point
39 Country on the south side of Mount Everest
42 Chinese philosopher __-tzu
43 Lopez with the 1963 hit "If I Had a Hammer"
44 Spanish artist El __
45 Colored part of the eye
47 Lead-in to maniac or surfing
48 1960s–'70s Ford Company model
52 Microscopic blob
55 West Coast travel hub, informally
56 "Largemouth" fish
57 By way of
60 Number in an octet
64 Many a line on a flight route map

65 Milky Way bars and others
68 With 53-Down, a coffee-flavored liqueur
69 Some marbles
70 Book before Nehemiah
71 Floppy rabbit feature
72 Refuses to acknowledge
73 River across the French/German border

DOWN

1 116, in ancient Rome
2 Clarinet or sax
3 Actress Hathaway
4 Wisconsin city
5 What an M.A. might go on to earn
6 Regret
7 Bullets, informally
8 Walk or trot
9 Open with a key
10 Fairness-in-hiring inits.
11 Polytheistic
12 Blue Grotto's island
13 Fundamental
18 Use a swizzle stick
22 Indian instrument
24 E.R. workers
26 Period after Shrove Tuesday
27 Be in a 32-Down, e.g.
28 Taiwan-based computer giant
29 Genre
30 Archaeologist's find
31 Japanese port
32 Group in church robes
36 "Carpe __"
37 Playwright William

38 Hilarious one
40 High points
41 Richard __, Clarence Darrow defendant
46 Word part: Abbr.
49 Wreak havoc on
50 Battle of Normandy city
51 Rust and lime
52 Diminish
53 See 68-Across
54 __ the Grouch
58 Modern Persia
59 Italian wine city
61 Egyptian pyramid city
62 Wife of Zeus
63 Old Russian despot
65 "What, me worry?" magazine
66 So-so grade
67 Donkey

by John R. O'Brien

ACROSS

1 Chews the fat
5 Fiona, e.g., in "Shrek"
11 Hula-Hoops or Furbys, once
14 500 sheets of paper
15 Geronimo's tribe
16 Fury
17 Hankering
18 One knocked off a pedestal
20 Pasture
22 Course guide?
23 C.E.O.'s job: Abbr.
24 Paid postgraduate position at a university
27 Black-eyed __
28 Cry after hitting a hammer on one's thumb, say
29 Morocco's capital
31 "Much __ About Nothing"
34 Uncooked
36 Beethoven's "Für __"
39 Solve a crossword, e.g.?
44 Greeted and seated
45 __-lacto-vegetarian
46 Old Navy alternative
47 Harnessed, as oxen
50 Mother of Don Juan
53 "You said it, sister!"
55 Put a spade atop a spade, say
60 Barn dance seat
61 Miami locale: Abbr.
62 Cake words in "Alice in Wonderland"
63 Illegal wrestling hold
67 Newswoman Paula
68 "__ You Experienced" (Jimi Hendrix's first album)
69 Sean who wrote "Juno and the Paycock"
70 Like show horses' feet
71 Tavern
72 Walked purposefully
73 Tiny hill dwellers

DOWN

1 Harsh and brusque
2 Eaglet's nest
3 Breakfast order with a hole in it
4 Like gym socks
5 Dunderhead
6 4.0 is a great one: Abbr.
7 Kramden of "The Honeymooners"
8 Cream-filled pastry
9 Mount Everest guide
10 McCain or McConnell: Abbr.
11 Squirming
12 Kitchen magnet?
13 Shoulder muscles, for short
19 African antelope or Chevrolet
21 Jane or John in court
25 Threadbare
26 Hit, as a fly
30 __ Paese cheese
31 C.I.O.'s partner
32 Repeated cry when sticking a stake in a vampire
33 1957 Disney dog movie
35 "__ Let the Dogs Out"
37 Cousin of calypso
38 Mind reading, for short
40 Big name in toy trains
41 Tattoos, slangily
42 Dastardly
43 Pro __ (like some law work)
48 Cause's partner
49 Avis rival
51 Ram's mate
52 One of the Gabor sisters
53 Beeb comedy
54 Actress Tierney of "ER"
56 Catch, as a dogie
57 Salt Lake City native
58 "Can we turn on a fan or something?!"
59 Manages, as a 71-Across
64 Denials
65 Brit. reference work
66 Bill the Science Guy

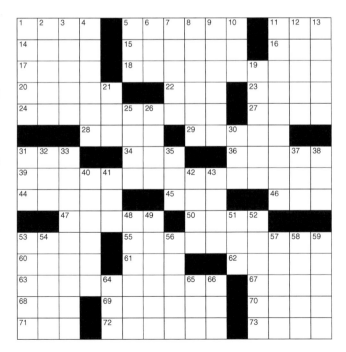

by Andrea Carla Michaels and Michael Blake

Note: When this puzzle is done, the circled letters, reading from left to right and top to bottom, will reveal who wrote the seven songs in the theme.

ACROSS

1 Piquancy
5 Feel in one's __
8 Sycophants, slangily
15 ¹/₁₂ of a ruler
16 Durham sch.
17 South Pacific region
18 Nebraska tribe
19 "__ Beso" (Paul Anka hit)
20 1970 song with the lyric "Whisper words of wisdom"
21 1965 song with the lyric "Isn't he a bit like you and me?"
24 Wealthy Brits
25 Fictitious
26 Chow down
28 1969 song with the lyric "Once there was a way to get back homeward"
33 Common people
34 Lament loudly
35 Sick
37 Singer DiFranco
38 1965 song with the lyric "These are words that go together well"
42 Low island
43 Election mo.
44 "Am __ late?"
45 Heredity unit
46 1965 song with the lyric "Think of what you're saying"
52 Bear: Sp.
53 Nebraska neighbor
54 McCarthy-era attorney Roy
57 1968 song with the lyric "We all want to change the world"
61 1968 song with the lyric "Remember to let her into your heart"
64 Suffix with zinc
65 "Amos 'n' __"

66 Candid, as a photo
67 Pecan or cashew
68 Some HDTV screens
69 Slip-ups
70 Car rte. displayer
71 Comfort

DOWN

1 Jewish homeland
2 Inner: Prefix
3 Garbage boat
4 One of filmdom's Avengers
5 "C'est la __"
6 Invisible
7 Cartoonist Nast
8 German cathedral city
9 Cold cube
10 Sink, as the sun
11 Jeanne d'Arc, e.g.
12 "Do __ others . . ."
13 Mr. __ (soft drink)
14 Mailing encls.
22 Conclusion

23 "For __ know . . ."
26 Disney's "__ and the Detectives"
27 Up to the task
28 First Moody Blues hit
29 Martini garnish
30 Delta competitor: Abbr.
31 Houston sch.
32 Bias
33 Enthusiast
36 Soapmaking stuff
38 Unaccounted-for G.I.'s
39 "Pay __ mind"
40 Mooer
41 Physicist with a law
45 Lose freshness
47 Scam
48 Stark __ mad
49 Get tense and hard, as a muscle
50 Archipelago bits
51 Letter after sigma
54 Common bait fish

55 Wine: Prefix
56 Syringe, for short
57 Cherry and ruby
58 Ancient Peruvian
59 Bookies give them
60 Big Board inits.
62 Troop-entertaining grp.
63 "In excelsis __"

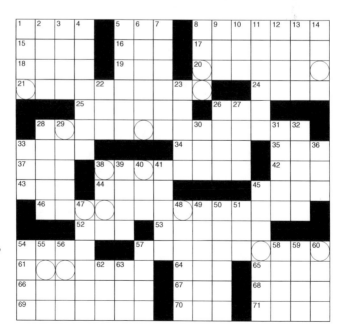

by Peter A. Collins

ACROSS

1 California's ___ Woods
5 Equipment for deep diving
10 Radio switch
14 The "A" of A.D.
15 Kind of saw in a workshop
16 Tilt-A-Whirl or bumper cars
17 Volcano output
18 Tennis great Chris
19 Exam for an aspiring atty.
20 Santa Claus facial feature
23 Have a meal
24 Misfortunes
25 Until now
28 Like an idol for a teen girl, say
30 Apple computer
33 The Cowboys of the Big 12 Conf.
34 Goes out with
35 Aid for night photos, once
37 "___ sorry"
40 Actress Catherine ___-Jones
41 Oil change chain
45 First, second or reverse
49 Toothpaste-evaluating org.
50 Doughnut shapes
51 Seed on many a bun
53 Mess up
55 Pop music's Bee ___
57 E.R. workers
58 Drink made with crystals
62 Golden arches for McDonald's, e.g.
64 Nebraska city or tribe
65 ___ Lund of "Casablanca"

66 Very dry, as Champagne
67 Cicero or Caesar
68 Mets' league: Abbr.
69 ___-Ball (arcade game)
70 English river through Nottingham
71 1974 Sutherland/Gould spoof

DOWN

1 Fountain treats
2 Paying no attention
3 Private party attender
4 Gray-sprinkled horse
5 Reeking
6 Well-mannered
7 Fork or spoon
8 Titanic's undoing
9 Johnson of "Laugh-In"

10 French city where van Gogh painted
11 1978 Rolling Stones hit
12 Medicine-approving org.
13 Ran into
21 Actress Basinger
22 Millionaire's boat, maybe
26 Class for newcomers to America, for short
27 Place for a soak
29 "Yeah, like that'll ever happen"
31 Labyrinth
32 Enzyme suffix
35 Quartet number
36 Luggage
38 Yeti and the Loch Ness monster
39 ___-mo

41 Elbow poke
42 Wedding words
43 Tiredness
44 Headliner
46 One of two on a winter cap
47 Forgiveness
48 Closes tightly again
51 Trigonometric ratio
52 That: Sp.
54 10 sawbucks make one
56 Actor Hawke
59 Libel or slander
60 Caesar's love
61 Fish propellers
62 Ozs. and ozs.
63 Home planet of Mindy's mate in an old sitcom

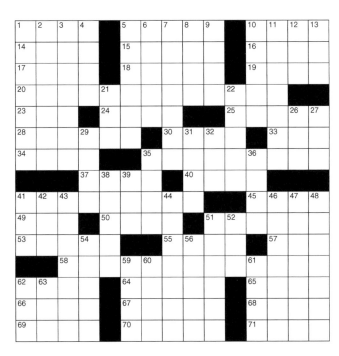

by Nancy Kavanaugh

ACROSS

1 Lighted sign over a doorway
5 Dam on the Nile
10 Back of the neck
14 Famous ___ cookies
15 Stiller's partner in comedy
16 Plow pullers
17 "Bye for now"
18 Like George W. vis-à-vis Jeb Bush
19 Backside
20 French writer's apprehension by the police?
23 1970s TV's "___ Ramsey"
24 Tech company spun off from Time Warner
25 French writer's state of drunkenness?
32 Leafy vegetable
33 "That's clear"
34 Offering from Lil Jon or Fat Joe
36 Pig sound
37 Abuses, as a fraternity pledge
39 Rain gutter site
40 Sack
41 Run a towel over
42 Adjust, as a hem
43 French writer's two-under-par holes?
47 Burnt part
48 LeBron James's org.
49 French writer's boardwalk booth operator?
56 Actor Bridges of "The Big Lebowski"
57 Crème-filled cookies
58 Prefix with disestablishmentarianism
60 ___ of Sandwich
61 Swap
62 Saddam Hussein's land
63 "Iliad" locale

64 Double curves
65 "___ is more"

DOWN

1 Have a meal
2 Dec. 25
3 Tiniest bit of the Greek alphabet?
4 Former St. Petersburg royal
5 Ovid's book of love poetry
6 Choose
7 Hunks of chewing tobacco
8 Locale
9 Gives an account
10 Useless
11 Germany, Italy and Japan, in W.W. II
12 Cooped (up)
13 Conclusion
21 Sound of a heavy fall

22 Womanizer
25 Small lab container
26 Where cowboys once sang "Oh, give me a home"
27 Mork's birthplace, on TV
28 Small, medium and large
29 NNW's opposite
30 Speechify
31 Parties that might have glow-in-the-dark freebies
32 Corn on the ___
35 The "p" in r.p.m.
37 It may be hit by a soprano
38 Zoo animal that beats its chest
39 90° turn
41 "What ___ thinking?!"

42 Actor John of "Sands of Iwo Jima"
44 Run-scoring hit that puts the batter out
45 Put in a secret language
46 Humiliates
49 Backside
50 Jackson 5 hairdo
51 Blunders
52 Caribbean and Mediterranean
53 Finger's tip
54 Concerning, on a memo
55 Flight board postings, for short
56 MetLife Stadium footballer
59 Figs. for geniuses

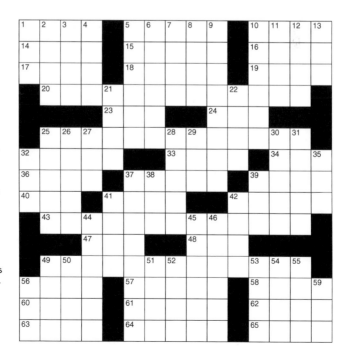

by Bernice Gordon

ACROSS

1 Birthstone that was the name of a Hitchcock film
6 "___ in there!"
10 Writer James
14 Relative of a giraffe
15 ___ vera
16 ___ beetle
17 Attorney-to-be
19 Refute
20 Unit of force
21 "Arabian Nights" bird
22 Erects
24 Transaction at Chase or Wells Fargo
26 "Is that so?!"
30 Lab eggs
31 Speed skater ___ Anton Ohno
32 Identical
34 Field cover during a rain delay
38 Rachel Maddow or Rush Limbaugh
41 Queen with a "lace"
42 Often-illegal turns, in slang
43 Scent
44 Letters on a Cardinal's cap
45 Kind of disk
46 Def Jam or EMI
52 2009 film that grossed over two billion dollars
53 Shack
54 Beans or wheat
58 Let off steam
59 You might carry a bucket to one at a hotel
62 Art Deco artist
63 Kind of tide
64 Western, in old slang
65 What to do after adding cream or sugar

66 Sneakers brand
67 Intermission . . . or what you can do to the starts of 17-, 24-, 38-, 46- and 59-Across

DOWN

1 Let the cat out of the bag
2 "Fine with me!"
3 Lowly chess piece
4 Cathedral area
5 Acne spot
6 Wore
7 Smart ___ (wise guy)
8 Oui's opposite
9 Settles the score
10 Build on
11 Jeans brand with a question mark in its logo
12 Ho-hum feeling
13 Sphinx site
18 Russia's ___ Mountains
23 Green org.
24 Political coalition
25 Tops of some stadiums
26 Comic Carvey
27 Unfurl
28 Village
29 "Anything ___?"
32 Scent
33 Poehler of "Parks and Recreation"
34 Poi source
35 Resting on
36 Frolic
37 Recite the rosary, e.g.
39 Hold one's liquor better than
40 Like basketball centers
44 Madrid Mrs.

45 Cheese in a Greek salad
46 All-night parties
47 Chris who won six U.S. Opens
48 "Is that a dare?"
49 Playful swimmer
50 Leading
51 Hits in dodgem cars
54 Blacken on the grill
55 Bar mitzvah or communion
56 Prime draft classification
57 Company car or key to the executive bathroom
60 So-so grade
61 Inner part of a corn ear

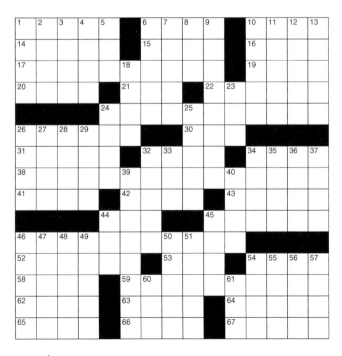

by C. W. Stewart

ACROSS

1 Holy city of Islam
6 Pieces of luggage
10 Cracked open, as a door
14 Surrounding glows
15 Leave the auditorium
16 A few
17 Husband's status symbol, possibly
19 Part of the leg that's often kicked
20 Bunny movements
21 Toward sunrise
22 Cable network specializing in "real life" shows
23 Reagan's "evil empire," for short
25 Attorney general Holder
26 General Mills baking product
32 Swim meet divisions
33 Stir-fry vessels
34 Italian "a"
35 Writer Tan and singer Grant
36 "Rolling in the Deep" singer, 2010
38 Ready-for-the-weekend cry
39 Chinese Chairman
40 Cedar or cypress
41 Brooklyn's ___ Institute
42 Panel for a complex legal case
46 Activity in which the police may beat down a door
47 Air port?
48 Release one's grip
50 Nabisco cookie
52 "60 Minutes" correspondent Logan
56 One on a pedestal
57 Popular Canadian whisky
59 "The African Queen" screenwriter James
60 Final Four org.
61 Occurrence
62 Complete foul-up
63 ___ a one
64 Italian sauce

DOWN

1 "Do the ___" ("You figure it out")
2 Replacement for the mark and franc
3 Clip, as a photo
4 Swallowable medicine units
5 Bit of volcanic fallout
6 "Watch out!"
7 W.W. II enemy
8 Present
9 Sault ___ Marie, Mich.
10 Attack
11 "Hurts So Good" singer, 1982
12 In the thick of
13 Russo of "Thor"
18 "O.K." from Huck Finn
22 Pekingese sounds
24 '60s teach-in organizer: Abbr.
25 Actress Sommer
26 Egyptian president Nasser
27 1936 Rodgers and Hart musical that incorporated jazz in its score
28 Dork
29 "You've got mail" co.
30 Oneness
31 Huck Finn's transport
32 Follower of Mary, in a nursery rhyme
36 Parched
37 Belle of the ball, for short
38 One and only, in romance
40 Quartet minus one
41 Bedwear, informally
43 Philadelphia gridders
44 Like a street with an arrow sign
45 Lunch time
48 Neeson of "Taken"
49 Rim
50 Killer whale
51 Lion's sound
53 Votes in favor
54 Blow a gasket
55 Voice below soprano
57 Where to see Anderson Cooper
58 Sales agent, informally

by Randall J. Hartman

ACROSS

1 Rounded cathedral feature
5 Undue speed
10 Bowled over
14 Miller ___ (low-calorie beer)
15 Banks in the Baseball Hall of Fame
16 Sheltered bay
17 Equipment to help a patient breathe
19 Regatta group
20 Prince who became Henry V
21 "___ I care"
22 Jules who wrote "Twenty Thousand Leagues Under the Sea"
23 Floor measurements
25 "Sorry to hear that"
28 Breath mint in a roll, informally
30 Events with baying hounds
31 Foray
34 Small bit, as of cream
35 Lab eggs
38 H. G. Wells novel . . . with a hint to this puzzle's circled words
42 Pea holder
43 Completely
44 In recent days
45 Trees that sway in a hurricane
48 Religious offshoot
49 Went to pieces
52 "Beauty is truth, truth beauty" poet
56 Resell unfairly, as tickets
57 First-rate
59 Flapper's neckwear
60 Musical sound
61 Vishnu or Shiva

64 Fashion designer Cassini
65 "It's ___ of the times"
66 Some poems from 52-Across
67 Tennis's Sampras
68 Broadway honors
69 Captain in "Twenty Thousand Leagues Under the Sea"

DOWN

1 ___ State (Hawaii's nickname)
2 Film studio behind "Toy Story" and "Up"
3 Fashion
4 Brain wave readout, for short
5 "Cluck, cluck" makers
6 Monet or Manet
7 Megamistake
8 Sn, to a chemist
9 Mouse spotter's cry
10 Say yes to
11 Troubling
12 Datebook notation
13 "___ Defeats Truman" (famous 1948 headline)
18 Enter slowly and carefully, as a parking spot
22 Many an airport shuttle
24 Play opener
26 Spiced tea
27 Telescope serviced by astronauts
29 Change significantly
31 Big inits. in fuel additives
32 "Well, whaddya know!"
33 Mars, with "the"

34 Web access inits.
36 Kilmer of "The Doors"
37 One or more
39 Rick's beloved in "Casablanca"
40 Was without
41 Suffix with major
46 Declare to be true
47 Swimming unit
48 Hardly hip
49 Camera lens setting
50 Place to learn in Lille
51 Carted off to jail
53 Tolerate
54 Emblem carved on a pole
55 Permission
58 Convent residents
61 Place for a rabbit in a magic act
62 Equal: Prefix
63 Immeasurably long time

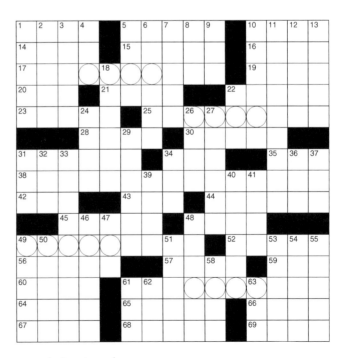

by Lynn Lempel

ACROSS

1 Translucent mineral in sheets
5 Telephone wire, for a bird
10 Trudge
14 Santa ___ (hot desert winds)
15 Hodgepodges
16 Prefix with plane
17 Alternative name for 42-Down
19 Buzzing annoyance
20 Greek god of the ocean
21 Go together perfectly
22 Buddy
23 "___ the twain shall meet"
24 Capital of the Philippines
25 Prefix with lateral
26 QBs pass for them
27 Treat, as leather
28 Moon landing vehicle, for short
29 Upside-down six
31 Mustachioed plumber of Nintendo games
33 Alternative name for 42-Down
39 Having pricked ears
40 Like 2, 4, 6, 8, etc.
42 Twice, in music
45 Foxlike
46 Insult, slangily
49 "Am ___ blame?"
50 Middle part of a Shakespearean play
52 What an aphrodisiac may produce
53 Schlep
54 Call playful names, say
55 Topple
57 Central
58 Alternative name for 42-Down
60 Farming prefix
61 Green military cap
62 Geese flying formations
63 Robin's haven
64 Numerical data
65 Opposite of subtracts

DOWN

1 "What, me worry?" magazine
2 Hysterical
3 Area between Georgia and Virginia
4 Questions
5 Paid (up)
6 Says "o'er" for "over," e.g.
7 Severity
8 Lawyer Roy of the McCarthy hearings
9 F.D.R.'s successor
10 Carl who hosted "Cosmos"
11 Protein-rich vegetarian soup
12 Future revealer
13 Hometown of 42-Down
18 ___ State (Ohio university)
21 Craze
22 So-called "lowest form of humor"
24 Fourth rock from the sun
27 Letter after sigma
30 Eco-friendly org.
31 Actor with the catchphrase "I pity the fool!"
32 Poem of praise
34 ___ the Cow (mascot)
35 Store where you might take a number
36 Weep
37 Glaring malevolently
38 Didn't keep, as a gift
41 Eggy Christmas drink
42 Comics debut of 1939
43 Big freeze
44 Flight between floors
46 Melodious
47 Keys
48 Stash
51 "War ___ the answer"
52 First lady before Michelle
55 Worry
56 "___-voom!"
58 Air gun ammo
59 Road curve

by Rosemarie Dolan and Christopher Geach

32

ACROSS
1 What a slob makes
5 Start of a play
9 House, in Havana
13 Poker pot starter
14 Animal used for Davy Crockett's cap
15 Ancient doctor known for his work on anatomy
16 *Big gamble
18 Daytime host DeGeneres
19 Good-looker
20 Impressive accomplishment
22 Scarfed down
23 Commencement
24 *Election Day receptacle
26 Blabs
28 Former Chevy subcompact
29 Doofus
32 Poses (for)
34 Pass, as a law
37 *Result of a financial panic
40 *Tight braid
42 Hogs
43 Desserts good for a hot day
45 "CSI" evidence, often
46 D.C.-based agents
48 Adams who photographed Yosemite
51 *Series of changes from birth to death
54 Criticize in good fun
58 Low-ranking U.S.N. officer
59 Petrol brand
60 Visitor to a confessional
61 Lagoon encircler
63 *Precipitous drop in cost
65 Like Cinderella's stepsisters
66 Verdi's opera slave girl
67 Sign of things to come
68 Loathe
69 Gas in a DINER sign
70 Uncool sort

DOWN
1 Like he-men
2 Energy giant that went bankrupt in 2001
3 Rebounds per game and others
4 Two trios plus one
5 Pine (for)
6 Murmur lovingly
7 Over the speed limit
8 Big maker of microchips
9 Baseball's record-setting Ripken
10 Train conductor's shout
11 Take care of
12 Building wing
15 Recover from
17 Web locale
21 Pie ___ mode
24 Russian pancakes
25 It's south of Ky.
27 Baton Rouge sch.
29 Belly muscles
30 Tool a magician uses in a woman-in-a-crate act
31 Detects like a bloodhound
33 Movie snippet
35 Pro's opposite
36 Old "We're up to something good" carrier
38 Leg joint
39 Blood component that contains hemoglobin
41 W.W. II spy org.
44 ___ counter (dieter)
47 Part of CBS: Abbr.
49 Lake between Ohio and Ontario
50 2012 Olympics locale, with a hint to the ends of the answers to the six starred clues
51 Dissolve and wash away, as minerals
52 The "I" of IM, sportswise
53 Network for political junkies
55 Genre of the "Pokémon" TV series
56 Break off
57 General way things are going
60 Read carefully
62 General at Appomattox
64 Words that have a certain ring to them?

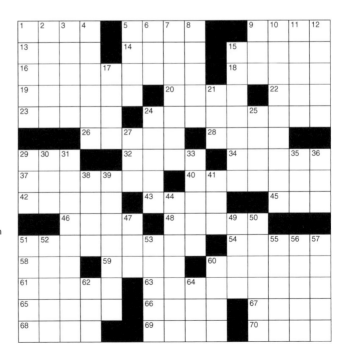

by Lynn Lempel

ACROSS

1 "Shoo, kitty!"
5 Minus item on a balance sheet
10 "Man, that was close!"
14 One's equal
15 Harden (to)
16 Jewish wedding dance
17 Et ___ (and others)
18 Luxury craft crossing the Atlantic, say
20 Hog's food
21 ___ sequitur
22 Give the most votes
23 Paris cabaret
27 Hog's home
28 Weapon for fencing
29 Shekel : Israel :: ___ : Mexico
31 Letter before iota
34 ___ Mustard (Clue character): Abbr.
35 Not naughty
39 Good grounding
43 Building block of molecules
44 Gibbon, for one
45 Heavy zoo critter
46 Lack of hardships
48 Employee's pay
50 Recipe amt.
53 Spooned-out Nestlé product
58 Many a South Seas island
60 By way of
61 Slangy greeting
62 What this crossword is, in a way?
65 "Step ___!" ("Hurry up!")
66 Having settled the score
67 Planet invaded in "The War of the Worlds"
68 Given for a time
69 Cincinnati team
70 Full of nerve
71 Exploring the bounds of propriety, as humor

DOWN

1 Involuntary twitch
2 Instrument played with a bow
3 Vowel run
4 Rhythm for a minuet or waltz
5 "Walk On By" singer Warwick
6 "Again! Again!"
7 Good, in Granada
8 Levin or Gershwin
9 "Perfect" number
10 Punxsutawney ___ (annual spring forecaster)
11 Sharpens
12 Posture-perfect
13 Like a witch's nose
19 Cask dregs
24 Portable Apple device
25 "___ my honor!"
26 Desex, as a stallion
30 Considered from all sides
31 Org. conducting airport searches
32 On a streak
33 "Livin' Thing" rock grp.
34 Pool stick
36 "East" on a grandfather clock
37 Jailbird
38 Rock producer Brian
40 Burkina ___ (African land)
41 Oil cartel
42 Jason's ship
47 Rights grp.
48 What belts wrap around
49 Lack of interest
50 Circus employee with a whip
51 Barrel support
52 Prodded with a finger
54 In broad daylight
55 Enjoyed a banquet
56 Looking at
57 Run-down
59 Periscope part
63 Item to hang your hat on
64 Greek cross

by Gareth Bain

34

ACROSS

1 City square
6 Thing on a cowboy's boot
10 Arrow-shooting Greek god
14 Overhauled
15 Man, in Roma
16 "See for yourself!"
17 Almost round
18 ___ platter (order at a Polynesian restaurant)
19 Word before Susan or Sunday
20 Help for newbies
23 Prior to, in verse
24 Swiss river to the Rhine
25 Med. care options
26 There's no such thing as this, according to a saying
31 Evening event
34 Kiev's land: Abbr.
35 1964 Pontiac debut
36 ___ tube
37 Sandra of "Gidget"
38 Craft with a paddle
40 Columbo and others: Abbr.
41 "Ta-ta"
42 Graduation cap attachment
43 Really strong
47 Sound heard before an MGM film
48 Weekend NBC staple, for short
49 Be a thespian
52 First woman to sit in the British House of Commons
56 Six-sided solid
57 Home of Lima and Toledo
58 Not straight, as a street
59 The Bruins of the N.C.A.A.

60 The Who's "___ Get Fooled Again"
61 Parisian girlfriends
62 Barely made, with "out"
63 Caustic alkalis
64 "I came, I saw, I conquered," e.g.

DOWN

1 Government investigation
2 Prying bar, e.g.
3 "Honesty is the best policy," e.g.
4 Large-tubed pasta
5 Former German chancellor Konrad
6 A-one
7 Rain cats and dogs
8 Officials on a diamond
9 Not as gentle

10 Broadway's "Billy ___"
11 Stop, Yield and No U Turn
12 Move like molasses
13 Wild blue yonder
21 Identify
22 Verbal hesitations
26 Rap's Dr. ___
27 Elizabeth I or II
28 Hawaiian instrument, for short
29 Oklahoma tribe
30 Christmas song
31 River deposit
32 Latch ___
33 Like a car or home, to State Farm
37 Prefix with functional
38 Arrange for transport to the airport, perhaps

39 Donkey
41 Nocturnal rodent hunter on a farm
42 Wee
44 Stop working, as a car battery
45 Farm bale
46 Broad ties
49 Heart chambers
50 Quiet places along a shore
51 Meeting for Romeo and Juliet
52 Word that can follow the starts of 20-, 26-, 43- and 52-Across
53 Chips ___!
54 Number of "lives" a cat has
55 Kind of wrestling
56 Pool ball striker

by Robert Cirillo

ACROSS

1 Unwanted e-mail
5 Top spot
9 Stupid jerk
14 Attire for Caesar
15 Get-out-of-jail money
16 Toward the back
17 Writer Waugh
18 "Coffee, Tea ___?" (1960s best seller)
19 Light bulb holders
20 "Vanilla Sky" actress
23 Young 'un
24 "I Like ___"
25 Carryall
29 Dead-on
31 How often Santa checks his list
33 Pie ___ mode
34 "I found it!"
36 Tic-tac-toe win
37 One who's closemouthed
38 Maiden voyage preceder
43 City near Osaka
44 Live
45 "___ the ramparts . . ."
46 Human's cousin
47 Old-time oath
49 1960s tripper Timothy
53 Best Picture of 1997
55 3 on a sundial
57 Grassy area
58 Ballpark maintenance groups
61 Pulitzer winner ___ Jefferson
64 Unaccompanied
65 Bush's ___ of Evil
66 Be of use
67 Swear
68 Nothing more than
69 Crown sparkler
70 Zany Martha
71 Waterfront walkway

DOWN

1 Paper clip alternative
2 Medieval weapon
3 Meeting plan
4 Nutmeg spice
5 "You can't judge ___ by its cover"
6 Wall-to-wall installation
7 Charades player
8 November event
9 Military action?
10 Fad
11 Skirt stitching
12 Atlas page
13 Hosp. areas
21 Supple
22 Highly ornate
26 "___ Ha'i"
27 "Oh, woe!"
28 Charades, e.g.
30 Wedding reception centerpiece
32 Impressed, and how!
35 Slowly, to a conductor
37 Medical breakthrough
38 It's played with a deck of 32 cards
39 Arizona Indian
40 Aid in crime
41 Delphic
42 Thing from the past
47 Sign up
48 Actor Poitier
50 Soviet leader ___ Kosygin
51 Provide with new cable
52 Late P.L.O. head Arafat
54 Texas A&M athlete
56 Grenoble's river
59 Popular PBS science series
60 Interstate exit
61 Rank below lt. col.
62 "___ Maria"
63 Like crunchy carrots

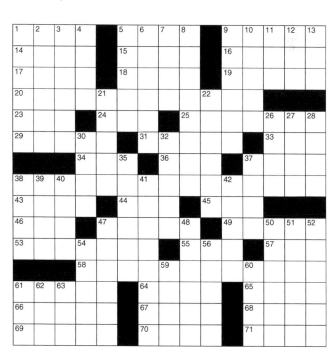

by Allan E. Parrish

ACROSS

1 Birds' homes
6 Order (around)
10 Quaint cry of shock
14 Not bottled, as beer
15 Choir voice
16 Knot
17 Writer ___ Rogers St. Johns
18 Nay opposers
19 Coin opening
20 Nursery rhyme bakery item
23 Rap's Dr. ___
24 Theater alert
25 More down and out
27 Omaha's home: Abbr.
30 Burden
33 Letters and packages
34 Make, in arithmetic
35 Reception with open arms
39 Was a passenger
41 Play on the radio
42 Supply-and-demand subj.
43 Tidy Lotto prize
48 Mary ___ cosmetics
49 Sweet Spanish dessert
50 Suffix with kitchen
51 Railroad stop: Abbr.
52 Once-fashionable card game
55 Pan Am rival
57 Doctors' org.
58 Scarce consolation
64 Pompeii, e.g., today
66 Writer Ephron
67 Anouk of "La Dolce Vita"
68 Capital NNW of Copenhagen
69 Slaughter of the 1940s–'50s Cardinals
70 ___ fatty acid

71 Taking the blue ribbon
72 Fall mo.
73 Elephant groups

DOWN

1 Ark builder
2 Prefix with derm
3 Leave in, as text
4 Bathroom powders
5 Songbird
6 Seabiscuit and Citation, e.g.
7 Barcelona cheers
8 Pierces
9 Flip response to a complaint
10 Naval rank: Abbr.
11 Famous bed tester
12 Love to pieces
13 Keep (from)
21 Mrs. Chaplin

22 Patricia who won an Oscar for "Hud"
26 Backgammon equipment
27 Drug cop
28 Suffix with switch
29 Not the most comfortable place to sleep
31 Russia's ___ Mountains
32 Grin
36 Lawyer's document
37 Palace protector
38 "A Day Without Rain" singer, 2000
40 Singer Fitzgerald
44 Fem. opposite
45 Recites
46 Germany's ___ von Bismarck
47 Educational innovation of the 1960s

52 Tree with pods
53 Entertain
54 By oneself
56 Blazing
59 Let go
60 Play group?
61 Bridge master Sharif
62 Tear
63 "___ of the D'Urbervilles"
65 Word in most of the Commandments

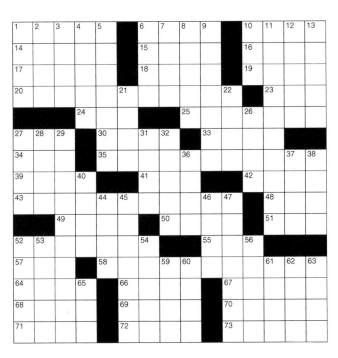

by Kurt Mengel

ACROSS

1 Layers
7 Sound of a lightning bolt
10 Cut the hair of
14 Main argument
15 Frank Sinatra's "___ Fool to Want You"
16 Top-notch
17 Losses, in accounting
18 Charlie Rose's network
19 Serving with chop suey
20 Jonathan Swift pamphlet about Ireland
23 To be given away
24 Court
25 The whole shebang
26 Twisty turn
27 See 29-Across
29 With 27-Across, get hitched
31 Cigarette residue
34 Ukr., once
35 Flight paths
37 Reason for turning down an invitation
41 Capulet rival
42 Stars and Stripes land
43 Ocean
44 Guess: Abbr.
45 Film director Craven
46 Nightwear, for short
49 Helios' Roman counterpart
51 Calf's mother
53 Jai ___
54 2003 teen comedy
59 Practice, as skills
60 Apply
61 Territory
62 In addition
63 Spy novelist Deighton
64 Show clearly
65 Spelling contests
66 "Acid"
67 Caught, as fish

DOWN

1 Machine-gun by plane
2 One's wife, slangily
3 Changes the décor of
4 Actor's whisper
5 Point at the dinner table?
6 Implores
7 Nothin'
8 Olympian repast
9 El ___, Tex.
10 Noel
11 Clark Kent's gal
12 Ancient Peruvian
13 Speed away, with "out"
21 Number of teeth Goofy has
22 Popular discount shoe store
27 Tel Aviv native
28 Worthless part
30 Bandy words
32 Capitol Hill V.I.P.: Abbr.
33 President after F.D.R.
34 Drunkard
35 Get better, as wine
36 Drs.' group
37 Afternoons and evenings, briefly
38 Caviar
39 Kinda
40 Wackos
45 Internet start-up?
46 Flexible
47 Actress Rule
48 Like finished contracts
50 Nabisco cookies
52 Continuously
53 Come clean
54 Ishmael's captain
55 Spy
56 Select
57 First lady's residence
58 Hawk's opposite

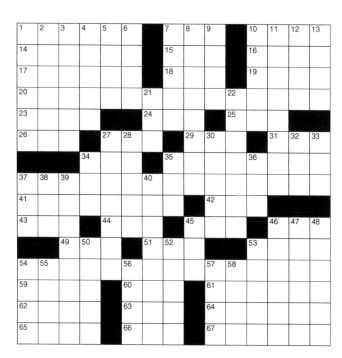

by Zach Jesse

38

ACROSS

1 Manila envelope closer
6 Computer screen image
10 "Spare tire"
14 Dominican Republic neighbor
15 Italia's capital
16 Interlude
17 Luggage clip-on
18 "Amo, amas, ___ . . ."
19 Prod
20 It made Leary bleary
22 Rizzuto of the 1940s–'50s Yankees
24 Fire, as from a job
25 Unruffled
28 Laid on generously
30 Tot's wheels
32 Hwy. mishap respondent
33 Med school subj.
34 Driveway occupant
36 Becomes a domehead
40 Skirt that shows off legs
41 Pasture
43 Forsaken
44 Fossil fuel blocks
46 Harry Potter's lightning bolt, e.g.
47 Suffix with buck
48 Piercing site
50 Exceed the bounds of
52 Summary holder?
56 With resolute spirit
57 WSW's opposite
58 Party for lei wearers
59 ___ Lanka
60 ___ Jay Lerner of Lerner & Loewe
62 Jolt
64 Jazz's James and Jones
68 Fall's opposite

69 Sea eagle
70 System utilizing grates
71 Editor's mark
72 Space capsule insignia
73 Rulers before Lenin

DOWN

1 Greek X
2 Boy
3 River island
4 Downers?
5 Farm pen
6 Tax deferral means: Abbr.
7 Connectors?
8 Nebraska city
9 Not an emigré
10 Winter ailment
11 Leave in the ___
12 Pond growths
13 Mix
21 Joe that won't keep you up
23 Arm or leg
25 Envelope sticker
26 Bert's Muppet pal
27 Late Princess of Wales
29 Uppers?
31 San ___ Obispo, Calif.
35 Norway's patron saint
37 Peter of "Casablanca"
38 Slobber
39 Like a winter wonderland
42 Wine residue
45 Comedian Mort
49 Sandwich with sauerkraut
51 Least seen
52 Closes in on
53 Dark
54 Pull one's leg
55 Mrs. Bush
61 Volleyball equipment
63 Small coal size
65 Intl. flier, once
66 ___ Lingus
67 Last year's jrs.

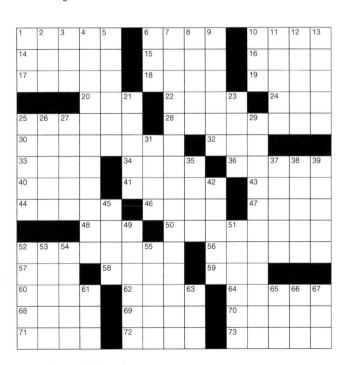

by Patrick Merrell

ACROSS

1 Homebuilder's strip
5 Bruins of the Pac 10
9 Unflashy
14 "Can you hear me? . . . hear me? . . . hear me?"
15 Horse in a '60s sitcom
16 Ralph ___ Emerson
17 "What a shame!"
18 Laser light
19 Go in
20 Overly florid writing
23 Acorn maker
24 Before, to Byron
25 Recharges one's batteries, so to speak
27 Bucky Beaver's toothpaste, in old ads
31 Switchblade
33 Weapons of ___ destruction
37 Pesos
39 Prefix with metric or tonic
40 Author Ferber
41 1951 Alec Guinness film, with "The"
44 City west of Tulsa
45 Night before
46 Go on Social Security, maybe
47 One-and-only
48 Mouth off to
50 September bloom
51 Frisbee, e.g.
53 Some univ. instructors
55 "I knew it!"
58 The 1890s
64 Reaction to the Beatles, once
66 Flying: Prefix
67 Pitch
68 "Git ___ Little Dogies"
69 Section of seats
70 58-Across and others
71 "Death Be Not Proud" poet John
72 North Carolina college
73 Hourly pay

DOWN

1 ___ year (2004, e.g.)
2 Legal rights grp.
3 In that direction, to a whaler
4 The "H" in "M*A*S*H": Abbr.
5 Brownish
6 Thin pancakes
7 "All in the Family" producer Norman
8 Call on the carpet
9 Clean the carpet
10 Brownish
11 Choir voice
12 Notion
13 Social misfit
21 Memorize
22 ___-faire
26 Gets the lead out?
27 Runs in neutral
28 Upright or baby grand
29 Blacksmith's block
30 Had to have
32 Root beer brand
34 Fess up to
35 Sound of slumber
36 Cavalry blade
38 Texas oil city
42 Clear out, as before a hurricane
43 Renter's paper
49 Alternative to mono
52 Likeness
54 Decorate
55 "Diary of ___ Housewife" (1970 film)
56 Angel's headwear
57 Unattributed: Abbr.
59 Bridal wear
60 Grind with the teeth
61 Distinctive quality
62 Quarter-mile race, e.g.
63 In addition
65 Holiday ___

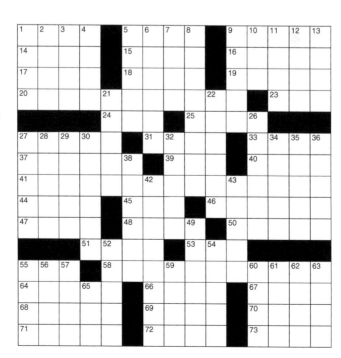

by Gregory E. Paul

ACROSS

1 People who make you yawn
6 Tibetan monk
10 British fellow
14 Crème de la crème
15 Had payments due
16 Part of a Valentine bouquet
17 Greek marketplace
18 Glenn Miller's "In the ___"
19 Leave out
20 Testifier in a court case
23 Sea eagles
24 "___ will be done . . ."
25 Event with floats
29 Female in a pride
33 Hebrew prophet
34 Be enraptured
36 Animal that beats its chest
37 Pleasant excursion
41 Golf peg
42 Abominates
43 Gillette razor
44 Regards highly
46 Mother of Joseph
48 Wayne film "___ Bravo"
49 Prayer's end
51 Top of a tall building, maybe
59 After-bath powder
60 Former Fed chairman Greenspan
61 Harold who composed "Over the Rainbow"
62 Gait faster than a walk
63 Film part
64 Cotton thread
65 Disastrous marks for a gymnast
66 Gardener's spring purchase
67 Outpouring

DOWN

1 Smile widely
2 Korbut of the 1972 Olympics
3 Very funny person
4 Raison d'___
5 Charred
6 Fictional salesman Willy
7 M.P.'s hunt them
8 Pussy's cry
9 Building wing
10 Actor Hume
11 Where the heart is, they say
12 Sale tag caution
13 Dogs, but rarely hogs
21 Anger
22 Daring bikini
25 Stickum
26 French girlfriends
27 Synonym man
28 Cigarette's end
29 Colleague of Clark at The Daily Planet
30 Our planet
31 Steeple
32 Flower part
34 Film designers' designs
35 Tiny
38 Not our
39 Tea urns
40 Tic-___-toe
45 Builds
46 ___ Speedwagon
47 Chronicles
49 "It is ___ told by an idiot": Macbeth
50 Dug up
51 ___ the Great (10th-century king)
52 Building near a silo
53 ___ gin fizz
54 ___ vera
55 What icicles do
56 Lohengrin's love
57 Boston cager, informally
58 Leg's middle

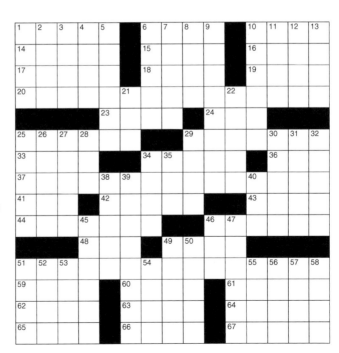

by Robert Dillman

ACROSS

1 Chances
5 Wires on a bicycle wheel
11 Tavern
14 In ___ of (substituting for)
15 One of Jerry's pals on "Seinfeld"
16 Down Under bird
17 Bejeweled president?
19 Mo. of Presidents' Day
20 "Much ___ About Nothing"
21 Dine
22 Planet
24 Pale, aging president?
28 Most elderly
31 Hang around for
32 Place to store valuables
33 Hair colorer
34 ___ and hearty
38 Devoted follower
40 Demolisher
42 More's opposite
43 Opening for a tab
45 Zeal
46 Burning up
48 Disinfects
49 Comic president?
53 Wheel turners
54 Tint
55 Historic period
58 Compete (for)
59 Hirsute president?
64 Mont Blanc, e.g.
65 Money earned
66 Communicate by hand
67 Tennis court divider
68 Check receivers
69 Neighborhood

DOWN

1 Gymnast Korbut
2 Stopped working, as an engine
3 Showroom model
4 Total
5 Trigonometric ratio
6 Ancient Greek thinker
7 Paddle
8 Set of tools
9 WSW's reverse
10 Composer Rachmaninoff
11 Obscure
12 Tiny creature
13 "American Idol" winner ___ Studdard
18 Frothy
23 One using lots of soap
24 Object of a dowser's search
25 Reclined
26 Lived
27 Like hen's teeth
28 The White House's ___ Office
29 Delicate fabric
30 Performing twosomes
33 "We love to fly, and it shows" airline
35 Alan of "M*A*S*H"
36 Ponce de ___
37 Goofs
39 Nicholas I or II
41 Appraiser
44 "___ the land of the free . . ."
47 Send again
48 Slides
49 From Jakarta, e.g.
50 Kick out of the country
51 Snoozed
52 Lemon ___ (herb)
55 Kuwaiti ruler
56 Fury
57 "___ and the King of Siam"
60 Santa ___ winds
61 Wintry
62 Shad product
63 Land between Can. and Mex.

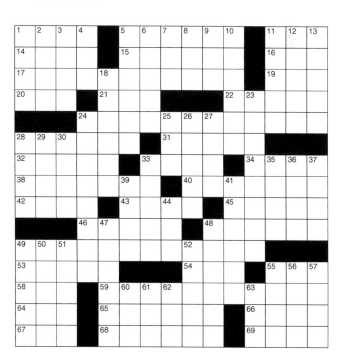

by Charles Barasch

ACROSS

1 Shade trees
5 Consent (to)
10 Baby bottle contents
14 "See you later!"
15 Senior dances
16 Assert
17 Flimflam
19 Roman cloak
20 ___ of a kind
21 Warp-resistant wood
22 Temptress
23 One who went to tell the king the sky was falling
26 Not just ask
29 Commotions
30 Family data
31 Juicy tropical fruit
33 Watering hole
36 Perform a dance with a shake
40 WNW's opposite
41 Hackneyed
42 Wall Street inits.
43 Wearisome one
44 Archipelago parts
46 Some messing around
49 Narrative
51 The "A" of ABM
52 Just great
55 Royal attendant
56 Mishmash
59 Asia's shrinking ___ Sea
60 County north of San Francisco
61 Where a stream may run
62 Lots of
63 Clay pigeon shoot
64 Final word

DOWN

1 Talk back?
2 Big cat
3 Nutmeg relative
4 Not worth a ___
5 Tack on
6 Bad pun response
7 Having lots of ups and downs
8 Cousin of an ostrich
9 Road curve
10 Morning prayers
11 Off-white
12 Theater section
13 Skating champ Michelle
18 British gun
22 Busybody
23 Dish of leftovers
24 Group of jurors
25 Jittery
26 Florida's Miami-___ County
27 Selves
28 Apportion, with "out"
31 Miser's hoarding
32 Alias
33 ___ terrier
34 Nuisance
35 One side of a vote
37 Jet black
38 "Listen!"
39 Exclusively
43 By the skin of one's teeth
44 Purpose
45 Omit
46 Title colonel in a 1960s sitcom
47 Military chaplain
48 Actress Dickinson
49 Unsolicited e-mail
50 "Gone With the Wind" estate
52 Man cast out of paradise
53 Girl-watch, e.g.
54 Sharp
56 ___ Pinafore
57 Acorn's source
58 Reproductive cells

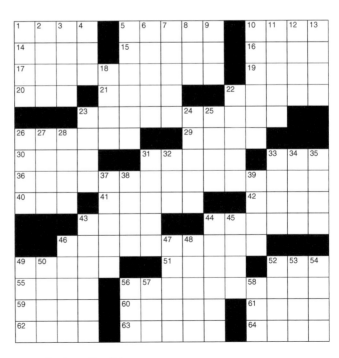

by Anne Garelick

ACROSS

1 Continental currency
5 Give off
9 Assumed name
14 Jazz's Kenton
15 Go (over) carefully
16 Officer's shield
17 Easy wins
19 With 62-Across, a possible title for this puzzle
20 Long sandwich
21 Regarding
23 Word after ready or petty
24 Web addresses, for short
26 List-ending abbr.
28 Young hospital helpers
33 Capone and Capp
34 Always, poetically
35 Predicament
37 Where a car may end up after an accident
40 Have dinner
42 Talent
43 Says "cheese"
45 Part of a baseball uniform
47 Tic-___-toe
48 Credits for doing nice things
52 The writing ___ the wall
53 Choir voice
54 Play parts
57 Fishhook feature
59 Corporate money managers: Abbr.
62 See 19-Across
64 Some USA Today graphics
67 The "V" of VCR
68 "Good grief!"
69 "Uh-huh"
70 Snoozer's sound
71 Old salts
72 Italia's capital

DOWN

1 PC key
2 The Beehive State
3 Yard tool
4 Small winning margin, in baseball
5 Ecol. watchdog
6 Baked beans ingredient
7 Bothers
8 Teacher, at times
9 Middle muscles, for short
10 Legal assistant
11 Brainstorm
12 Mellows, as wine
13 Adam's third
18 Basic dictionary entry
22 Soul singer Redding
25 Caustic substance
27 Rental units: Abbr.
28 Get to the top of
29 Up and about
30 It may be called on the battlefield
31 Singer Bonnie
32 "___ Marner"
33 Computer pop-ups
36 R.N.'s forte
38 Religious site
39 Chops
41 Goldilocks sat in his chair
44 Snooty person
46 Campaigner, in brief
49 All worked up
50 Hankering
51 "That's cheating!"
54 Ones heading for the hills?: Abbr.
55 Nickel or dime
56 Commotion
58 Latvia's capital
60 Approximately
61 Flower stalk
63 Tiller's tool
65 S&L offerings
66 Baltic or Bering

by Gail Grabowski

ACROSS

1 Fed. food inspectors
5 Raindrop sound
9 Songwriters' grp.
14 Lecherous look
15 Cleveland cagers, briefly
16 Weigher
17 Co-star of 36-Down
19 Jabs
20 It's heard on the grapevine
21 I. M. Pei, for one
23 Red flag, e.g.
24 Lyricist Lorenz ___
25 See 41-Down
29 Online film maker
33 Star of 36-Down
38 Stallone title role
39 Out of port
40 January in Juárez
42 "___ delighted!"
43 Brouhahas
45 Co-star of 36-Down
47 Knock over
49 Fencing blade
50 The "Y" of B.Y.O.B.
52 Barge's route
57 100% incorrect
62 Whooping ___
63 '50s candidate Stevenson
64 Setting for 36-Down
66 ___ breath (flower)
67 "Guilty" or "not guilty"
68 Flex
69 Boffo show
70 Gardener's bagful
71 Counts up

DOWN

1 Part of UHF
2 Capital of South Korea
3 Film director Jonathan
4 Shady spot
5 Alternatives to Macs
6 Syllables in "Deck the Halls"
7 Finished
8 Intimidate, with "out"
9 Person with goals
10 Co-star of 36-Down
11 Wedding reception centerpiece
12 Writer Waugh
13 Exterminator's target
18 Garden products name
22 "Hee ___"

26 ___-inspiring
27 Lois of "Superman"
28 "___ Jacques" (children's song)
30 Naval leader: Abbr.
31 "Dancing Queen" quartet
32 Big name in water faucets
33 Makeshift river conveyance
34 Norway's capital
35 Certain tide
36 TV series that premiered in 1974
37 Cause for a plumber
41 With 25-Across, 50%
44 Molasseslike
46 Muhammad's birthplace
48 Where Switz. is

51 Easy wins
53 Popular Caribbean island
54 Sans clothing
55 Put ___ to (halt)
56 English city NE of Manchester
57 Applies lightly
58 Dutch cheese
59 "Duchess of ___" (Goya work)
60 Cairo's river
61 Elation
65 Mouthful of gum

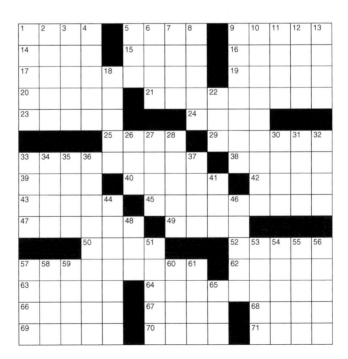

by Allan E. Parrish

ACROSS

1 Opposite of highs
5 Big stingers
10 Concert blasters
14 Hawaiian island
15 Maximum poker bet
16 Bob who lost to Bill Clinton
17 Warner's statement after the fact
19 "Roots" author Haley
20 "Julius Caesar," e.g.
22 ___-fi
23 Bird's home
24 Fire leftover
27 Eve's predecessor
30 Tortilla chip dip
34 Fateful day in a 20-Across
38 Ringer
39 Not so good
40 Egg: Prefix
41 Baseball hit just beyond the infield
42 Bard of ___
43 Fateful day in a 20-Across
45 Pays a landlord
47 Require
48 "I get it!"
49 Guys-only
52 Cry to a mouse
54 "Et tu, Brute? Then fall, Caesar!," e.g.
62 Building beam
63 One who warned Caesar
64 Bronx cheer
65 Golfer Palmer, familiarly
66 Liberals, with "the"
67 ___-bitsy
68 Fabric colorers
69 Schnauzer in Dashiell Hammett books

DOWN

1 ___ Lane, admirer of Superman
2 Inauguration Day recital
3 Command to a horse
4 Broods
5 Land next to a road
6 Crooked
7 Turn on a pivot
8 Resident near the Leaning Tower
9 Make a nighttime ruckus
10 Not limited to one use
11 Gangster's gal
12 Defendant's declaration at an arraignment
13 Alluring
18 The '60s or '70s, e.g.
21 Road section requiring caution
24 Battling
25 Rudely push
26 Long-billed wader
28 ___ this minute
29 "The Jeffersons" theme "___ On Up"
31 Hotelier Helmsley
32 Laziness
33 Omega's opposite
35 Feels no remorse
36 Drum accompanier
37 John Philip Sousa offering
41 Moistens with droplets
43 "Little Women" family name
44 Grows chewers
46 VW predecessors?
50 Syrian president
51 "Mine eyes have seen the ___..."
53 Australian "bear"
54 Land SW of Samoa
55 Assist in crime
56 Fannie ___ (securities)
57 Top-notch
58 Mix (up)
59 Deli loaves
60 Adept
61 Sp. miss

by Patrick Merrell

ACROSS

1 1953 Leslie Caron title role
5 Water pitcher
9 Companion for Snow White
14 Garden of ___
15 Bad habit
16 At the proper time
17 Meteorologist's favorite movie of 1939?
20 Longtime buddy
21 Metals from the earth
22 Drunk's problem
23 One of the Jackson 5
25 Quaker ___
27 "Pow!"
30 "___ the night before Christmas . . ."
32 Lumberjack's "Heads up!"
36 Lotion ingredient
38 "Now it all makes sense!"
40 Dinero
41 Meteorologist's favorite movie of 1952?
44 Tennis champ Chris
45 London district
46 Jazz singer ___ James
47 Dislike with a passion
49 Writer Philip
51 "Game, ___, match!"
52 Kite part
54 Trade
56 Co. that merged with Time Warner
59 Consider
61 Meeting schedule
65 Meteorologist's favorite movie of 2000?

68 Miss America's crown
69 Scotch ___
70 Forest unit
71 Sing in the Alps
72 Speak unclearly
73 [Been there, done that]

DOWN

1 Toy block company
2 TV's "American ___"
3 Give temporarily
4 Bumbling
5 Easily-blamed alter ego
6 Mental quickness
7 Canyon effect
8 Fashionably outdated
9 Chills in the cooler
10 ESE's reverse
11 Etching liquid
12 Little squirt
13 Government agents
18 "Hold on!"
19 Miami basketball team
24 Desert resting place
26 Campfire treat popular with Scouts
27 ___ on a true story
28 Full of energy
29 "Water Lilies" painter Claude
31 Mexican mister
33 Marina sights
34 Cream of the crop
35 Charged
37 Everglades wader
39 Cultural values
42 Words with a handshake
43 Deep trouble
48 Seating level
50 Crones

53 About half of all turns
55 Trifling
56 Lawyer: Abbr.
57 Birthplace of seven U.S. presidents
58 Its symbol is Pb
60 Breakfast, lunch or dinner
62 Author Ephron
63 Sketched
64 "You can say that again!"
66 Opposite of post-
67 PC core: Abbr.

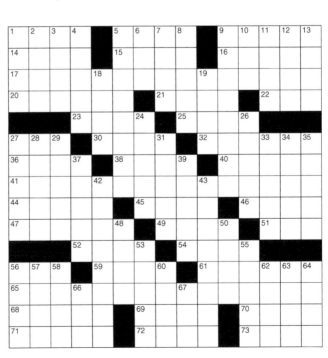

by Kyle Mahowald

ACROSS

1 Apple computers
5 1:00, e.g.
9 Eye color
14 Hideous
15 In ___ (actual)
16 New York's ___ Fisher Hall
17 Time for a Wild West shootout
18 "Excuse me . . ."
19 Pointing device
20 Fancy term for a 36-Across
23 Hornswoggled
24 Tetley product
25 Regretted
26 London's Big ___
27 Shopping place
28 Quick punch
31 Self-evident truth
34 ___ fide
35 Coke or Pepsi
36 Puzzling person?
39 Goldie of "Laugh-In" fame
40 Party giver
41 Atlas blow-up
42 Needle hole
43 Yappy dog, briefly
44 Colorado native
45 Kodak product
46 Explosive letters
47 Put down, slangily
50 Fancy term for a 36-Across
54 Secluded valleys
55 Actress Winslet
56 Stage part
57 W.W. II vessel
58 Split personalities?
59 Think tank output
60 Hairy-chested
61 Edges
62 Work station

DOWN

1 Chew (on)
2 Ancient marketplace
3 Cirrus or cumulus
4 Lip-___ (not really sing)
5 Realm for St. Peter
6 Actor Milo
7 One who takes drugs, e.g.
8 "The Night Watch" painter
9 Tiny village
10 Steer clear of
11 Mount Olympus chief
12 Formerly, once
13 Caustic substance
21 Tabloid twosomes
22 Surrounding glows
26 Cap'n's mate
27 Samuel with a code
28 Scribbles (down)
29 Cream ingredient
30 Quarterback Starr
31 Flu symptom
32 Picture of health?
33 "___ Russia $1200" (Bob Hope book)
34 Gambling professional
35 Art movie theater
37 Overcome utterly
38 "Same here!"
43 Boar's abode
44 Except if
45 Important exam
46 ___ pole
47 Electron tube
48 Cruise stopovers
49 T-bone, e.g.
50 Site of Napoleon's exile
51 Light on Broadway
52 Prepare for takeoff
53 Lines on a radar screen
54 Doublemint, e.g.

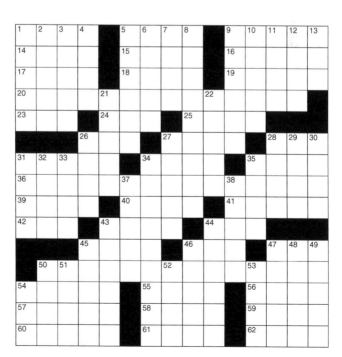

by Barry C. Silk

ACROSS

1 Tough spots to get out of
5 City leader
10 Ego
14 Old radio word for the letter O
15 "___ there yet?"
16 Half a sextet
17 Charlton Heston epic, with "The"
20 Ratfink
21 Ray of the Kinks
22 Essential
25 Witherspoon of "Legally Blonde"
26 "Holy smokes!"
29 Marked, as a survey square
31 Whodunit board game
32 New Guinea native
34 C.E.O.'s degree
37 Home for Pooh and Tigger
40 Baseballer Mel
41 Large system of newsgroups
42 Smog
43 Unappetizing dishes
44 Try to pick up, as at a bar
45 Laissez-___
48 Join forces (with)
51 Popular Honda
53 Runs full speed
57 Chain in the upper St. Lawrence River
60 Ages and ages
61 False move
62 Jazzy improv style
63 One bit of medicine
64 Hot dog picker-upper
65 Amerada ___ (oil giant)

DOWN

1 Writes (down)
2 Assist in wrongdoing
3 Pre-stereo sound
4 Supported, as a motion
5 Mrs. Eisenhower
6 Like gunmen and octopuses
7 Nay's opposite
8 Possess
9 Foxx of "Sanford and Son"
10 Filmmaker Spielberg
11 Bert's roommate on "Sesame Street"
12 Reduced-calorie beers
13 "All That Jazz" choreographer Bob
18 Bullfight cheers
19 Corps member
23 Wide area
24 Two of cards
26 Sound in a big, empty room
27 Excess supply
28 Uncle's partner
30 It's thrown at a bull's-eye
32 Mexican money
33 Good (at)
34 Castle encircler
35 Old TV clown
36 Chief Yemeni port
38 Kings and queens
39 Auto accident injury
43 Complain
44 Hockey great Bobby
45 Destined
46 Sound preceding "God bless"
47 Desktop pictures
49 Growing older
50 Sail supports
52 Loony
54 Formerly
55 Some handhelds: Abbr.
56 Speedy fliers, for short
58 Modern: Prefix
59 Kipling's "Gunga ___"

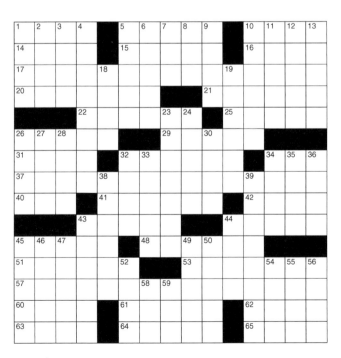

by Jim Hyres

ACROSS

1 Subdued color
7 Lift in Aspen
11 Height: Abbr.
14 Title girl in Kay Thompson books
15 "Othello" villain
16 Pastoral place
17 Golf locale
19 Prohibit
20 Letters on a Cardinal's cap
21 Rock musician Brian
22 Diving board's part of a swimming pool
24 Ambles (along)
27 Johnson of "Laugh-In"
28 Thom ___ shoes
30 Extremely low, as prices
34 Strokes on a green
36 Game authority
37 Brays
40 Views, as through binoculars
44 Online correspondence
46 Quick bite
47 Informal group discussion
52 Choir voice
53 Roundish
54 Walks about looking for prey
56 Frog's seat
60 Figure skater Midori ___
61 ___ Lingus
64 On the ___ (fleeing)
65 Pivoting span on a river
68 Summer in Montréal
69 Encl. with a manuscript
70 Give, as duties
71 One side in checkers
72 Little 'un
73 Tyrannical leader

DOWN

1 Chest muscles, briefly
2 Tremendously
3 One's special person in life
4 ___ Lizzie (Model T)
5 ___ Park, Colo.
6 Loewe's partner on Broadway
7 The first O of O-O-O
8 Like Yul Brynner or Telly Savalas
9 Tropical fever
10 Justice's attire
11 Queen Victoria's prince
12 Shack
13 Two-trailer rig
18 Toy that does tricks
23 Fatherly
25 Furtively
26 Jr. high, e.g.
28 Speedometer letters
29 Billiards rod
31 Keystone officer
32 Automatic tournament advance
33 Bullring hurrahs
35 Identical
38 "What ___ I saying?"
39 ___-boom-bah
41 Spicy chip topping
42 Malfunction, with "up"
43 Bout ender, for short
45 Place for gloss
47 Hair salon item
48 Fly
49 Picked up stealthily
50 It goes on a photocopier: Abbr.
51 "Pretty good!"
55 Poorer
57 "Hey, you!"
58 Not at home
59 Part of the spine
62 Frozen waffle brand
63 Apartment payment
66 Previously named
67 Magazine no.

by Gail Grabowski

ACROSS

1 Timber wolf
5 Gymnast Comaneci
10 Little tricksters
14 Grad
15 Addicts
16 One who nabs 15-Across
17 Nothing more than
18 Eats elegantly
19 French cheese
20 Like some Christians
22 Four-door
23 Do cross-country
24 When the stomach starts grumbling
26 Air conditioner capacity, for short
29 Co. name completer
31 Boar's mate
32 Not behaving conservatively
39 Genesis garden
40 French sea
41 Dublin's land
42 Not just gone
47 ___ Jima
48 Science guy Bill
49 CD predecessors
50 Does a U-turn
55 Place to relax
57 Enlighten
58 Utterance that sums up 20-, 32- and 42-Across
63 Misshapen citrus
64 Chicago airport
65 "A Clockwork Orange" protagonist
66 Unload, as stock
67 Voting machine part
68 5,280 feet
69 Dutch cheese
70 Clothe
71 Quaker ___

DOWN

1 Gentle animal
2 Toast spread
3 Famous duelist
4 Black cats, traditionally speaking
5 Prodding
6 One side of the Urals
7 Overalls material
8 "Me, Myself & ___" (2000 flick)
9 Ninny
10 Not on one side or the other
11 ___ Gras
12 Trojan War king
13 Verona, in "Romeo and Juliet"
21 Related
22 ___ gin fizz
25 Arson aftermath
26 Ran, as colors
27 Seashore washer
28 Eye layer
30 Deep sleep
33 Sundance entry, informally
34 Actor Beatty
35 1982 Disney film
36 Use a rotary phone
37 Basic of golf instruction
38 Lampreys, e.g.
43 Twisted
44 Letters of distress
45 Dish sometimes served "on the half-shell"
46 Officials elected for two yrs.
50 Employ again
51 Nosed (out)
52 Mediterranean estate
53 Old-fashioned anesthetic
54 Trim
56 Site of an 1836 massacre
59 Son of Zeus
60 Russian gold medalist ___ Kulik
61 Had emotions
62 Alimony receivers
64 On in years

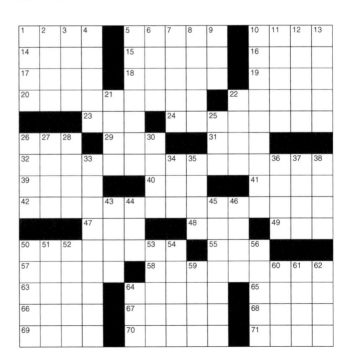

by Michael Doran

ACROSS

1 Casino game
5 Symbol on a "one way" sign
10 Numbered musical work
14 Patron saint of Norway
15 "Yeah"
16 Prefix with physical
17 Homeless child
18 Mother ___ stories
19 Checkbook record
20 Mother in a 1960s sitcom
23 Web address: Abbr.
24 Naturalness
25 Sen. Feinstein
27 Go away
30 Mississippi city
32 Arkansas's ___ Mountains
33 Be in harmony (with)
34 Diner sign
37 Vessel for ashes
38 Thirst quenchers
41 Poker prize
42 Historical
44 Pinnacle
45 Port-au-Prince's land
47 It's a bore
49 Los Angeles baseballer
50 Golden period
52 Drop of sweat
53 "Hold On Tight" band
54 1965 Natalie Wood title role
60 Emcee's need
62 Big African critter
63 Opposite of 15-Across
64 France's Côte d'___
65 Fund contributor
66 Laced up
67 Partner of rank and serial number
68 Gushes
69 Lyric poems

DOWN

1 Chickens and turkeys
2 Jai ___
3 Train transport
4 Extended slump
5 Month without a national holiday
6 River of Lyon
7 Greek R's
8 Un-elect
9 Apple-polisher
10 Meditative sounds
11 Merrie Melodies "co-star"
12 Reversal
13 Valuable fur
21 Pre-euro German money
22 ___ Bravo
26 Paul Bunyan's tool
27 Arrange, as the hair
28 Book before Nehemiah
29 "Li'l Abner" mother
30 Gang member, maybe
31 Wild goat
33 Make sport of
35 Lug
36 Recipe direction
39 Holders of referee whistles
40 River hazard
43 Small amount
46 Extend, as a house
48 Roll of bills
49 Styles
50 Charles Atlas, for one
51 "My Fair Lady" lady
52 Already
55 Breakfast restaurant chain
56 Trig function
57 Empty space
58 Fencing blade
59 Wines that aren't whites
61 Afore

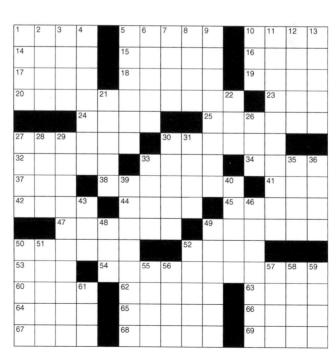

by Merle Baker

ACROSS

1 Did laps in a pool
5 Foolhardy
9 "She loves me . . . she loves me not" flower
14 "Horrors!"
15 "Cómo ___ usted?"
16 Blast from the past
17 Spick-and-span
18 Genesis twin
19 F.B.I. worker
20 Achieve initial success
23 Singletons
24 Bullfight cheer
25 Suffix with lion
28 Oar-powered ship
31 Like a fiddle
34 "Scratch and win" game
36 Pub brew
37 Sweep under the rug
38 Estimates
42 Intl. oil group
43 Take to court
44 Use crib notes
45 Cheyenne's locale: Abbr.
46 Kind of underwear
49 Foxy
50 "___ Drives Me Crazy" (Fine Young Cannibals hit)
51 Western tribe
53 Completely mistaken
60 Improperly long sentence
61 Risk-free
62 Number not on a grandfather clock
63 Space shuttle gasket
64 With warts and all
65 Elm or elder
66 ___ Park, Colo.
67 Camper's cover
68 Hankerings

DOWN

1 Spiritual, e.g.
2 Cry on a roller coaster
3 Med. school class
4 E pluribus unum, for instance
5 "___ Madness" (1936 antidrug film)
6 Whence St. Francis
7 Night twinkler
8 Düsseldorf dwelling
9 Within one's power
10 Pond buildup
11 March 15, e.g.
12 Trig term
13 "Are we there ___?"
21 In first place
22 Marisa of "My Cousin Vinny"
25 Arm joint
26 Unrinsed, maybe
27 Fifth-century pope
29 Autumn yard worker
30 Santa's little helper
31 Pink-slips
32 Perfect
33 Short-tempered
35 Nurse's skill, for short
37 "What'd you say?"
39 Gray
40 Feel sorry about
41 Symbol at the head of a musical staff
46 First ___ first
47 Breakfast bread
48 Swear (to)
50 Masonry
52 Nearing retirement age, maybe
53 Yours and mine
54 The "U" in I.C.U.
55 Future atty.'s exam
56 Facilitate
57 Dublin's land
58 Legal claim
59 Goes kaput
60 Salmon eggs

by Gregory E. Paul

ACROSS

1 Likely
4 Hot dish with beans
9 Bridge maven Charles
14 Justice Sandra ___ O'Connor
15 Appealingly shocking
16 Licorice flavoring
17 Antique auto
19 Frank of rock's Mothers of Invention
20 Vegetable oil component
21 The "S" of CBS
23 Black currant
25 Humiliated
29 Tea server's question
33 Out of one's mind
36 Van Susteren of Fox News
37 Alternative to a nail
38 "That's ___!" (angry denial)
40 Conductor's stick
42 Long-eared hopper
43 Neuters
45 Danger
47 Fashion inits.
48 Cause of an out
51 Refuses
52 Smoothed
56 Drops
60 Baghdad resident
61 ___ Mongolia
64 Small frosted cake
66 Item confiscated at an airport
67 Goofy
68 Wrestler's locale
69 Seasoned sailors
70 Parachute pulls
71 They: Fr.

DOWN

1 ___ committee
2 Newswoman Zahn
3 Varieties
4 Asexual reproduction
5 Where spokes meet
6 Showy flower
7 Showy flower
8 "Beware the ___ . . ."
9 Park shelters
10 Parading . . . or a hint to this puzzle's theme
11 ___ Van Winkle
12 Psychic's claim
13 Educator's org.
18 Japanese soup
22 Punch out, as Morse code
24 Kosovo war participant
26 Not stay on the path

27 Pitchers
28 Wooden pin
30 Bounded
31 Absolute
32 New Zealand native
33 A brig has two
34 ___ male (top dog)
35 Locked book
39 Command to people who are 10-Down
41 "Just do it" sloganeer
44 Gentlemen of España
46 An original tribe of Israel
49 Scatter, as seeds
50 Feudal figure
53 Ashley's country-singing mother
54 Sweet'N Low rival

55 Mud, dust and grime
57 Like "The Lord of the Rings"
58 It's north of Carson City
59 Movie rating unit
61 Approves
62 Spanish article
63 Up to, informally
65 Polit. maverick

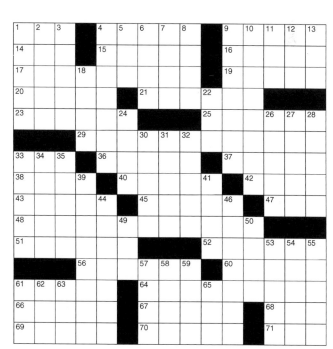

by Joy M. Andrews

ACROSS

1 Boeing 747's and 767's
5 The Monkees' "___ Believer"
8 "Am not!" rejoinder
14 Forced out
16 Wash receptacles
17 With 56-Across, lawyer who argued in 19- and 49-Across
18 Pre-Mexican Indians
19 With 49-Across, noted decision made 5/17/54
21 Buying binge
24 Musical talent
25 Eight: Fr.
26 Stuart queen
29 Went after congers
34 Aged
35 On the briny
36 Curious thing
37 Decision reversed by 19- and 49-Across
40 One sailing under a skull and crossbones
41 Locust or larch
42 Spanish aunt
43 Belgian painter James
44 Chief Justice ___ Warren, majority opinion writer for 19- and 49-Across
45 Rolodex nos.
46 Select, with "for"
48 Stanford-___ test
49 See 19-Across
55 Sitting room
56 See 17-Across
60 Groups of starting players
61 Forebodes
62 Former vice president Dick
63 Ave. crossers
64 Mary ___ Lincoln

DOWN

1 Stick (out)
2 Book after Galatians: Abbr.
3 Capote, for short
4 Iced dessert
5 Langston Hughes poem
6 Cat's cry
7 Annex: Abbr.
8 Addis ___, Ethiopia
9 Symbol of sharpness
10 "Cómo ___ usted?"
11 Echelon
12 How a lot of modern music is sold
13 Secret W.W. II agcy.
15 Brute
20 Flying geese formation
21 Quaint establishment
22 Arrive, as by car
23 Passengers
26 "___ sow, so shall . . ."
27 Reno's state: Abbr.
28 U.S./Can./Mex. pact
30 University URL ending
31 Pay attention
32 French star
33 Ruler by birth
35 Houston landmark
36 Pitcher Hershiser
38 ___ Paulo, Brazil
39 Go off track
44 And so forth
45 Soldier's helmet, slangily
47 Short-winded
48 Bruce Springsteen, with "the"
49 ___ of office
50 Gratis
51 Flair
52 Concert equipment
53 Pucker-inducing
54 Angers
55 ___-Man (arcade game)
57 Past
58 Was ahead
59 "Acid"

by Ethan Cooper

ACROSS

1 Dreadful, as circumstances
5 One not of high morals
10 Spanish house
14 TV's "American ___"
15 Come back
16 Shakespeare, the Bard of ___
17 1970 Richard Thomas film adapted from a Richard Bradford novel
20 Mao ___-tung
21 Hula shakers
22 To no ___ (uselessly)
23 Outlaws
24 Wall Street business
26 Jumped
29 Long baths
30 Ayatollah's land
31 Kunta ___ of "Roots"
32 Duo
35 1975 Al Pacino film
39 Lamb's mother
40 Landlord payments
41 Shrek, for one
42 Slight hangups
43 Reveries
45 Oilless paint
48 Cure
49 Lily family plants
50 Arias, usually
51 King topper
54 1941 Priscilla Lane film whose title was a #1 song
58 Advance, as money
59 Lollapalooza
60 Bridle strap
61 Football positions

62 "I'm innocent!"
63 Poet ___ St. Vincent Millay

DOWN

1 Earth
2 Midmonth date
3 Was transported
4 Raised railroads
5 Difficult
6 Harvests
7 Intermissions separate them
8 Silent
9 ___-am (sports competition)
10 Sail material
11 Birdlike
12 ___ boom
13 Corner
18 Mongol title
19 Fouler

23 Wedding reception staple
24 Type assortments
25 "I can't believe ___ . . ." (old ad catchphrase)
26 Lateral part
27 Ship's front
28 Fury
29 Sorts (through)
31 Australian hopper, for short
32 "Gladiator" garment
33 Fish bait
34 Halves of a 32-Across
36 James of "Gunsmoke"
37 Wine vintage
38 Christmas song
42 Zips (along)
43 X out
44 Cause for umbrellas

45 Billiards furniture
46 Actress Burstyn
47 Knoll
48 Yawn-inducing
50 Yards rushing, e.g.
51 Elderly
52 Goatee site
53 Sicilian volcano
55 Son of, in Arabic names
56 Recent: Prefix
57 Fury

by Frederick J. Healy

ACROSS

1 Gun-toting gal
5 ___ vu
9 Put forth, as a theory
14 Singer Brickell
15 Greek counterpart of 27-Down
16 Wonderland girl
17 Mediocre
18 "___, vidi, vici" (Caesar's boast)
19 Ohio birthplace of William McKinley
20 Bridge
23 Widespread
24 April 15 deadline agcy.
25 Fond du ___, Wis.
28 Take the witness stand
31 Classic muscle car
34 Caribbean resort island
36 "___ we having fun yet?"
37 Conclude, with "up"
38 Bridge
42 Spew
43 Washington's ___ Stadium
44 Below
45 Young fellow
46 Feature of Texaco's logo, once
49 Period in history
50 Sawbuck
51 Periods in history
53 Bridge
61 Ancient Greek marketplace
62 Prayer's end
63 Govern
64 Laser printer powder
65 Left, at sea
66 Vicinity
67 War horse
68 Some Father's Day callers
69 Sign of boredom

DOWN

1 Flat-topped hill
2 Reason to say "pee-yew!"
3 "Schindler's ___"
4 Sainted ninth-century pope
5 Concoct
6 Puts up, as a tower
7 Mitchell who sang "Big Yellow Taxi"
8 India's locale
9 Kitchen closet
10 Miscellanies
11 Building next to a barn
12 Noted rapper/actor
13 Radio host John
21 Deadly
22 Prisoner who'll never get out
25 Sports jacket feature
26 Inviting smell
27 Roman counterpart of 15-Across
29 Bulletin board stickers
30 Savings for old age: Abbr.
31 Exam mark
32 Worker with circus lions
33 "La Bohème," e.g.
35 Except that
37 Chicago-based Superstation
39 Where the action is
40 TV's "Mayberry ___"
41 German engraver Albrecht
46 Offer on a "Wanted" poster
47 Alehouse
48 C.I.A. operatives
50 Number of points for a field goal
52 Deodorant type
53 Stetsons, e.g.
54 Gershwin's "___ Rhythm"
55 Sold, to an auctioneer
56 Puppy sounds
57 1847 Melville novel
58 Mysterious quality
59 Whole bunch
60 Actor Connery

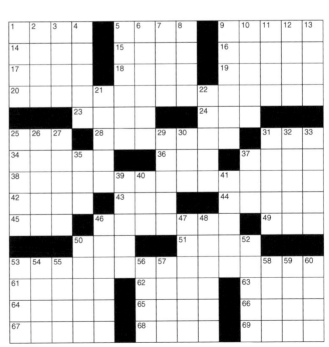

by Gregory E. Paul

ACROSS

1 True-blue
6 Toy gun poppers
10 Smooch
14 "Good Night" girl of song
15 Arthur ___ Stadium in Queens
16 Peak
17 River triangle
18 Signify
19 Horn's sound
20 Logic
23 ___ capita
24 Buffalo's lake
25 Money in the bank, e.g.
30 Declare
33 Seizes without authority
34 Old what's-___-name
35 George W. Bush's alma mater
36 Michael who starred in "Dirty Rotten Scoundrels"
37 Snorkeling accessory
38 Wolf calls
39 Broadway hit with 7,000+ performances
40 With it
41 Immobilize
42 Swelling reducer
43 Highway stops
45 Ritzy
46 Little rascal
47 Question of concern, with a hint to 20-, 25- and 43-Across
54 Corner square in Monopoly
55 Den
56 Unsophisticated
57 Loafing
58 Dublin's home
59 Lyrics accompany them

60 2000 "subway series" losers
61 Toy used on hills
62 Commence

DOWN

1 Eyeball covers
2 Nabisco cookie
3 Shout
4 Against
5 Weapon in the game of Clue
6 Tripod topper
7 On the open water
8 Adds gradually
9 Mexican misters
10 Couric of daytime talk
11 Computer symbol
12 Haze
13 Movie backdrop
21 Commies
22 Tiny criticism

25 Emmy-winner (finally!) Susan
26 Author ___ Bashevis Singer
27 Truly
28 Vases
29 Harbor sights
30 Took care of
31 Totally tired
32 Sí and oui
35 Quotable Yank
37 Swerve back and forth, as a car's rear end
38 Very short shorts
40 Big bothers
41 Soccer star Mia
43 Caught
44 In layers
45 Sees a ghost, maybe
47 Walk through water
48 Sword handle
49 Put on the payroll

50 Tightly stretched
51 Turner who sang "I Don't Wanna Fight"
52 At any time
53 Sabbath activity
54 ___-dandy

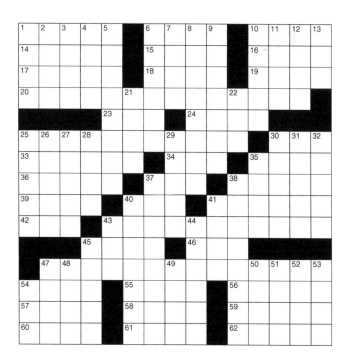

by Lynn Lempel

ACROSS

1 Literature Nobelist Bellow
5 Slender
9 Gregorian music style
14 Port or claret
15 Left a chair
16 Edmonton hockey player
17 Vicinity
18 Out of the wind
19 Handsome wood design
20 Place to pull in for a meal
23 Seafood in shells
24 Site of one-armed bandits
27 Place for a pig
28 New York ballplayer
29 Ryan of "When Harry Met Sally"
30 Four-star officer: Abbr.
31 F.D.R. radio broadcast
34 As well
37 Responses to a masseur
38 German chancellor ___ von Bismarck
39 Highest-priced boxing ticket
44 It may be served with crumpets
45 Snoop around
46 Old cable inits.
47 "Sesame Street" broadcaster
50 Modern affluent type
52 Teen meeting place
54 Kindly doctor's asset
57 Setting for Theseus and the Minotaur
59 Plumb crazy
60 Skin outbreak
61 Broadcasting
62 Whiskey drink
63 Display
64 Desires
65 Statement figures: Abbr.
66 "Bonanza" brother

DOWN

1 Groups of bees
2 Clear of stale smells
3 Apprehensive
4 Clues, to a detective
5 Movie preview
6 Not change course
7 "Gotcha"
8 Must-have item
9 Just-made-up word
10 Actor/dancer Gregory
11 O.K.
12 Org. that funds exhibits
13 Have a go at
21 Big rig
22 Decorated, as a cake
25 Well-groomed
26 Not fooled by
29 Fail to qualify, as for a team
31 London weather, often
32 That girl
33 Barracks bunk
34 Bohemian
35 In ___ of (replacing)
36 Vegetable in a crisp pod
40 Tarantulas, e.g.
41 Angers
42 Captivates
43 Tennis star Kournikova
47 Pullover raincoat
48 ___ Aires
49 Scatters, as petals
51 Mini, in Marseille
53 Grind, as teeth
55 Rick's love in "Casablanca"
56 Fate
57 It may be put out to pasture
58 Genetic stuff

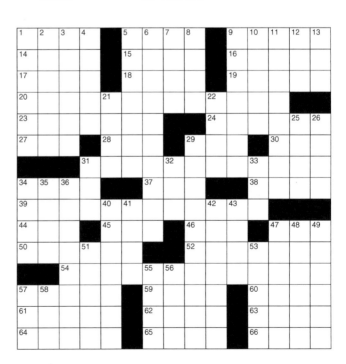

by Craig Kasper

ACROSS
1 End-of-week cry
5 Makes, as tea
10 Wise ___ owl
14 Folk singer Guthrie
15 Soprano Callas
16 Popular building block
17 1959 Doris Day/Rock Hudson comedy
19 Actress Singer of "Footloose"
20 Victor's entitlement
21 Errors
23 See 24-Across
24 With 23-Across, Neptune, e.g.
26 Back street
27 Clearance item's caveat
29 Wrestler's win
30 Had a bite
31 Disposable pen maker
32 Davenport
33 Church official
37 What a full insurance policy offers
40 Bronze and stainless steel
41 Bed size smaller than full
42 ___ Paul's seafood
43 Spider's prey
44 Conger or moray
45 Mosquito repellent ingredient
46 First lady after Hillary
49 Put two and two together?
50 California's Big ___
51 Evidence in court
53 Tetley competitor
56 Radio tuner
57 Piano player's aid
60 France, under Caesar

61 "___ Doone" (1869 novel)
62 Not us
63 Building additions
64 Vote into office
65 Jekyll's alter ego

DOWN
1 Bugler's evening call
2 Hang on tight?
3 Not according to Mr. Spock
4 Shakespearean volumes
5 Some luxury cars
6 Squealer
7 Time in history
8 "The Flintstones" mother
9 Pseudonym of H. H. Munro
10 Post-danger signal

11 1988 Olympics host
12 Be of one mind
13 Clamorous
18 Outdated
22 Lustrous fabric
24 Go (through), as evidence
25 Made into law
27 "Mamma Mia" pop group
28 Window box location
29 Verse-writing
30 Tablet with ibuprofen
32 Bygone space station
34 Averse to picture-taking
35 Meanie
36 Home in a tree
38 Without any extras

39 Was beholden to
45 University of Minnesota campus site
46 Overhang
47 Like some symmetry
48 Mover's rental
49 Playwright ___ Fugard
50 Uncle ___
52 Ireland, the Emerald ___
53 Ballpark figure?
54 Went out, as a fire
55 Pinnacle
58 Before, in 29-Down
59 Business letter abbr.

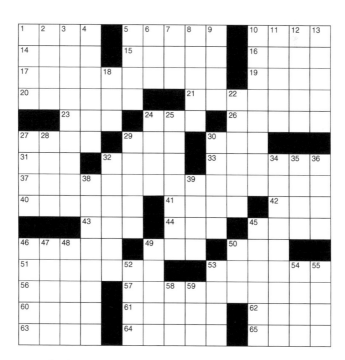

by Craig Kasper

60

ACROSS
1 Crossword pattern
5 Dinner and a movie, perhaps
9 No longer fresh
14 Prefix with space
15 Sharif of "Funny Girl"
16 Swatch competitor
17 Convention group
18 Sitarist Shankar
19 Christopher of "Superman"
20 Polyester, e.g.
23 Battering device
24 Words before tear or roll
25 Astroturf, e.g.
34 Everest or Ararat
35 Comic strip orphan
36 Country singer Brenda
37 Johnson of "Laugh-In"
38 Vision-related
39 Darn, as socks
40 Lunar New Year
41 Grand Canyon transport
42 Contemptible person
43 Oleomargarine, e.g.
46 Airport monitor abbr.
47 Blonde shade
48 Fake 50, e.g.
57 Throng
58 Banjo-plucking Scruggs
59 Hand lotion ingredient
60 Indy-winning Al Jr. or Sr.
61 Canal of song
62 It's trapped on laundry day
63 Sirs' counterparts
64 Give temporarily
65 Falls behind

DOWN
1 Chews the fat
2 Depend (on)
3 "Pumping ___"
4 Marxism, for one
5 Starting notes in music
6 Amo, amas, ___ . . .
7 Rikki-tikki-___
8 Guitarist Clapton
9 Eerie
10 Item of men's jewelry
11 From the United States: Abbr.
12 Jeans purveyor Strauss
13 Business V.I.P.
21 Sword handle
22 ___ acid (B vitamin)
25 Maker of precious violins
26 Composer/author Ned
27 ___-frutti
28 Isle in the Bay of Naples
29 Emcee's spiel
30 Negatively charged particle
31 Alaskan native
32 "Common" thing that's not always common
33 Passover feast
38 Bizarre
39 Closet larvae repellent
41 Does deals without money
42 Earthy desire
44 Bicycle for two
45 Tried to save a sinking boat
48 Buddy
49 One of the O'Neills
50 ___ Major
51 Rod's partner
52 Price of a ride
53 "___ go bragh"
54 Pelvic bones
55 Beyond the end line
56 Answer to "Shall we?"

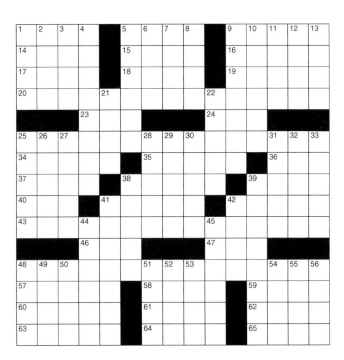

by Sarah Keller

ACROSS

1 What a surfer rides
5 Do agricultural work
9 Pre-euro German money
14 Violinist Leopold
15 Side squared, for a square
16 When added up
17 Porn classification
19 AM/FM device
20 Rainbow's shape
21 Attractive
23 Nova ___
26 Battle exhortations
27 Followers of the Vatican
29 Dockworker's org.
30 Postponed
31 Driver entitled to free maps, perhaps
37 Sprinted
38 Grp. battling consumer fraud
39 Genetic letters
40 Big shoe request
44 Accumulate
46 Lumberjack's tool
47 Binds, as wounds
49 Sign-making aids
54 Gets the soap off
55 Part of a grandfather clock
56 "Then what . . . ?"
57 Handy ___ (good repairmen)
58 English king during the American Revolution
63 Feed, as a fire
64 Jazz's Fitzgerald
65 Horse color
66 Customs
67 Leave in, to a proofreader
68 At the ocean's bottom, as a ship

DOWN

1 Floor application
2 Secondary, as an outlet: Abbr.
3 Annoy
4 Inconsistent
5 Wealthy sort, slangily
6 ___ Ben Canaan of "Exodus"
7 Extend a subscription
8 ___ cum laude
9 Act of God
10 Horrid glances from Charles Grodin?
11 Hub projections
12 Kevin of "A Fish Called Wanda"
13 Wades (through)
18 Stand up
22 Bad, as a prognosis
23 Mold's origin
24 Something not really on Mars
25 Hypothesize
28 Kemo ___ (the Lone Ranger)
32 Pres. Lincoln
33 Help in crime
34 Button material
35 Follow
36 Metal filers
41 Beard named for a Flemish artist
42 Forgives
43 Astronaut Armstrong
44 Imitating
45 Darners
48 Mount where an ark parked
49 Charley horse, e.g.
50 ___-one (long odds)
51 Witch of ___
52 Olympic sleds
53 Refine, as metal
59 Bullring call
60 Debtor's note
61 Writer Fleming
62 It's kept in a pen

by Patrick Merrell

ACROSS

1 Food lover's sense
6 Home for alligators
11 "Open ___ 9" (shop sign)
14 Pays to play poker
15 Talk show group
16 Early afternoon hour
17 "Pronto!"
19 Tribe related to the Hopi
20 Historic times
21 Use a hose on, as a garden
23 Rev. William who originated the phrase "a blushing crow"
27 "What so ___ we hailed . . ."
29 Singer Don of the Eagles
30 Opt for
31 Parking lot posting
32 Dahl who wrote "Charlie and the Chocolate Factory"
33 Subject of "worship"
36 Sound in a cave
37 Pocketbook
38 Ditty
39 Itsy-bitsy
40 Free-for-all
41 "I do" sayer
42 "Tom ___" (#1 Kingston Trio hit)
44 Smashed and grabbed
45 Adds up (to)
47 "___ keepers . . ."
48 Boxing matches
49 Skin soother
50 Sphere
51 "Pronto!"
58 Gibson who was People magazine's first Sexiest Man Alive
59 Hair-raising

60 Dickens's ___ Heep
61 "Later!"
62 Coral ridges
63 Shindig

DOWN

1 Bar bill
2 At ___ rate
3 Mudhole
4 Golf ball support
5 Ancient Jewish sect
6 Javelin
7 The "W" in V.F.W.
8 Plus
9 "Oh, give ___ home . . ."
10 Layered building material
11 "Pronto!"
12 Computer chip company
13 Suspicious
18 Card below a four
22 "The Sound of Music" setting: Abbr.
23 Nagging sort
24 Result of a treaty
25 "Pronto!"
26 Skillet lubricant
27 Moon stage
28 Part in a play
30 Actor Feldman
32 Contest specifications
34 Below
35 Requires
37 Hit with snowballs, say
38 Walked on
40 Loch Ness dweller, they say
41 Studies hard
43 Ump's call
44 Animal with a cub
45 Mushroom cloud maker

46 Amsterdam of "The Dick Van Dyke Show"
47 Goes by jet
49 "___ I care!"
52 Part of a giggle
53 Bad temper
54 ___-la-la
55 Atmosphere
56 Turner who led a revolt
57 "___ will be done"

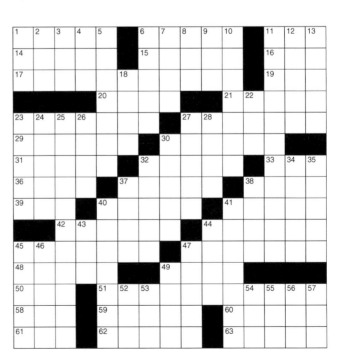

by Gregory E. Paul

ACROSS

1 Big blowout
5 Vehicles with meters
9 Like some committees
14 Charles Lamb's nom de plume
15 Cookie with creme inside
16 Takes a card from the pile
17 Where to order egg salad
18 Flintstone fellow
19 Designer Karan
20 Practically gives away
23 Whole lot
24 Restless
27 Bandleader Shaw
29 Big galoots
31 "Vive le ___!"
32 Faint from rapture
33 Waterless
34 Mulligatawny, for one
35 Starts telling a different story
38 Theme park attraction
39 Bringing up the rear
40 Magician's rods
41 Gallery display
42 One who's suckered
43 Voting districts
44 Pushed snow aside
46 Saucy
47 Prepares to be punished
53 Desperately want
55 Homeboy's turf
56 Hurry up
57 Macho guys
58 English princess
59 River in an Agatha Christie title
60 Apply, as pressure

61 Not the original color
62 Meal in a pot

DOWN

1 People retire to these spots
2 Toward the sheltered side
3 Window feature
4 Dangerous bit of precipitation
5 Morning eyeopener
6 Turn signal
7 Brewski
8 Word after baking or club
9 Extras
10 Speak in a monotone
11 Loiter
12 Part of B.Y.O.B.
13 Jefferson Davis org.

21 David's weapon, in the Bible
22 Soft leather
25 Pings and dings
26 "Holy mackerel!"
27 Spinning
28 Celebrity's upward path
29 Cropped up
30 Pub offering
32 Throw out
33 "On the double!"
34 Bravura performances
36 Escape the detection of
37 Bunch of bees
42 Not half bad
43 Pulled dandelions, say
45 Be indecisive
46 Give a buzz
48 Certain herring

49 Chichi
50 Clubs or hearts
51 Capri, for one
52 Enjoy some gum
53 Friend of Fidel
54 Mystery author Stout

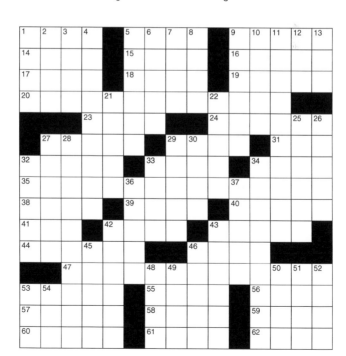

by Nancy Salomon and Kendall Twigg

ACROSS

1 Musical genre pioneered by Bill Haley and His Comets
5 Cove
10 Partner of ready and willing
14 Unattractive tropical fruit
15 Voting site
16 Hit with the fist
17 Sunbather's award?
19 Sandwich fish
20 Still
21 Before, in poetry
22 Interpret without hearing
24 1051 on monuments
25 Edward who wrote "The Owl and the Pussycat"
26 Temples in the Far East
30 Assassinating
33 Old-time actress Massey
34 Join, in woodworking
36 La Paz is its cap.
37 President after Tyler
38 Sun-bleached
39 "__ Ben Adhem," Leigh Hunt poem
40 Finish
41 Duelist Burr
42 Was bright, as the sun
43 Mark for misconduct
45 Gas ratings
47 Kuwaiti leader
48 Sun or planet
49 Depot baggage handlers
52 Actress Joanne
53 Next-to-last Greek letter
56 Wings: Lat.
57 Romantics' awards?
60 1/500 of the Indianapolis 500

61 Have a mad crush on
62 Colorful gem
63 [No bid]
64 Changed direction, as a ship
65 Actor Billy of "Titanic"

DOWN

1 Slippers' color in "The Wizard of Oz"
2 Shrek, for one
3 Blood problem
4 One of the same bloodline
5 Portugal and Spain together
6 Snout
7 Auction unit
8 List-ending abbr.
9 Tickled pink
10 Off course
11 Sad person's award?
12 Moon goddess
13 Old-time exclamation
18 Mrs. F. Scott Fitzgerald
23 Nectar source
24 Neurotic TV detective played by Tony Shalhoub
26 Spoke (up)
27 On one's own
28 Big recording artists' awards?
29 Brainy
30 Dictation taker
31 Nary a soul
32 Affixes (to)
35 Wedding 58-Down
38 Good sportsmanship
39 "Moby-Dick" captain
41 Song for a diva
42 Olympic gymnast Kerri

44 Roasts' hosts
46 __ beef
49 Entrance to an expressway
50 Director Kazan
51 Scotch's partner
52 Dreadful
53 Insect stage
54 Go across
55 __ of Man
58 See 35-Down
59 Family relation, for short

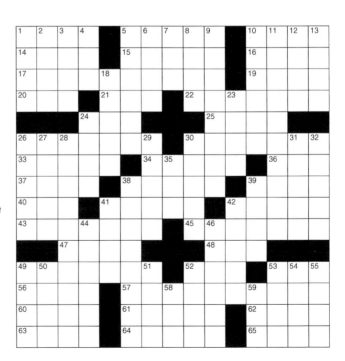

by Bernice Gordon

ACROSS

1 Mall component
6 Genesis twin
10 Fly like an eagle
14 Hiker's path
15 Goatee's locale
16 Time for eggnog
17 Having no entryways?
19 A.A.A. recommendations: Abbr.
20 Left on a map
21 How some ham sandwiches are made
22 Letter after theta
23 Disney World attraction
25 Opposite of whole, milkwise
27 "French" dog
30 "I'm ready to leave"
32 Down Under bird
33 Britannica, for one: Abbr.
35 "Thanks, Pierre!"
38 Squeal (on)
39 ___ standstill (motionless)
40 City that Fred Astaire was "flying down to" in a 1933 hit
42 "Dear old" family member
43 Jogs
45 Looks sullen
47 Poetic palindrome
48 Tributary
50 Word before Nevada or Leone
52 Hold back
54 Give a benediction to
56 Ball field covering
57 Motionless
59 Campaign funders, for short
63 Buffalo's lake
64 Having no vision?

66 Submarine danger
67 Number between dos and cuatro
68 Weird
69 Habitual tipplers
70 Gumbo vegetable
71 Modify to particular conditions

DOWN

1 Put in the hold
2 "___ Grit" (John Wayne film)
3 Quaker ___
4 Ran amok
5 Santa's little helper
6 Commercial prefix with Lodge
7 In a moment
8 Bright and breezy
9 Still in the out-box, as mail
10 Injection selection
11 Having no commandment?
12 Prince Valiant's wife
13 Plopped down again
18 Museum guide
24 Delighted
26 Gradual absorption method
27 Saucy
28 Bradley or Sharif
29 Having no typeset letters?
31 Stocking shade
34 Where to watch whales in Massachusetts, with "the"
36 Writer John Dickson ___
37 Inkling
41 "The only thing we have to fear is fear ___": F.D.R.

44 Prairie homes
46 It goes around the world
49 Mississippi River explorer
51 Caught sight of
52 Agenda details
53 The first part missing in the author's name ___ Vargas ___
55 The second part missing in the author's name ___ Vargas ___
58 Istanbul resident
60 Taj Mahal locale
61 Intel product
62 Typesetting mark
65 Poseidon's domain

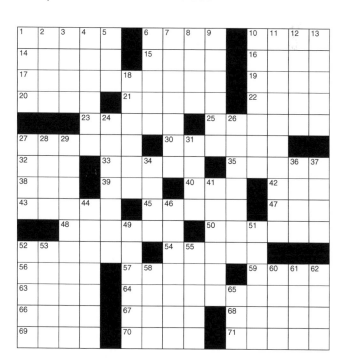

by Holden Baker

ACROSS

1 Pitches four balls to
6 Cain's brother
10 Insurrectionist Turner and others
14 Not reacting chemically
15 Muse of history
16 Monogram part: Abbr.
17 Pilfer
18 Kitchen gadget that turns
20 "Faster!"
22 No great ___
23 Iced tea flavoring
26 Full complement of fingers
27 Sob
30 Before, in poetry
31 Classic gas brand
34 Composer Rachmaninoff
36 Midsection muscles, for short
37 "Faster!"
40 Knight's title
41 Rat or squirrel
42 Dye containers
43 Western Indian
44 Linear, for short
45 Rope-a-dope boxer
47 Fixes
49 1960s–'70s space program
52 "Faster!"
57 Cramped space
59 Rich cake
60 Primer dog
61 Sharif of film
62 Gives an audience to
63 Band with the 1988 #1 hit "Need You Tonight"
64 Monthly payment
65 Birds by sea cliffs

DOWN

1 Bit of smoke
2 Contrarians
3 Bloodsucker
4 Volcano that famously erupted in 1883
5 Acts of the Apostles writer
6 Bank holdings: Abbr.
7 Dull
8 Mozart's "a"
9 Circle
10 Daughter of a sister, perhaps
11 Ben Stiller's mother
12 Bit of business attire
13 Narrow water passage: Abbr.
19 Washed-out
21 Money for retirement
24 What a satellite may be in
25 Digs with twigs?
27 Kennel club info
28 "Son of ___!"
29 Had a cow
31 ___ salts
32 Luxury hotel accommodations
33 Safe
35 Mahler's "Das Lied von der ___"
38 Snowman of song
39 Villain
46 Can't stand
48 Amounts in red numbers
49 Notify
50 Ship's navigation system
51 Weird
53 Norse thunder god
54 Terse directive to a chauffeur
55 Panache
56 "___ of the D'Urbervilles"
57 Popular TV police drama
58 The WB competitor

by M. Francis Vuolo

ACROSS

1 Poi source
5 "The Thin Man" dog
9 Rum-soaked cakes
14 Stench
15 Where an honoree may sit
16 Friend, south of the border
17 Rocket scientist's employer
18 Prefix with potent
19 Alpine song
20 Not much
23 ___ glance (quickly)
24 Center of activity
25 Grammys, e.g.
29 Tip for a ballerina
31 Aide: Abbr.
35 Funnel-shaped
36 Craze
38 Hurry
39 Activities that generate no money
42 Surgery spots, for short
43 Indians of New York
44 Jack who ate no fat
45 Seeded loaves
47 Dog-tag wearers, briefly
48 Choirs may stand on them
49 Overly
51 Loser to D.D.E. twice
52 Boatswains, e.g.
59 R-rated, say
61 Poker payment
62 Confess
63 Tutu material
64 Rude look
65 Peru's capital
66 Back tooth
67 Slips
68 Fizzless, as a soft drink

DOWN

1 Cargo weights
2 Sandler of "Big Daddy"
3 Painter Bonheur
4 Face-to-face exam
5 Takes as one's own
6 Pago Pago's land
7 Salon application
8 Where Nepal is
9 Louisiana waterway
10 Microscopic organism
11 Bridge declarations
12 Questionnaire datum
13 Note after fa
21 Scottish beau
22 "A League of ___ Own" (1992 comedy)
25 Cast member
26 "What, me ___?"
27 Liqueur flavorer
28 Speed (up)
29 Blackmailer's evidence
30 Burden
32 English county
33 Ravi Shankar's instrument
34 Checkups
36 1052, in a proclamation
37 St. Francis' birthplace
40 Lingo
41 Raises
46 "A Streetcar Named Desire" woman
48 Directs (to)
50 Stream bank cavorter
51 "___ you" ("You go first")
52 Clout
53 Connecticut campus
54 Unique individual
55 Ranch newborn
56 Diabolical
57 Capital south of Venezia
58 Whack
59 Bank amenity, for short
60 Pair

by Joy C. Frank

68

ACROSS

1 Tree that people carve their initials in
6 Pepper's partner
10 Author Dinesen
14 Stevenson of 1950s politics
15 Dunkable cookie
16 Plot parcel
17 "Dee-licious!"
19 Alum
20 Carson's predecessor on "The Tonight Show"
21 Surgeon's outfit
23 Play parts
26 Goes to sleep, with "off"
29 Skirt lines
30 Bangkok native
31 Like snow after a blizzard, perhaps
33 Corrosions
35 Eyelid problem
36 Spanish aunt
39 Crying
42 Evangeline or Anna Karenina, e.g.
44 What candles sometimes represent
45 "Very funny!"
47 Animal nose
48 Show biz parent
52 Go left or right
53 Petri dish filler
54 Where the Himalayas are
55 Not in port
56 Main arteries
58 Den
60 High spirits
61 "Dee-licious!"
67 Fanny
68 Certain woodwind
69 Pitcher Martínez
70 Painting and sculpting, e.g.
71 Yards advanced
72 Animal in a roundup

DOWN

1 San Francisco/ Oakland separator
2 School's Web site address ender
3 Shade tree
4 Where a tent is pitched
5 "Howdy!"
6 Grow sick of
7 Quarterback's asset
8 Moon lander, for short
9 Santa's sackful
10 "Amen!"
11 "Dee-licious!"
12 Saudis and Iraqis
13 Classic sneakers
18 American, abroad
22 Bar "where everybody knows your name"
23 Skylit lobbies
24 Newswoman Connie
25 "Dee-licious!"
27 ___ Moines
28 Genesis son
32 Color, as an Easter egg
34 African desert
37 Get used (to)
38 MetLife competitor
40 Scandal sheet
41 Where the Mets could once be met
43 Perfectly precise
46 Mornings, briefly
49 Spuds
50 Some Texas tycoons
51 "Just the facts, ___"
53 One who hears "You've got mail"
56 Taj Mahal site
57 Urban haze
59 Little devils
62 Entrepreneur's deg.
63 "Who, me?"
64 "___ to Joy"
65 Mine find
66 "Le Coq ___"

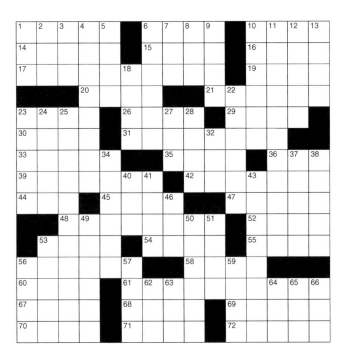

by Nancy Salomon and Kyle Mahowald

ACROSS

1 Tow
5 From County Clare, e.g.
10 ___ pet (onetime fad item)
14 "The Thin Man" pooch
15 Off-limits
16 "Crazy" bird
17 Manual transmission
19 "What've you been ___?"
20 Politely
21 High-spirited horse
23 Swap
24 From one side to the other
26 Shade of beige
28 Warwick who sang "Walk On By"
32 Tree branch
36 Makes a row in a garden, say
38 "Hasta la vista!"
39 Operatic solo
40 Academy Award
42 Fighting, often with "again"
43 Goes off on a mad tangent
45 With 22-Down, Korea's location
46 Bone-dry
47 Moose or mouse
49 Perlman of "Cheers"
51 Upstate New York city famous for silverware
53 Twinkie's filling
58 Versatile legume
61 Entraps
62 Jai ___
63 Lakeshore rental, perhaps
66 Lass
67 Between, en français
68 Taking a break from work

69 One of two wives of Henry VIII
70 Hem again
71 Loch ___ monster

DOWN

1 Lacks, quickly
2 Up and about
3 Ancient city NW of Carthage
4 Tied, as shoes
5 ___-bitsy
6 Shout from the bleachers
7 There: Lat.
8 Until now
9 Souped-up car
10 Standard drink mixers
11 Arizona tribe
12 Tiny amount
13 Shortly
18 Swiss artist Paul ___

22 See 45-Across
24 Came up
25 What a TV host reads from
27 Funnywoman Margaret
29 Evening, in ads
30 Dark film genre, informally
31 Villa d'___
32 "___ Croft Tomb Raider" (2001 film)
33 Tehran's land
34 Prefix with skirt or series
35 Transportation for the Dynamic Duo
37 Bird's name in "Peter and the Wolf"
41 Numbered rd.
44 Of sound mind
48 Frog, at times

50 Unappealing skin condition
52 Idiotic
54 1990s Israeli P.M.
55 Wear away
56 Breakfast, lunch and dinner
57 Kefauver of 1950s politics
58 The "Star Wars" trilogy, for one
59 Actress Lena
60 Folksy tale
61 Whole bunch
64 Alcoholic's woe
65 Rapper Dr. ___

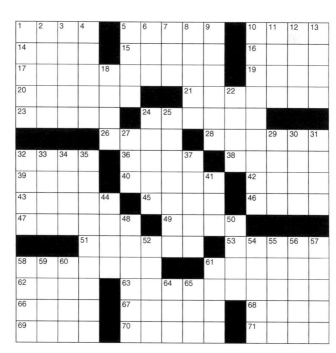

by Jeffrey Harris

ACROSS

1. Child by marriage
8. Downtown Chicago
15. Percentage listed in an I.R.S. booklet
16. "Good shot!"
17. Woman who's "carrying"
19. Anger, with "up"
20. Summer: Fr.
21. Coin opening
22. Lottery player's exultant cry
23. Obstreperous
26. Wash
27. Put on board, as cargo
28. ___ constrictor
29. Bits of land in la Méditerranée
30. Ogled
31. Yankee Stadium locale, with "the"
33. Role
34. "Vive ___!" (old French cheer)
35. Trail
39. Uncles' mates
40. Shakespearean king
44. On the ocean
45. Schubert's Symphony No. 8 ___ Minor
46. Wheel turner
47. Pie pans
48. Patronizes a library
51. Italian resort on the Adriatic
52. Founded: Abbr.
53. Bill Clinton's relig. affiliation
54. New-___ (devotee of crystals and incense)
55. Traditional end of summer
60. Lenders, often
61. International alliance
62. Summed
63. Appetizer

DOWN

1. Germless
2. What a plane rolls along
3. Go off, as a bomb
4. Dressed up in a fussy way
5. Anatomical pouch
6. Playful aquatic animal
7. "Pretty amazing!"
8. Boom producer, for short
9. "She Done ___ Wrong"
10. Environmental prefix
11. Accidentally reveal
12. "Sexy!"
13. Bogey, in golf
14. Most cheeky
18. Maternity ward arrival
24. Start of a forbiddance
25. Vertical line on a graph
31. Former British P.M. Tony
32. Get together with old classmates, say
35. Kneecap
36. "Let me repeat . . ."
37. Covered place to sleep
38. Committed, as an act
40. Staples Center player, for short
41. Requiring immediate attention
42. Somewhat firm, as pasta
43. Organize differently, as troops
49. 1920s vice president Charles
50. Paid out
56. Wand
57. R&B band ___ Hill
58. Nile viper
59. Greek letter

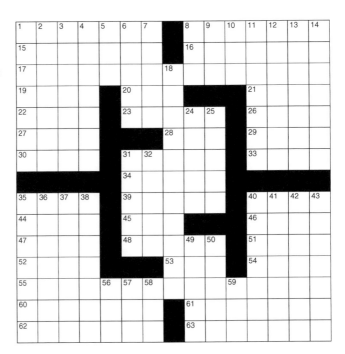

by Michael Shteyman

ACROSS

1 Raindrop sound
5 Sgt., e.g.
8 Present for a teacher
13 Kelly of morning TV
14 Marlboro alternative
15 Shine
16 Son of Isaac
17 Metal that Superman can't see through
18 On again, as a candle
19 Fashionable London locale
21 Ardor
22 Big containers
23 Filmmaker Spike
24 G.M. sports car
27 Whitewater part of a stream
30 Fireplace accessory
32 U.K. record label
33 Cast member
36 Hits head-on
37 Get help of a sort on "Who Wants to Be a Millionaire"
41 Wriggling fishes
42 Place
43 Tit for ___
44 Teems
47 Zoo denizens
49 Something "on the books"
50 Motorists' grp.
51 Skier's transport
52 Quick job for a barber
54 Sweater
58 To no ___ (purposelessly)
60 Classic artist's subject
61 Sandwich spread, for short
62 Oscar who wrote "The Picture of Dorian Gray"
63 Popular shirt label

64 Certain stock index
65 Los Angeles cager
66 Craggy hill
67 Agile

DOWN

1 Make ready, for short
2 Elvis's daughter ___ Marie
3 Milky gem
4 1960s–'70s pontiff
5 December songs
6 Fuel from a mine
7 Bygone
8 Consented
9 Bit of begging
10 Educational assistance since 1972
11 China's Chou En-___
12 Expert in resuscitation, in brief
14 Coffee gathering
20 Angry with
21 ___ state (blissful self-awareness)
23 Lash of old westerns
25 Frisky feline
26 Beginnings
27 Statute removal
28 Itsy-bitsy creature
29 Bedtime gab
31 Anger
34 Actress Allen of "Enough"
35 Cheerios grain
38 Baton Rouge sch.
39 Tried a little of this, a little of that
40 Rarely-met goal
45 Hammer user
46 Hoover ___
48 Scents
51 Henry VIII's family name
53 Travel on horseback
54 Mario who wrote "The Godfather"
55 Seductress
56 Witness
57 Classic theater name
58 Leatherworker's tool
59 By way of
60 Annual hoops contest, for short

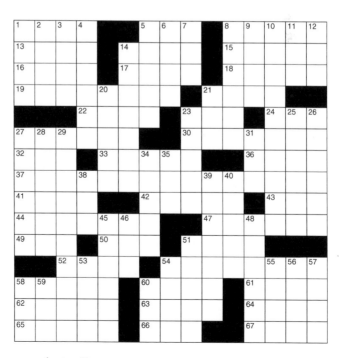

by Jay Giess

72

ACROSS

1 Go to sea
5 Feet above sea
level: Abbr.
9 Boston's airport
14 Stubborn
animal
15 Ear part
16 Ex-Mrs. Trump
17 Fitzgerald who
sang "I'm Making
Believe"
18 University V.I.P.
19 Car parker
20 Decreed
23 ___ foil
24 Before, in verse
25 Fleming of 007
fame
26 Bad mark
28 Discontinued
29 Lacking muscle
33 Writer Welty
35 Throng
36 Document of legal
representation
40 Liqueur flavoring
41 Armadas
42 Nary a soul
43 Injection units, for
short
44 Relaxed
48 Tree swinger
49 Joanne of "Sylvia,"
1965
50 1959 hit song
about "a man
named Charlie"
51 Children's game
56 Easy gallops
57 Bad place to drop a
heavy box
58 Landed (on)
59 Florida city
60 Advantage
61 Ready for
picking
62 Like sea air
63 Flagmaker Betsy
64 1930s boxer
Max

DOWN

1 Refines, as metal
2 How some café is
served
3 "Fighting" Big Ten
team
4 Starring role
5 Fabled New
World city
6 "Camelot"
composer
7 Israel's Abba
8 Open the
windows in
9 Jazz up
10 Running track
11 Festive party
12 Again
13 ___ King Cole
21 Shy
22 "This ___ better
be good!"
27 Honkers
28 Rigorous exams
29 On the downslide
30 Sea eagle
31 Lemon or lime drink
32 C minor, for one
34 Unbalanced
35 Spa feature
36 Criticize, as a movie
37 Plastic ___ Band
38 Victory
39 Fragrant flowers
43 Overseer of co.
books
45 Earhart who
disappeared over the
Pacific
46 Skunk feature
47 It immediately follows
Passiontide
48 Examine, as ore
49 Bottom of the barrel
51 ___-Cola
52 Iridescent stone
53 Skin
54 One slow on
the uptake
55 Cutting remark
56 The "L" of L.A.

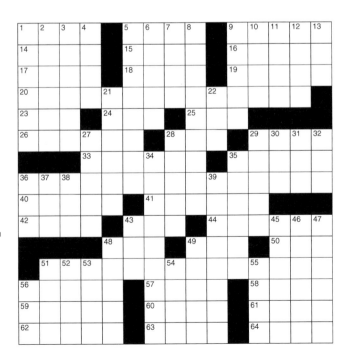

by A. J. Santora

ACROSS

1 Leaf's support
5 Knife
9 Wood for chests
14 Like a lemon
15 Medal of honor recipient
16 "Stayin' ___" (disco hit)
17 Prison sentence
18 Therefore
19 Without a stitch on
20 Eventually
23 The "M" in MSG
24 Calif.'s northern neighbor
25 Ewe's mate
28 Main school team
31 Valedictorian's pride, for short
34 Make amends (for)
36 Ubiquitous bug
37 QB Tarkenton
38 Daring bet
42 Whom Ingrid played in "Casablanca"
43 Pea container
44 Many a John Wayne film
45 Spanish cheer
46 Most sore
49 Tricky
50 Title car in a 1964 pop hit
51 Have to have
53 Availability extremes
59 Alaskan islander
60 Lifeguard's watch
61 "___ honest with you . . ."
63 The vowel sound in "dude"
64 That girl, in Paris
65 Problem with a fishing line
66 Excited, with "up"
67 Funnyman Foxx
68 Stringed toy

DOWN

1 Jet decommissioned in '03
2 They may get stepped on
3 Continental "dollar"
4 1983 role reversal film
5 The Ramones' "___ Is a Punk Rocker"
6 Extreme fear
7 Jason's ship, in myth
8 Unmannered fellow
9 Bird in a cage
10 Gladden
11 Dutch embankment
12 Swear to
13 Bloodshot
21 "The Catcher in the Rye," e.g.
22 Game with a drawing
25 The "R" of NPR
26 Polynesian island
27 Cat's quarry
29 Noted New York restaurateur
30 A home away from home
31 Southern breakfast dish
32 Discussion group
33 Incensed
35 Hoops grp.
37 Home loan agcy.
39 Disney's ___ Center
40 "That feels good!"
41 Carving on a pole
46 Offered for breeding, as a thoroughbred
47 Wrap up
48 Made airtight
50 Measuring tool
52 Scatterbrained
53 Ice sheet
54 Start of a counting-out rhyme
55 0 on a phone: Abbr.
56 Play part
57 Talking on a cell phone during a movie, e.g.
58 Online auction house
59 Chemical base: Abbr.
62 Swellheadedness

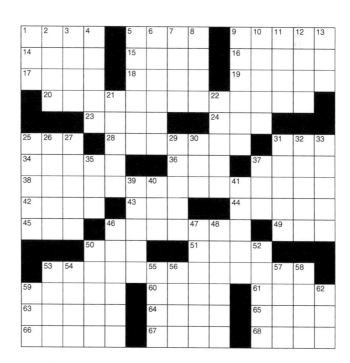

by Gregory E. Paul

ACROSS

1 Used a broom
6 Opened just a crack
10 Doesn't guzzle
14 Place for a barbecue
15 "Uh-uh"
16 Threaded fastener
17 Proverb
18 Managed, with "out"
19 ___ avis (unusual one)
20 Bathroom fixture sales representative?
23 Way to the top of a mountain
26 Stave off
27 Hanging sculpture in Alabama?
32 Alleviated
33 Words said on the way out the door
34 E.M.T.'s skill
37 Pub drinks
38 Gasps for air
39 "Scram!"
40 Dashed
41 Sunday newspaper color feature
42 Continue downhill without pedaling
43 Warsaw refinement?
45 G-rated
48 Accustoms
49 Majestic summer time?
54 Solar emissions
55 Really big show
56 Lubricated
60 Victim of a prank
61 Choir voice
62 State fund-raiser
63 Retired fliers, for short
64 Spinks or Trotsky
65 Company in a 2001–02 scandal

DOWN

1 Hot springs locale
2 Bankroll
3 When a plane should get in: Abbr.
4 Dirty places
5 Initial progress on a tough problem
6 From a fresh angle
7 Wisecrack
8 Copycat
9 Cincinnati team
10 Endeavored
11 Dumbstruck
12 Less adulterated
13 Sudden jump
21 Be behind in payments
22 50-50 share
23 Besmirch
24 Down Under critter
25 "A Doll's House" playwright
28 Dolphins' venue
29 Onetime Dodges
30 Mess up
31 Contingencies
34 Committee head
35 Search party
36 Some I.R.A.'s, informally
38 One in the legislative biz
39 "Eureka!" cause
41 Swindles
42 TV cabinet
43 Purposes of commas
44 Little, in Lille
45 Deck of 52
46 Hawaiian feasts
47 "Aïda" setting
50 Bluish green
51 Car rod
52 "What've you been ___?"
53 Hired thug
57 Epistle: Abbr.
58 W.W. II arena
59 Underworld boss

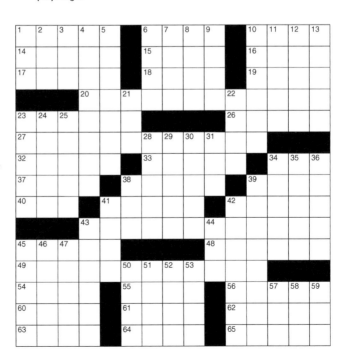

by Seth A. Abel

ACROSS

1 The "D" of D.J.
5 Huge hit
10 Nile reptiles
14 Great Salt Lake's state
15 Cosmetician Lauder
16 Junk e-mail
17 "The Price Is Right" phrase
19 Trig function
20 Eugene O'Neill's "___ for the Misbegotten"
21 Some necklines do this
23 Flatters, with "up"
26 Egypt's capital
27 2004 Olympics city
28 Made a cashless transaction
31 Accomplisher
32 Up, on a map
33 Chicago-to-Atlanta dir.
34 Factory-emissions testing grp.
35 "The Weakest Link" phrase
37 Photo ___ (picture-taking times)
38 Cotton ___
39 Bassoon's smaller cousins
40 Et ___ (and others)
41 Protective wear for airborne toxins
43 Wonder to behold
45 Nursery supplies
46 "___ Gump"
47 Oreo fillings
49 Wonderland cake message
50 Loooong sandwich
51 "Family Feud" phrase
56 Wading bird
57 Painting stand
58 Cafeteria carrier
59 Space shuttle launcher
60 Attire
61 "The ___ the limit"

DOWN

1 French nobleman
2 "How was ___ know?"
3 ___ Adams, patriot with a beer named after him
4 One peeking at answers on a test
5 Spanish gents
6 1980s PCs ran on it
7 Lots and lots
8 Finish, with "up"
9 All-female get-together
10 State confidently to
11 "Wheel of Fortune" phrase
12 Sign of hunger
13 "Peter Pan" pirate
18 Future indicator
22 Like a ballerina's body
23 No-goodnik
24 Paradise
25 "Jeopardy!" phrase
26 Atkins diet concerns, briefly
28 ___ well (is a good sign)
29 Glimpses
30 Make potable, as sea water
32 Partner of crannies
35 Flip out
36 Fanatical
40 Handcuffs
42 Brunch cocktail
43 Roadside stops
44 The Cadets, in college sports
46 Ones you just adore
47 Goatee's locale
48 Singer McEntire
49 Gaelic tongue
52 Former Mideast grp.
53 Noah's craft
54 Palindromic cheer
55 Part of CBS: Abbr.

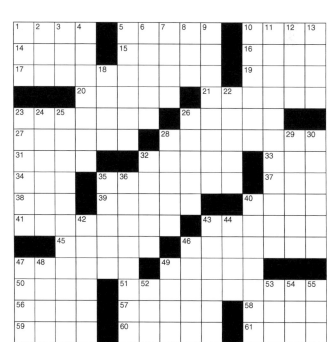

by Jim Hyres

ACROSS

1 How ham may be served in a sandwich
6 Popular kitchen wrap
11 Tiny bit, as of hair cream
14 Oscar Mayer product
15 Skip to the altar
16 Billy Joel's "___ to Extremes"
17 The Bard
19 Judges administer it
20 Hammed it up
21 Thick urban air condition
23 City where "Ulysses" is set
26 Item carried by a dog walker
28 Columbus sch.
29 "Mona Lisa" features that "follow" the viewer
32 Years, to Cicero
33 Large bays
35 PIN points
37 Concept
40 Shopping ___
41 Theme of this puzzle
42 Shopping ___
43 ___ Romeo (Italian car)
44 G.M. car
45 Birth-related
46 Ancient South American
48 Meditative exercises
50 Spanish "that"
51 Lions and tigers and bears
54 Stage comments to the audience
56 Alternative
57 Safes
60 Turncoat
61 Very scary
66 Spanish cheer
67 Synthetic fiber

68 Continental money
69 Neither's partner
70 Mexican money
71 Gaucho's rope

DOWN

1 Delivery room docs, for short
2 "I don't think so"
3 Major TV brand
4 Bumpkin
5 Foes
6 Equinox mo.
7 Out of the wind, at sea
8 All of them lead to Rome, they say
9 Tax mo.
10 Liam of "Schindler's List"
11 Run-down
12 Staring
13 Shady garden spot

18 Major TV brand
22 One of the friends on "Friends"
23 Bedrock belief
24 Commonplace
25 Waver of a red cape
27 Throw, as dice
30 Count's counterpart
31 Pore over
34 Projecting rim on a pipe
36 Japanese soup
38 Wipe out
39 World book
41 Pillow filler
45 Not as nice
47 Drive-in restaurant server
49 Grand party
51 Element with the symbol B
52 Author Calvino

53 Lesser of two ___
55 It's debatable
58 Suffix with buck
59 Big coffee holders
62 With 64-Down, reply to "Am too!"
63 Tax adviser's recommendation, for short
64 See 62-Down
65 Fed. property overseer

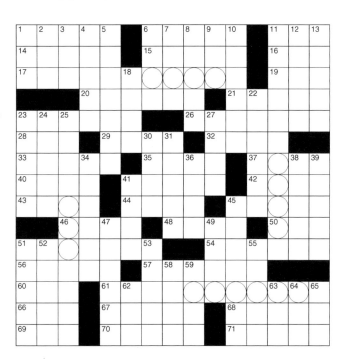

by Steve Kahn

ACROSS

1 "So long!"
5 Burden
9 Museo in Madrid
14 Death notice
15 It follows song or slug
16 Pine exudation
17 Gets together in person
20 "Blondie" or "Beetle Bailey"
21 Tennis champ Steffi
22 Vegetable that rolls
23 Narrow street
26 Jannings of old movies
28 Confronts, with "with"
34 "___ Baba and the 40 Thieves"
35 "Kiss me" miss
36 Tangle
37 Dietary no-no for Mrs. Sprat
39 Holds on to
42 Tiny weight
43 Former Argentine dictator
45 Actress Patricia of "The Subject Was Roses"
47 Drunkard's woe, for short
48 Returns a gaze
52 Ugandan tyrant Idi ___
53 Rules, shortly
54 Pres. Lincoln
57 Urges (on)
59 "Gesundheit!" preceder
63 Strolls, as with a sweetheart
67 1950s candidate Stevenson
68 B or B+, say
69 Nobelist Wiesel
70 Irish poet who wrote "The Lake Isle of Innisfree"
71 Lambs' mothers
72 Soaks

DOWN

1 Big gobblers
2 Aid and ___
3 Layer
4 Famous Hun
5 Not at work
6 Teachers' org.
7 Grp. that patrols shores
8 Sound system
9 Opposite of losses
10 Ump
11 "Quickly!"
12 Backgammon equipment
13 Prime draft status
18 Not spare the rod
19 Domesticate
24 Bismarck's state: Abbr.
25 Toward sunrise, in Mexico
27 Yearn (for)
28 Precipitation at about 32°
29 Crown
30 Itsy-bitsy
31 Late
32 Speak from a soapbox
33 Stately shade trees
34 Austrian peaks
38 Comic Dunn formerly of "S.N.L."
40 Person of equal rank
41 Fill up
44 Unbeatable foe
46 Boston airport
49 ['Tis a pity!]
50 Capture, as one's attention
51 Shun
54 Not home
55 Requested
56 Fitzgerald, the First Lady of Jazz
58 Precipitation below 32°
60 Robust
61 "Don't bet ___!"
62 Lyric verses
64 Krazy ___
65 Mother deer
66 They're checked at checkpoints, in brief

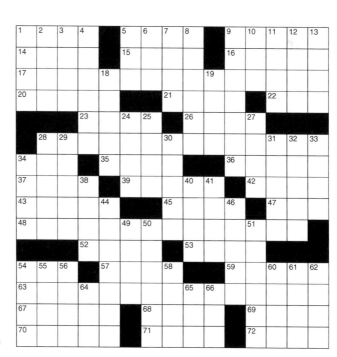

by Kurt Mengel and Jan-Michele Gianette

ACROSS

1 Strait-laced
5 It can make you sick
9 Raise a glass to
14 Mrs. Chaplin
15 Charles Lamb's nom de plume
16 Stan's sidekick in old comedy
17 Gulf sultanate
18 After-bath powder
19 Mexican coins
20 "Get rid of your inhibitions!"
23 Phoned
24 Lennon's lady
25 Mil. stores
26 Hard ___ rock
28 Very, in Vichy
31 Indy racer sponsor
33 Baseball scores
35 Without much thought
37 Cuban line dance
41 "Dance the night away!"
44 Big mug
45 18-wheeler
46 Lacking slack
47 Sgt., for one
49 Easy marks
51 Mad Hatter's drink
52 Univ., e.g.
55 Downs' opposite
57 Hairdo
59 "Party hearty!"
65 Label with a name on it
66 Stench
67 Drop from the eye
68 Home of Arizona State
69 "___ my lips!"
70 Glowing review
71 Sauna feature
72 Concludes
73 Gave a thumbs-up

DOWN

1 Betting group
2 The Eternal City
3 Spellbound
4 Craze
5 "Control yourself!"
6 Israeli airline
7 Small stream
8 Very virile
9 A-one
10 Designer Cassini
11 Journalist Joseph
12 Language of the Omahas
13 Midterms, e.g.
21 Cable TV choice
22 Partner of a ques.
26 Synagogue chests
27 Office wear
29 "Grand" ice cream brand
30 Tart fruits
32 Frost or Burns
34 Where pores are
36 City WSW of Phoenix
38 Compulsive cleaner
39 Stickum
40 "The Thin Man" dog
42 Diamond in the rough, e.g.
43 Parachutists' lifelines
48 Select, with "for"
50 Female pig
52 Barbecue rods
53 West Pointer
54 Blackjack request
56 Seashell site
58 Foreword, for short
60 California wine valley
61 Steinbeck's "East of ___"
62 Little hopper
63 Roof's edge
64 ___ Scott decision, 1857

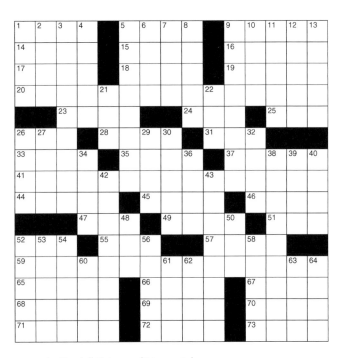

by Kendall Twigg and Nancy Salomon

ACROSS

1 Wildcat
5 "Hey . . . over here!"
9 Look without blinking
14 Smile proudly
15 Canyon sound
16 Artist's stand
17 Not crazy
18 Wander
19 The Little Mermaid
20 Pass along some football plays?
23 "The loneliest number"
24 Owl sound
25 Rots
29 Alexander ___, secretary of state under Reagan
30 Listening device
33 Texas battle site, with "the"
34 Does tailoring
35 McDonald's arches, e.g.
36 Begin to use wrestling feats?
39 Salt Lake City collegians
40 Sculls
41 Wall climbers
42 Club ___ (resort)
43 It turns at a pig roast
44 Dangerous African fly
45 Recipe direction
46 Tic-___-toe
47 Make time for aerobics classes?
54 Being from beyond Earth
55 Toward shelter
56 Not nerdy
58 Rain-snow mixture
59 Calendar span
60 Tackle box item
61 Jeans and khakis
62 Lushes
63 Side squared, for a square

DOWN

1 Dieters' units: Abbr.
2 "Right on!"
3 Mom's mom
4 Marvel Comics group
5 Eva and Juan
6 British biscuit
7 Old Iranian ruler
8 Weapons on the warpath
9 Veteran sailor
10 Cards for the clairvoyant
11 "Oh, that'll ever happen!"
12 Coral ridge
13 Building annexes
21 "___ want to dance?"
22 Cacophony
25 Informational unit
26 Overjoy
27 Like thick, dry mud
28 Iowa State's home
29 Valentine symbol
30 Namely
31 Moorehead of "Bewitched"
32 Sheriff's crew
34 Railing sites
35 Valentine subject
37 Stop by briefly
38 1970s–'80s musical craze
43 Periods on jobs
44 "Any ___?"
45 Trapshooting
46 Pick up the tab
47 Winged stinger
48 Earthen pot
49 It means nothing to the French
50 Bread spread
51 Sch. where Bill Walton played
52 What a band may have planned
53 Achy
57 Meadow

by Damon J. Gulczynski

ACROSS

1 Frozen treats
5 Soothing cream
9 Cursed
14 Chef's serving
15 Seller of his birthright, in Gen. 25
16 Hizzoner
17 ___'acte
18 Flexible, electrically
19 One with an amorous eye
20 Hidden advantage
23 "___ Doone" (romance)
24 Run-of-the-mill: Abbr.
25 Gentle ___ lamb
28 Lion, by tradition
33 Maybes
36 Den
37 Run for the ___ (Kentucky Derby)
38 Shingle site
40 Lady's title
43 Singer Horne
44 Farm measures
46 Dutch cheese
48 Yo-yo or Gobot
49 1950s–'60s game show
53 Neighbor of Syr.
54 Second letter after epsilon
55 Dough leavener
59 Start of a nursery rhyme
63 Actress Kim
66 Hobbling
67 Israel's Abba
68 Nitrous ___ (laughing gas)
69 Shade trees
70 Brooklyn hoopsters
71 Light sleeper
72 Affirmative votes
73 Understanding words

DOWN

1 Perfect
2 ___ de Mayo (Mexican holiday)
3 Fragrant compound
4 Psychiatrist, slangily
5 Regular drumming
6 Author Sholem
7 Put on board
8 Not quite all
9 Burn without a flame
10 What a worker earns
11 Popeye's Olive ___
12 Fish eggs
13 Mess up
21 It's on the tip of one's finger
22 Globe
25 Winning smile, they say
26 Dictation taker
27 Test mineralogically
29 "Platoon" setting
30 Actress Scala
31 Opposite of chaos
32 Netscape's owner
33 Baghdad resident
34 Concentrate
35 More achy
39 Lawyer's charge
41 Letters on a toothpaste tube
42 Irate
45 Athletic shoe
47 "___ help you?"
50 Agcy. that promotes fair competition
51 Markswoman Annie
52 Sana'a native
56 French clerics
57 List of candidates
58 Not relaxed
59 Green gem
60 Hay bundle
61 Jane Austen heroine
62 Loch ___
63 Sign of approval
64 Losing tic-tac-toe line
65 Namely: Abbr.

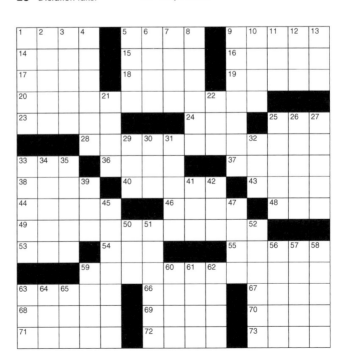

by Alison Donald

ACROSS

1 The "A" in I.R.A.: Abbr.
5 Chili con __
10 Do newspaper work
14 End of a fishing line
15 Sewing machine inventor Howe
16 Financial page inits.
17 Charles Lindbergh's feat across the Atlantic
19 Nameless, for short
20 Prehistoric
21 Marked down
22 "Friends, __, countrymen"
24 Antlered deer
25 The City of Witches
26 Thin, as oatmeal
29 Game show player
32 See eye to eye
33 "It takes two" to do this
34 When repeated, a ballroom dance
35 Explore the seven seas
36 Emphatic ending with yes
37 Tennis score after deuce
38 Uncle: Sp.
39 External
40 Three sheets to the wind
41 Oratorio performers
43 Fake ducks
44 Martini garnish
45 Golf shirt
46 Present to Goodwill, e.g.
48 Is no more, informally
49 "That's it!"
52 At the drop of __
53 Paul Scott tetralogy, with "The"
56 Formal ceremony
57 Rainbow __
58 Dory or ferry
59 Cousin of a frog
60 Eye sores
61 Memorial Day weekend event, briefly

DOWN

1 Mock words of understanding
2 In the 40s, say
3 In the 20s, say
4 Certain boxing win, for short
5 Stalk vegetable
6 Desirable party group
7 Fixes illegally
8 "I'd rather not"
9 Alienate
10 Tooth cover
11 Batman and Robin
12 The Rolling Stones' "Time __ My Side"
13 Hamilton bills
18 Marooned person's signal
23 Skillet lubricant
24 Rear of a sole
25 Less loony
26 "__ not, want not"
27 Once more
28 One of six Bach compositions
29 "Gay" city
30 Polished, as shoes
31 "Patton" vehicles
33 Sir or madam
36 Undermines
37 Sacramento's __ Arena
39 Leave out
40 Atlanta-based airline
42 Pleased as punch
43 Krispy Kreme products
45 Excite, as curiosity
46 Bull's-eye hitter
47 The Buckeye State
48 "A thing of beauty is __ forever"
49 Oodles
50 Noggin
51 Trial fig.
54 The "A" in MoMA
55 Baseball stat

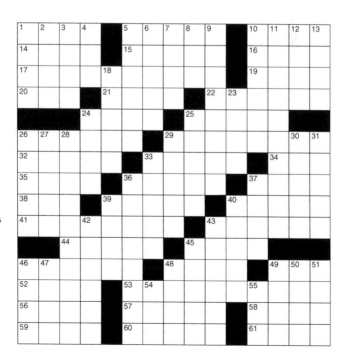

by Gregory E. Paul

82

ACROSS

1 Spats
6 Poker variety
10 Theda ___ of the silents
14 18-and-over
15 Sit for a shot
16 Catchall abbr.
17 Auto racer Andretti
18 Humorist Bombeck
19 K–12, in education
20 "If looks could kill" look
23 Dog sled driver
26 Former telecommunications giant: Abbr.
27 ___ Luis Obispo
28 Bickering
29 Racetrack fence
32 Courtroom pledge
34 Coarse file
35 Helping hand
36 Big inits. in trucks
37 Welcome that's not so welcoming
43 Vienna's land: Abbr.
44 Fitting
45 Meditation method
46 Hoodwinks
48 Close angrily
49 The "O" in S.R.O.
50 George W., to George
51 Shirt or sweater
53 Tickles the fancy
55 Snub
59 Merle Haggard's "___ From Muskogee"
60 Ponder
61 Not live
65 Just dandy
66 Away from land
67 Light on one's feet
68 Serve supper to
69 Geeky sort
70 Open the door to

DOWN

1 Tartan cap
2 Boise's state: Abbr.
3 Mink, for one
4 Pilot's pre-takeoff filing
5 Mink, for one
6 On ___ (without a contract)
7 Pop singer Amos
8 Label on a street-corner box
9 Handed out cards
10 Symbol of redness
11 "Finally!"
12 Gung-ho
13 Non-earthling
21 Lines up
22 Jazz dance
23 Artist Chagall
24 Great Salt Lake state
25 Mexican's assent
30 Ventilate
31 Standard of perfection
33 "Stop behaving like a child!"
36 Start to fume
38 Hungers (for)
39 Number cruncher, for short
40 Charged particles
41 Gawk at, as on the beach
42 Thumbs-down votes
46 Gingersnap, e.g.
47 Connected to the Internet
48 Marital partner
50 Speak derisively
52 "What now?!"
54 Rock music genre
56 Monopoly card
57 Exploitative type
58 Show the way
62 Peach center
63 Samuel's mentor
64 Comfy room

by Kendall Twigg and Nancy Salomon

ACROSS

1 Beginner
5 Ceiling support
9 Brass instruments
14 Crowd noise
15 The Bruins of the Pac-10
16 Take by force
17 Just twiddling one's thumbs
18 Diagram
19 Juliet's beloved
20 Navel
23 Louisville Slugger
24 French president's residence
25 Critical
27 "Oh my goodness!"
30 Hippie happening
33 One of the Bushes
36 Not completely dissolved, as a drink mix
38 Online auction house
39 Collect
41 "Dear" letter recipient
42 Guitar bars
43 Pickle flavoring
44 Copier of a manuscript
46 Wide shoe specification
47 Mama Cass ___
49 Dirties
51 TV host Winfrey
53 Shines
57 F.B.I. employee: Abbr.
59 The Midwest, agriculturally speaking
62 Bar mitzvah officiator
64 Fitzgerald of scat
65 It ebbs and flows
66 Approximately
67 "Whatcha ___?"
68 Dublin's land, in poetry
69 School readings
70 Gulp from a bottle
71 Mexican sandwich

DOWN

1 Arapaho or Apache
2 Alpine song
3 Come from behind
4 Ultimatum words
5 Hobgoblin
6 Off-white
7 Landed (on)
8 Fox comedy series
9 Seek help from
10 Bob Hope tour grp.
11 Big stinger
12 ___ code (long-distance need)
13 Parking place
21 Safecrackers
22 Slick
26 Profess
28 Frisbee, e.g.
29 Mixes
31 "Must've been something ___"
32 Nasdaq rival
33 Green gem
34 Silents star Jannings
35 Vote depository
37 Threesome
40 Lingerie item
42 Guy
44 Christmas tree topper
45 Cosmic explosion
48 Satellite paths
50 Last six lines of a sonnet
52 Obeys
54 Director Kurosawa
55 Doc
56 Meeting transcriber
57 Smell ___ (be leery)
58 Kotter of "Welcome Back, Kotter"
60 Strike ___ blow
61 552, in old Rome
63 Except

by Barry C. Silk

ACROSS

1 Drug buster, for short
5 Apartments
10 Arizona city
14 Mishmash
15 Scoundrel
16 Kuwaiti leader
17 Group voting the same way
18 Car from Japan
19 It may be carried with a guitar
20 Unexpectedly
23 Dismal, in poetry
24 Not just anger
28 "___ out!" (ump's call)
29 Mine finds
33 Grassy Argentine plains
34 Gap and Toys 'R' Us, e.g.
36 Verb not in the king's English
37 Unexpectedly
41 Pro ___ (proportionally)
42 Followed smoothly
43 Natural to a creature
46 Rocker David Lee ___
47 Sup
50 "Saturday Night Fever" group, with "the"
52 "Where the deer and the antelope play"
54 Unexpectedly
58 Shoot (by)
61 Decree
62 Family rooms
63 Detest
64 Delay leaving
65 Stow cargo
66 Reason to put a clothespin on your nose

67 Earl of ___, favorite of Queen Elizabeth I
68 Pitching stats, for short

DOWN

1 Opposite of everyone
2 That certain something
3 Violent troublemaker
4 Beverage with a marshmallow
5 Pledges' group, for short
6 ___ Ness monster
7 Flulike symptoms
8 Supercharged engine
9 Close tightly
10 Parking ticket issuer
11 Flightless Australian bird
12 Break a Commandment
13 "___ you there?"
21 Foam
22 Actress Hagen
25 Neat as ___
26 Jets or Sharks, in "West Side Story"
27 Not an exact fig.
30 Howard of "Happy Days"
31 Archer of myth
32 Waste conduit
34 Telescope user
35 Palm starch
37 Decrease gradually
38 "Can ___ true?"
39 Same old same old
40 Kind of jacket
41 "Spare" item at a barbecue
44 Snakelike fish
45 Erase

47 Make lovable
48 Slate
49 Present and future
51 Ice cream concoctions
53 Confuse
55 Some evergreens
56 Land unit
57 River to the underworld
58 Group with the rock opera "Tommy," with "the"
59 Owned
60 Judge Lance of the O. J. Simpson case

by Sarah Keller

ACROSS

1 God of love
5 Diehard
9 Give the heave-ho
14 Audition goal
15 Pet on "The Flintstones"
16 Bravery
17 Start of a Yogi Berra quote
19 Online periodical, briefly
20 "This is only ___"
21 Ear part
23 Off the wall
24 Susan who wrote "Illness as Metaphor"
26 Peruvian beast
28 End of 17-Across
33 Russian leader of old
36 Knock the socks off of
37 African fly
38 ___ Lilly & Co.
39 Alternative to dial-up Internet: Abbr.
40 "Quiet!"
41 Cheerios ingredient
42 The "r" of "πr²"
44 When a plane is due to take off: Abbr.
45 B&B's
46 Start of a Yogi Berra quote
49 Mild cigar
50 New Haven collegians
54 Prefix with bytes or bucks
57 Out of control
59 Spice of life
60 Spend, as energy
62 End of 46-Across
64 Ditch digger's tool
65 Plant's start
66 Slightly

67 Play (around)
68 Bookie's quote
69 Telescope part

DOWN

1 Diva performances
2 "Live Free or Die," for New Hampshire
3 Mary-Kate and Ashley ___ (celebrity twins)
4 Antares, e.g.
5 Modifying word: Abbr.
6 Small container for liquids
7 Entail
8 Two-base hit
9 Christmas ___
10 The 1920s
11 Pen name for Charles Lamb
12 It's south of Mass.

13 Deuce topper
18 And others: Abbr.
22 Environmentalists' celebration
25 Boxer's weak spot
27 Beat to a pulp
29 Harry Potter's messenger bird Hedwig, e.g.
30 Lots and lots
31 "No man ___ island . . ."
32 Brooklyn hoopsters
33 Actress Garr
34 Venetian blind part
35 Gives a hand
39 Old-fashioned showdown
40 TV classic "The ___ Erwin Show"
43 What bouncers check

44 Went from apes to humans
45 Prohibited
47 Melodious
48 Volcano flow
51 Seeing red
52 Big name in bottled water
53 Mails
54 Net material
55 Giant fair
56 Cyclist's choice
58 Monopoly card
61 Golf peg
63 Hwys.

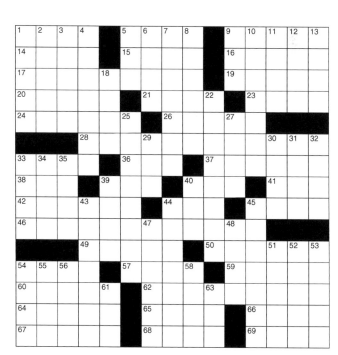

by Kyle Mahowald

ACROSS

1 Hatch plots
7 Busy activity
11 Little devil
14 Broadway musical based on Dickens
15 In the thick of
16 Lao-tzu principle
17 Gets noticed, as an actor?
19 Mustache site
20 Paradises
21 ___ Kong, China
22 Hawkeye player on "M*A*S*H"
23 "The Nutcracker" attire
25 Resentful
27 Cable film channel
30 Gets noticed, as an acrobat?
33 Newspaperman William Randolph ___
35 Book before Job
36 "It was ___ mistake!"
37 Tiny hill builder
38 Tizzy
41 Noisy insect
44 Harmonize
46 Gets noticed, as a chef?
49 "Harper Valley ___"
50 Napping
51 Count ___, villain in Lemony Snicket books
53 Neighbor of Niger
54 Get ___ a good thing
57 Telegraph pioneer
61 Do-it-yourselfer's purchase
62 Gets noticed, as an artist?
64 Sign after Cancer
65 Period after dark, in ads
66 Shabby
67 Go wrong
68 Ever and ___
69 Causing goosebumps

DOWN

1 Not all
2 Dressed
3 Nature walk
4 Super Bowl or the Oscars, e.g.
5 Boo-boos
6 Mesozoic, for one
7 Mexican serving
8 Mysterious sign
9 Nutcake
10 Poetic tribute
11 "We'll find it"
12 Whom a dragon threatens in a fairy tale
13 Certain 1960s paintings
18 Synagogue
22 Swear (to)
24 When repeated, "For shame!"
26 Suffix with devil
27 "Now I see!"
28 Gibson who directed "The Passion of the Christ"
29 Texas Instruments product
31 Horne and Olin
32 Grounded jet, for short
34 Reared
37 Org. for tooth doctors
39 Bankbook abbr.
40 Drink with one lump or two
42 Middle grade
43 Headache queller
44 Have headaches, say
45 Trolley
46 Witch's laugh
47 More grayish
48 Truck scale units
52 Blacksmith's workplace
55 Defense grp. since 1949
56 Actor Wilson of "Shanghai Noon"
58 Monotonous learning
59 Give this for that
60 Nervously irritable
62 Paternity identifier
63 Bowlike line

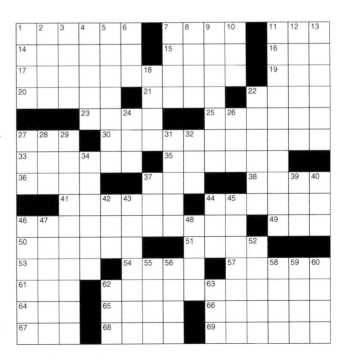

by Levi Denham

ACROSS

1 Actor Baldwin
5 Go a mile a minute, say
10 Canaanite god
14 Length between mini and maxi
15 Uptight person
16 Peter ___, classic cartoonist for The New Yorker
17 One's equal
18 Dances at Jewish weddings
19 Alliance since '49
20 1852 book
23 Old Italian money
24 Long, long time
25 1944 play
31 Trap
32 Low-cal
33 Miner's find
35 Egyptian fertility goddess
36 Takes a turn on "Wheel of Fortune"
38 Unadulterated
39 "Queen of denial" for Queen of the Nile
40 Ollie's partner in old comedy
41 Wild
42 1992 movie
46 Actor Chaney
47 Classical paintings
48 1970s TV show with a literal hint to 20-, 25- and 42-Across
55 Feeling that makes you say "Ow!"
56 Biblical spy
57 When repeated, a court cry
59 For men only
60 The Little Mermaid
61 The "N" of N.B.
62 "Dear God!"
63 Pee Wee who was nicknamed the Little Colonel
64 Quick cut

DOWN

1 Unit of current, informally
2 In ___ of (instead of)
3 Home for Adam and Eve
4 Vultures, at times
5 Globe
6 For the time being
7 Currency that replaced 23-Across
8 Dutch cheese
9 Puddings and pies, e.g.
10 Snack for a monkey
11 Saudi, e.g.
12 Not for
13 Crazy as a ___
21 Fertilizer ingredient
22 Arrive
25 "To recap . . ."
26 Wet, weatherwise
27 Thin pancakes
28 "Ich bin ___ Berliner"
29 Grieve
30 Lineup
31 Taste, as wine
34 Sushi fish
36 Vehicle that does crazy tricks
37 ___ de deux
38 Funds for retirees
40 Shortly
41 What soap may leave
43 Tight, as clothes
44 Bank's ad come-on
45 Practical, as a plan
48 Lhasa ___ (dog)
49 Homebuilder's strip
50 Actor Neeson
51 Long-eared leaper
52 Nobelist Wiesel
53 City on the Rhône
54 Abominable Snowman
58 Microwave

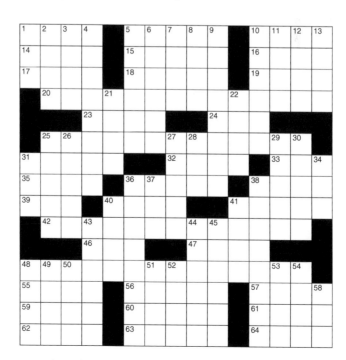

by Linda Schechet Tucker

88

ACROSS

1 Freighter or whaler
5 Read cursorily
9 Chick's cries
14 Window section
15 Prefix with sphere
16 Uncredited actor
17 Rocketeer
19 Writer Joyce Carol ___
20 Cheerleader's cheer
21 Novelty dance spawned by a 1962 #1 hit
23 CD player
25 Freudian ___
26 Reach by foot
29 Certain fir
33 "I love," in France
35 "___ perpetua" (Idaho's motto)
37 Raison d'___
38 Holder of funerary ashes
39 What the ends of 21- and 57-Across and 3- and 30-Down all name
42 Leading pitcher
43 Close by, in poetry
45 Words of enlightenment
46 Goose egg
48 Less difficult
50 Have high hopes
52 Nickname for Dallas
54 Fiats
57 Party bowlful
62 "___ la la!"
63 Lenin's middle name
64 Big business-related
66 Small recess
67 "What is to be done?!"

68 Kind of tea
69 "___ With Love" (1967 hit)
70 Wild hog
71 Units of resistance

DOWN

1 Poles on a 1-Across
2 Attacks
3 Waiting just out of sight
4 The "p" of m.p.h.
5 Dope
6 New Jersey's ___ University
7 Don of talk radio
8 Hands, in slang
9 Central Illinois city
10 Case in point
11 Blues singer ___ James
12 F.D.R. or J.F.K.
13 Window frame

18 Dish often served with home fries
22 Rudely poke
24 St. Louis gridder
27 "___ of the D'Urbervilles"
28 Actor Milo
30 Old West transport
31 St. Louis landmark
32 Get together
33 Beaver's mom on "Leave It to Beaver"
34 Opera highlight
36 "Little piggies"
40 Sign of late summer
41 Declared
44 Small patio grill
47 Mentalist Geller
49 A choice word
51 Jalapeño, to name one
53 1983 Mr. T flick

55 Pole carving
56 Outbuildings
57 Blood donation, maybe
58 Mishmash
59 Tiny spasms
60 Popular cream-filled cake
61 "My Friend ___" of old radio/TV
65 Brazilian getaway

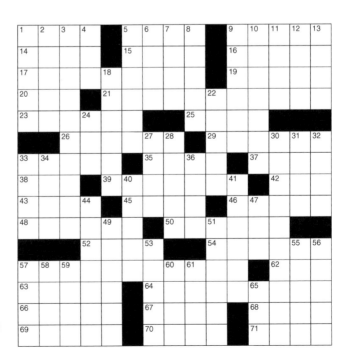

by Allan E. Parrish

ACROSS

1 Persistent annoyer
5 Upper or lower bed
9 Monastery head
14 Author Wiesel
15 Geometry calculation
16 Does a prelaundry chore
17 Leader of an 1831 slave rebellion
19 "___ or treat?"
20 Rejects, as a lover
21 "That's ___" (Dean Martin classic)
23 1960s–'70s singer Hayes
24 Bottom line, businesswise
28 Dobbin's doc
29 Actresses Graff and Kristen
31 "___ number one!" (stadium chant)
32 Suffix with Brooklyn
33 Meat that's often served piccata
34 Tête topper
35 Faultfinder extraordinaire
38 1988 Summer Olympics city
41 It may be kicked in anger
42 Alt. spelling
45 Jai ___
46 Duds
48 Opposite WSW
49 "Slow down!"
51 Ban rival
53 African language
54 "Relax, soldier!"
55 Makes, as a salary
57 Müeslix alternative
60 "The final frontier"
61 Meadowlands pace
62 ___ fixe (obsession)
63 Belief
64 Trig function
65 Boys

DOWN

1 Deep in thought
2 Goes by, as time
3 Put in place
4 Prefix with -hedron
5 Jail cell parts
6 Vase
7 Maiden name preceder
8 Activity with chops and kicks
9 Early fur trader John Jacob ___
10 Person using a library card
11 Less wordy
12 Stock page heading: Abbr.
13 "For shame!"
18 Rude
22 Brit. legislators
24 Semimonthly tide
25 Joins up
26 Rage
27 Lunar New Year
30 Tennis court call
34 Under
35 Pain in the neck
36 IOU
37 White wine cocktail
38 ___ Juan, P.R.
39 "Roll Over Beethoven" grp.
40 Healthful cereal grain
42 Front porch
43 Liqueur flavoring
44 Overnight flights
46 Back, at sea
47 Teases
50 Beginning
52 Lubricate again
54 Pot starter
55 N.Y.C. winter clock setting
56 King Kong, e.g.
58 Spoonbender Geller
59 Coal unit

by Sarah Keller

ACROSS

1 Martini garnish
6 Mrs. Dithers in "Blondie"
10 Colonel or captain
14 1976 Olympic gymnastics gold medalist ___ Comaneci
15 Assert
16 Away from the wind
17 OVALS
20 Words before roll or whim
21 Murder
22 "You're ___ talk!"
23 Affix one's John Hancock
24 On one's rocker?
26 K
32 Ship's crane
33 Needle parts
34 Évian, par exemple
35 Pizazz
36 Jazz instruments
38 ___ Strauss jeans
39 Be sick
40 Elisabeth of "Leaving Las Vegas"
41 Add a lane to, perhaps
42 STORY
46 "Lovely" Beatles girl
47 Bad news for a dieter
48 Assassinated
51 Atlantic Coast area, with "the"
52 Thrilla in Manila victor
55 X
59 Reverse, as an action
60 Commedia dell'___
61 Fit for a king
62 Gripe
63 Many a teenager's room
64 Alibi

DOWN

1 Aware of
2 Croquet area
3 Conception
4 Beaujolais, e.g.
5 Grovel
6 Checking out, as a joint
7 Kitchen hot spot
8 Gun, as an engine
9 "___ you kidding?"
10 Gilda of the early "S.N.L."
11 Soothing agent
12 Brilliantly colored salamander
13 Gambling game with numbers
18 Indian mystic
19 They're taboo
23 "Wheel of Fortune" turn
24 Eye sore
25 11's in blackjack
26 Actress Shire
27 Picture frames lacking corners
28 Under a spell
29 Must-haves
30 Icicle holders
31 Destroy
32 It may be new, raw or big
36 Gun blast
37 Mystique
38 Circus animal with a tamer
40 Hogs
41 Novelists
43 Son of Poseidon
44 Playing marbles
45 Alternative to check or charge
48 Pond gunk
49 Jay of late-night
50 Wing ___ prayer
51 Young 12-Downs
52 Jason's ship
53 Fibber
54 Without doing anything
56 Ewe's mate
57 Mine find
58 "___ lost!"

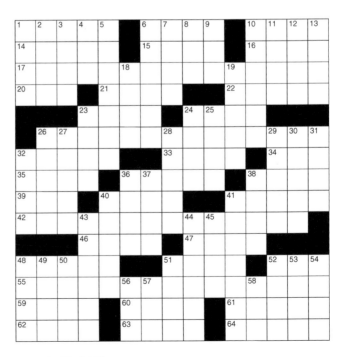

by Mark Milhet

ACROSS

1 Madam's counterpart
4 Resort island near Venice
8 Voodoo charms
13 Poem of praise
14 Stove part
15 Inventor's goal
16 Slangy negative
17 Renowned bandleader at the Cotton Club
19 "I have an idea!"
20 Go before
21 Androids
23 By way of
24 24-hr. banking convenience
27 Dernier ___ (latest thing)
28 Raisin ___ (cereal)
30 Suffix with buck
31 Belief
33 Beats a hasty retreat
34 Emilia's husband, in "Othello"
35 Chinese province
36 They're "easy" to find in 17- and 53-Across and 3- and 24-Down
37 Rural's opposite
38 High: Prefix
39 Muskogee native
40 Walks like an expectant father
41 Noticed
42 Stoop
43 With 45-Across, for the time being
44 Mess up
45 See 43-Across
46 Monkeylike animals
49 Tends, as a patient
52 Butterfly catcher's tool
53 Seize power
56 Road goo
57 Reap
58 Arnaz of "I Love Lucy"
59 Hwy.
60 Dizzy-making drawings
61 Ooze
62 Big fat mouth

DOWN

1 Submarine-detecting system
2 Just 45 miles of it borders Canada
3 Place to get clean
4 When said three times, a real estate mantra
5 Several Russian czars
6 Bankruptcy cause
7 "___ upon a time . . ."
8 Island country south of Sicily
9 15-Down tribe
10 Synagogue attender
11 Keep ___ short leash
12 Hog's home
15 Where the buffalo roamed
18 Like Calculus II
22 Confer holy orders on
24 Jordan or Iraq
25 Ancient Roman robes
26 Mars has two
28 Train stoppers
29 Apply, as cream
30 Military branch with planes
31 Pursue
32 12" stick
37 Mustache site
39 Fairy king, in Shakespeare
45 Silently understood
46 Not tied down
47 Rodeo rope
48 ___ throat
49 "Good buddy"
50 Regulations: Abbr.
51 Not tied down
53 Sporty Pontiac
54 Grandmaster Flash's music genre
55 Alias, for short

by Adam G. Perl

ACROSS

1 Healthful retreats
5 Cartoonist Thomas who attacked Boss Tweed
9 Sleeves cover them
13 Chair designer Charles
15 Addict
16 Outscore
17 "Ain't it the ___?!"
18 Computer info
19 River of Spain
20 Germfree armored vehicle?
23 Ruined
24 H, in Greece
25 Golf gadget
26 Jan. and Feb.
27 Bring forth
30 Looks lasciviously
32 It may be served à la mode
33 Motorist's org.
34 Order between "ready" and "fire"
35 Money for busting up monopolies?
41 Buck's mate
42 ___ Paulo, Brazil
43 Mentalist Geller
45 Peak
48 Reddish hair dye
50 Cambridge sch.
51 "For ___ a jolly . . ."
52 Mimic
54 Agree (to)
56 Vandalism or thievery?
60 Rung
61 Go no further
62 Embarrass
64 Sailors
65 Princes but not princesses
66 Frank ___, Al Capone lieutenant
67 Otherwise
68 Gaelic
69 Math subj. with angles

DOWN

1 Order between "ready" and "go"
2 "They're following me!" feeling
3 South Pole explorer Roald
4 Melee
5 Unclothed
6 Pronto, on memos
7 Couch
8 Blue eyes or dark hair, e.g.
9 Assist illegally
10 Money-back offer
11 George Eliot's "Silas ___"
12 Feeds, as a fire
14 Rise and ___
21 Tranquilize
22 Where L.A. and S.F. are
23 Caller of balls and strikes
28 Nasser's dream: Abbr.
29 Make happen
31 Bird more than five feet tall
34 Hard-to-hum
36 QB's scores
37 Bits
38 ___ Clemente
39 List from 1 to whatever
40 Toasts
44 Cousin ___ of "The Addams Family"
45 Modest
46 U-Haul truck, e.g.
47 Fragrant compounds
48 Victim of Achilles
49 Egyptian dam
53 Rapper's entourage
55 Edna Ferber novel
57 ___ dixit
58 Some Saturns
59 Cathedral recess
63 Her's partner

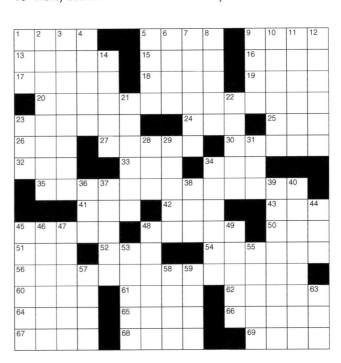

by Sheldon Benardo

93

ACROSS

1 Satisfying drink
6 Light bulb unit
10 Howled, as the wind
14 Graduation march composer
15 Type of textbook market
16 Four-star review
17 John who made plows
18 Grad
19 9:00–5:30 store sign
20 Amusement park ride with organ music
23 ___ Beta Kappa
26 Existed
27 Offers dessert, as to a dieter
28 Hero of a Virgil epic
30 Comedian Mort
32 Toy that bounces weirdly
34 Play divisions
38 Arduous journeys
39 Bolt attachment
40 Mensa-suitable
41 Concerning
42 Counterfeit cash
44 Skirt bottoms
45 Roof attachment seen less often these days
46 Take to a higher court
50 Having ridden one too many times on a 20-Across, say
51 Canonized mlle.
52 Seashore bird with a distinctive cry
56 Humorist Bombeck
57 Christmas carol
58 Not inner
62 Use the library
63 "Tickle me" doll
64 Complete reversal
65 "___ of the D'Urbervilles"
66 Not too great
67 Four: Prefix

DOWN

1 Letters after a proof
2 Suffix with sched-
3 What birthday candles signify
4 Old MacDonald's property
5 Most interstates
6 Has on
7 Partner in war
8 Hoodlum
9 Dalton who played 007
10 Janitor's tool
11 Receive with enthusiasm
12 Media attraction
13 Pursues, as one's way
21 Coarse file
22 Aunt or uncle, e.g.: Abbr.
23 Rotini or linguine
24 People named in wills
25 Small bay
29 Nevada county
30 Astonishes
31 Env. abbr.
33 E pluribus ___
34 Valentine's Day cherub
35 ___ Major
36 Bonbon, e.g.
37 Baroque or rococo
40 Detect with the nose
42 Cougars and such
43 River to Korea Bay
44 "Take that!"
46 Watchful
47 French city, in song
48 Cougars
49 "Oh, no!"
50 Eskimo dwelling
53 ___ contendere (court plea)
54 Stones on rings
55 Old instrument that's strummed
59 Boy king of ancient Egypt
60 "To ___ is human"
61 Genetic material, for short

by Janet R. Bender

ACROSS

1 Honda's home
6 Classic shark movie
10 Performed an aria
14 Lacking a partner
15 Toledo's lake
16 Dark doings
17 Bush cabinet member
20 Door opener
21 See 18-Down
22 Like presents
23 Feel aggrieved
26 Akin (to)
29 Like shopping done all in the same place
33 Intestinal bacteria
34 12 months in Madrid
35 Female with a wool coat
36 Hasn't a clue
41 "Kidnapped" author's inits.
42 Web address ending
43 Unexpected victory
44 "Make up your mind!"
47 Gary Cooper title role
49 Photographer's request
51 From the top
54 "Dies ___" (hymn)
55 Chiang ___-shek
58 What the last words of 17-, 23-, 36- and 49-Across might be
62 Neighbor of Java
63 Victor's cry
64 Chucklehead
65 Old radio's "___ 'n' Andy"
66 Mexican moolah
67 Square one, slangily

DOWN

1 "You don't know ___"
2 Burn soother
3 Youngster's mount
4 In addition
5 Post-Renaissance language
6 Expressed derision
7 Fight site
8 1975 musical set in Oz, with "The"
9 Utters, informally
10 Typographical embellishments
11 Tel ___, Israel
12 Not naughty
13 Secluded valley
18 With 21-Across, heartsick
19 James who wrote "The Morning Watch"
23 Dutch artist Frans

24 Globetrotting rock star/political activist
25 Sufficient, in verse
26 Put back in the kiln
27 French school
28 Windblown soil
30 Flirt with
31 Had title to
32 Annoyers
34 "Brokeback Mountain" director Lee
37 Theater award
38 McDonald's founder Ray
39 Fay Vincent's successor as baseball commissioner
40 Sporting sword
45 Egyptian god of the underworld

46 Rajah's mate
47 Fine sheep's wool
48 True-to-life
50 LP players
51 "Mamma Mia" quartet
52 Where America's Day Begins
53 Folk's Guthrie
55 Make bootees, e.g.
56 Obviously eager
57 "What ___ become of me?"
59 Visible part of an iceberg
60 Have bills due
61 Suffix with hydrox-

by Doug Peterson

ACROSS

1 More wet and cold, as weather
6 Puts behind bars
11 Maker of the Envoy and Yukon S.U.V.'s
14 End of ___ (notable time)
15 Open, as a bottle
16 Winter peril
17 Elated
20 Allow
21 Forest ranger?
22 Take offense at
23 One of 12 at Alcoholics Anonymous
25 Third son of Adam and Eve
28 Plowmaker John
29 Heart chambers
31 TV's "Star ___"
33 Eros, to Romans
34 Barbershop quartet members
36 Mine finds
38 "For ___ a jolly . . ."
39 Jubilant
42 Uncle with a cabin
44 Many-stringed instrument
45 Endangered cat
48 Word after rest or restricted
50 Garden invader
52 Volley of gunfire
53 Cultivates land
55 Small metric weight
57 Kojak, to friends
58 Home made with buffalo skin, maybe
60 ___ Paulo, Brazil
62 LAX posting: Abbr.
63 Ecstatic
67 Mel who played at the Polo Grounds
68 Dumbstruck
69 Like ghostly sounds
70 NNW's opposite
71 19th-century fur trade monopolist
72 Clothesline alternative

DOWN

1 Berates
2 Actress Bening
3 Brunch order with diced peppers, onions and ham
4 Afore
5 Talk like a madman
6 Paid-for trip
7 Opposite of syn.
8 "___ bin ein Berliner"
9 Lion player in "The Wizard of Oz"
10 Go 60, say, on city streets
11 1948 campaign cry
12 John who won tennis's U.S. Open four times
13 Midpoints
18 Chicago trains
19 Cruising
24 Subatomic particle
26 Actor on a tour
27 Cattle that all have the same brand
30 Curve, as the back
32 Numbers game with a card
35 Side order at KFC
37 Canine attack commands
40 Wash. neighbor
41 Fastidious
42 Pictures made in parlors
43 Points in the right direction
46 Cover
47 Specifically as one likes
49 Purina competitor
51 One of Santa's team
54 Old photo color
56 Old-time actress West
59 Ages and ages
61 Was in the red
64 Lard, essentially
65 What the "bi" in bicycle means
66 Anthem contraction

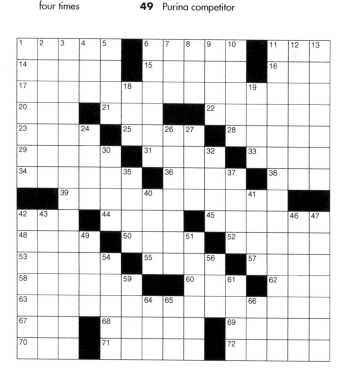

by Ed Early

ACROSS

1 Actor Jean-Claude Van __
6 Perry whose secretary was Della Street
11 L-1011, e.g.
14 Kind of address with @ in it
15 Do penance
16 Pie __ mode
17 Definition of a loser
20 Andrea __, ill-fated ship
21 Nobelist Wiesel
22 Gun owners' constitutional protection
28 Drs.' group
29 Victory sign
30 Kanga's baby in "Winnie-the-Pooh"
31 Doohickey: Var.
34 Standards of perfection
37 1950 #1 Anton Karas recording
41 Goes abroad for a baby, perhaps
42 Things
44 Lawyer, for short
47 Poet's "before"
48 Letter after sigma
49 Esperanto, for some
56 Quartet, after a defection
57 Everything being counted
58 Take apart to understand the design of
65 U-turn from WSW
66 Old Ford model named for a horse
67 German expression of appreciation
68 Poetic contraction
69 Hatfield adversary
70 Historic English county

DOWN

1 Dict. offering
2 French friend
3 Dent or scratch
4 Botch
5 John who sang "Candle in the Wind"
6 Madness
7 First-stringers
8 Boozehound
9 Musical Yoko
10 It's south of S.D.
11 Prisoner watcher
12 Pacific weather phenomenon
13 Like immediately
18 California's Fort __
19 Moon lander, for short
22 Droop
23 Give off
24 Money on hand
25 Makes level
26 "Dandy!"
27 Indian city of 13 million
32 "Mamma __!"
33 Hamburger with fries, e.g.
34 Spur
35 "Can't Help Lovin' __ Man"
36 Tennis division
38 "Dumb" girl of old comics
39 Prefix with physical
40 Webzine
43 Seek damages from
44 Course after the appetizer
45 Calm
46 Holder of arrows
50 Stocking stuffer?
51 Deceive
52 Bother
53 Old horse
54 Skate on ice
55 Radii's neighbors
59 Tach reading, for short
60 Cry to an attack dog
61 Env. insertion
62 Naval officer below lieut.
63 Barely make, with "out"
64 "Oedipus __"

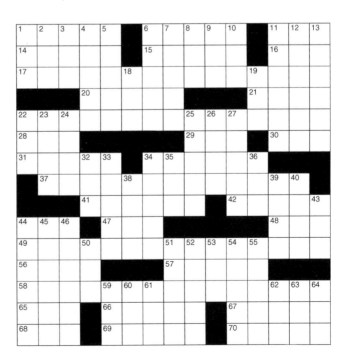

by Jack McInturff

ACROSS

1 Role to play
5 Poison ivy woe
9 In ___ (not yet born)
14 Worker in the garden
15 Connecting point
16 Word before and after say
17 "My Friend ___" of '50s TV
18 Mangled
19 Words before "So sue me!"
20 Vain
23 Hurried
24 It "has fleas" in an old ditty
25 A few
28 Forward flow
32 "That was bad of you!"
35 Claw
38 Pay the kitty
39 Vane
43 Alan of "M*A*S*H"
44 French cubist Fernand ___
45 Big ___ (circus)
46 Mischief-maker
49 Hornswoggle
51 Poet T. S. ___
54 Apportions, with "out"
58 Vein
62 Powdered cleaning agent
63 Guy with an Irish Rose, on old Broadway
64 Delete
65 Question to the Lord in Matthew 26
66 Shout
67 Prefix with scope
68 Goes a few rounds in the ring (with)
69 Not delete
70 Glimpsed

DOWN

1 Look for people to scam online
2 Major blood conveyor
3 Story-telling uncle
4 Pieces of land to develop
5 Put ___ words
6 Bugs Bunny or Wile E. Coyote
7 Computer information holder
8 Funnyman Youngman
9 A choir may sing in it
10 Old Western Union delivery
11 Foul doings
12 Where a yacht might run aground
13 City reg.
21 Capital of Japan before 22-Down
22 Old name for Tokyo
26 Homo sapiens
27 Airline to Tel Aviv
29 Condo, e.g.
30 Normandy invasion town
31 "S.O.S.!"
32 Nicholas II was the last one
33 Room in una casa
34 See 59-Down
36 Be in the red
37 "And stay by my cradle till morning is ___"
40 Mangle
41 Prefix with classical
42 Many an Arthur Miller work
47 One of the Carringtons on "Dynasty"
48 ___ Fail, Irish coronation stone
50 Son of Darius I
52 Green-lights
53 Lhasa's land
55 Hearty steak
56 Give the slip
57 Attack
58 Neither good nor bad
59 Cereal for 34-Down
60 Alexandria's river
61 Go soft, as butter
62 Baby's dinner neckwear

by Bernice Gordon

ACROSS

1 "No bid," in bridge
6 Settled, as a bill
10 Go after, as flies
14 BBC sci-fi classic
15 Shows on TV
16 Head, in France
17 Carouse, when young
20 Main arteries
21 Out, as a candle
22 Go gaga over
25 Volkswagen bug
26 "Who __ to argue?"
27 Place of refuge
30 Part of Ralph Kramden's laugh
31 The fifth letter of "garage," but not the first
33 Got up
36 Clinch the game
41 Occupied, as a lavatory
42 Them, to us
44 Buenos Aires's land: Abbr.
47 Zany
50 Sgt. or cpl.
51 Adds to, as a bar bill
54 Person from Pocatello
56 Colorful Apple computers
57 One of the Gabor sisters
59 "Now tell me something I don't know"
64 Transport on rails
65 Perched on
66 Blackmore's "Lorna __"
67 Concerning, in a memo
68 Mollycoddle
69 Came to a close

DOWN

1 Doorkeepers' demands, briefly
2 Paid player
3 "How adorable!"
4 Sand bar
5 "Darn it all!"
6 Danish or tart
7 Sony competitor
8 Colored eye part
9 High-speed Internet inits.
10 Sturdy wall composition
11 Riches
12 Historic Hun
13 Consumer Reports employee
18 Greek god of love
19 Scheduled to arrive
22 Notes after mis
23 Old Testament book
24 Prison sentence that may be "without parole"
25 Univ. class president, maybe
28 Washed up
29 Self-proclaimed psychic Geller
32 Prefix with night or light
34 Get out of the way
35 A billion years
37 Gas station fixture
38 Happy __ clam
39 City near Tahoe
40 1978 Village People hit
43 Over there, old-style
44 Competitor of Capitol and Epic
45 Water cooler tidbits
46 Bother horribly
48 U.S. operative
49 Wood-shaping tool
52 Doofus
53 Can./Mex. separator
55 Wears
57 Letter after epsilon
58 Neatnik's opposite
60 Key above caps lock
61 Silent acknowledgment
62 180° from WSW
63 Tie the knot

by Earl W. Reed and Nancy Salomon

ACROSS

1 Neatnik's opposite
5 Loathe
10 Pillage
14 ___ bean
15 Parisian pancake
16 Fashion magazine
17 Native Saudi
18 "Little Lulu," for one
19 Pre-1917 monarch
20 Actor's New York home?
23 Longtime West Virginia senator
24 Grp. that entertains troops
25 Unit of pearls
28 Rod at a pig roast
30 Brand of briefs
33 Calculators with beads
34 One who's just too funny
35 Phobia
36 TV host's Tennessee home?
39 Types
40 Decorative molding
41 Sign before Taurus
42 Overhead trains
43 Color tones
44 Opposite of liabilities
45 Groupie
46 Working without ___
47 Business mogul's Pennsylvania home?
55 Drops the ball
56 One of the Muses
57 Workplace watchdog grp.
58 Strike out, to a typesetter
59 Puerto ___
60 Rivers of Spain
61 N.Y.S.E. debuts
62 Sleep soundly?
63 Ogden who wrote "The Bronx? / No, thonx!"

DOWN

1 Refined waste
2 Old Italian money
3 Gen. Bradley
4 Some ribs
5 Honda model
6 Ones a mother hen mothers
7 Rope fiber
8 Aunt Bee's charge on "The Andy Griffith Show"
9 New arrivals at camp
10 Fight
11 In addition
12 Cat's scratcher
13 Jerome who composed "Show Boat"
21 Sour sort
22 Retired jet, for short
25 Hawkins of "Li'l Abner"
26 Govt. note
27 Ball holders in pool
28 Fathers on a farm
29 Jab
30 Contradict
31 A man's man
32 Gown
34 Fad
35 Heir to a throne, typically
37 Sun deck figures
38 Ming objects
43 Broadway's ___ Prince
44 Random person
45 Circuit breakers replaced these
46 Fragrant oil
47 "Star Wars" knight
48 Make ready, briefly
49 Guthrie who sang "City of New Orleans"
50 "___ go bragh!"
51 Stuffed tortilla
52 Voice of America grp.
53 Preceders of sigmas
54 Deep cut

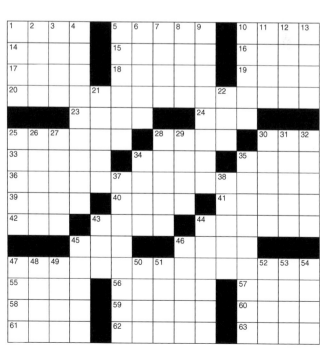

by Janice M. Putney

100

ACROSS

1 Glass container in a lab
5 Not fresh
10 Notre ___
14 Prefix with European
15 Resting place in a garden
16 Martinique et Guadeloupe
17 College professors travel in them
20 Sidekick, in the Southwest
21 The tiniest bit
22 Openings
25 Full of the latest happenings
26 Bead counters
30 Partner of "or"
33 ___ to go
34 Ballpark stat.
35 "You've got mail" co.
38 Fiancées wear them
42 "Fourscore and seven years ___ . . ."
43 Gossip
44 The "U" of UHF
45 Flat peppermint candy
47 Cold shower?
48 Name a criminal goes by
51 Juice drinks
53 Echo locations
56 Vetoes
60 Alternatives to stoplights
64 Cube inventor Rubik
65 Magna cum ___
66 Singer Guthrie
67 Not a natural blonde, say
68 Glowing remnant
69 Kennel cry

DOWN

1 By way of
2 Ancient Peruvian
3 One who raised Cain
4 Jersey city south of Paramus
5 Locale of a Margaret Mead study
6 Prefix with cycle
7 "Boston Legal" network
8 Bonkers
9 Dublin's home
10 More problematical
11 Let happen
12 Track events
13 Op-ed piece
18 Prodding
19 Mathematician Descartes
23 Let happen
24 Cold place to be banished to
26 Locale
27 Gun sound
28 Jason's ship
29 Spy org.
31 Like some windows
32 President after F.D.R.
35 Toss in a chip, say
36 Shrek, for one
37 Aspiring atty.'s exam
39 Summer hrs. in N.Y.C.
40 Where 24-Down is
41 Under the weather
45 Treat, at a restaurant
46 Starting from
48 Played on stage
49 King of TV
50 Cockamamie
52 Exit's opposite
54 Cairo's waterway
55 Rip-off
57 Like Superman's vision
58 Dublin's home
59 Dump, as stock
61 Massage
62 Poem titled "To a . . ."
63 Soak (up)

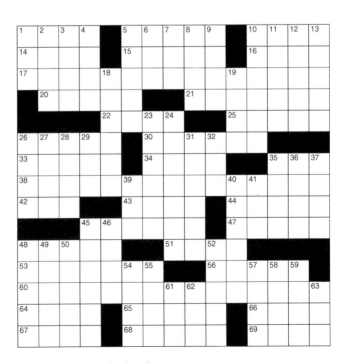

by Gary J. Whitehead

ACROSS

1 Club in "Casablanca"
6 Impel
10 Heading on a list of errands
14 Nerdy, say
15 Ballyhoo
16 Music box?
17 Acted incautiously
20 Sum up
21 Proceeds furtively
22 Letter after chi
24 Believer with a turban
27 Sees romantically
28 Jokes
31 Garlicky mayonnaise
33 When a plane is due in: Abbr.
34 Arab or Jew
36 Aquarium fish
38 Grew tired
42 Wash hard
43 Did fill-in work
45 "NCIS" airer
48 Muslim's holy book
50 Lose-weight schemes
51 Clock/radio feature
53 Creature that goes "ribbit!"
55 Fam. member
56 Bequest receivers
58 Low opera voices
61 Experienced trouble
66 Genesis garden
67 Praise
68 Look ___ horse in the mouth
69 Gives hue to a do
70 Unrestrained revelry
71 Big faux pas

DOWN

1 Moscow's home: Abbr.
2 It's more permanent than pencil marks
3 Personal magnetism
4 Toy with a tail
5 Design detail
6 Perfect world
7 Hollywood's Howard
8 Pit of the stomach
9 Ordinal endings
10 Skin problem
11 Drug that dulls the brain
12 Court calendar
13 City on the Black Sea
18 "___ Kapital"
19 Charged with a crime
22 Bedwear, informally

23 Futures analyst?
25 Unit of pressure
26 Horse's foot
29 Cookie containers
30 Cowboys
32 Endure
35 21st-century currency
37 Prefix with sphere
39 Gang land
40 Absinthe or ouzo
41 Parcel (out)
44 Alternate to dial-up, for short
45 Sponged
46 Red from an injury
47 Dakota tribe
49 Nonentity
52 Coachman's handful
54 Gangster's gun

57 Normandy town
59 Booty
60 Drawn-out drama
62 Crew member
63 "Welcome home" greeting
64 Grade below dee
65 Hwy.

by Larry Paul

ACROSS

1 First name in daytime talk
6 Expires
10 Has a part on stage
14 Carbon copy
15 Univ. military program
16 Abrupt
17 Quaker Oats cereal
19 Village Voice bestowal
20 Indian in the Four Corners states
21 Fraternity party staples
22 Entrance to a superhighway
24 Fixes, as old shoes
26 Hired hitman
27 One side in checkers
28 Good-looking
32 Whaling weapon
35 Seeger of the Weavers
36 Wharf
37 Threadbare
38 Passover meal
39 Lenin's land, for short
40 Entranced
41 Cribbage pieces
42 Wash oneself
43 Steep drop, as in prices
45 "___ better to have loved . . ."
46 Pickle-to-be, slangily
47 Ship's warning signal
51 What a 54-Across may do to a matador
54 Matador's foe
55 Cattle call
56 Doozy
57 Iced tea garnish

60 Awfully long time
61 "Heavens to Betsy!"
62 Tighten, as laces
63 Ritzy
64 Awfully long time
65 Acceptances

DOWN

1 Take place
2 Batter's place
3 Know the ___
4 Andy's raggedy pal
5 Audience troublemaker
6 What dispensaries dispense
7 Molecular bits
8 And so on, briefly
9 Large sailing vessel
10 Thanksgiving vegetable
11 It's south of Florida

12 Svelte
13 "___ lively!"
18 Oboe part
23 Silent assent
25 Soft drink that Norman Rockwell drew ads for
26 Fence openings
28 Property divider
29 Give the heave-ho
30 Turn into pulp
31 Brontë's "Jane ___"
32 "___ Lake"
33 Cartoon possum
34 Greek love god
35 Irk
38 "Do the Right Thing" director, writer and actor
42 Prejudice
44 Searched for buried treasure

45 Shredded
47 Supermarket offerings
48 Excludes
49 W.W. II's ___ the Riveter
50 Memory joggers
51 Applaud
52 "Les Misérables" author
53 Tavern mugfuls
54 I.R.S. agent, e.g.
58 Source of an attitude
59 Pint-sized

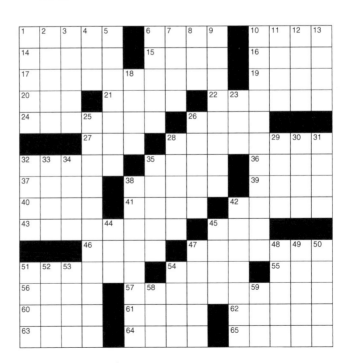

by Lynn Lempel

ACROSS

1 Beginning
6 What icicles do
10 Church recess
14 Baby grand, e.g.
15 Musical set in ancient Egypt
16 Lecherous look
17 Prevent legally
18 Bucks' mates
19 Riot spray
20 What a cadet won't do (or permit others to do), per the West Point honor code
23 Bale contents
24 Four years, for a U.S. president
25 "My gal" of song
28 Kind of torch on "Survivor"
31 Noshes
35 Old
37 Siestas
39 Spread around
40 TV title role for Pierce Brosnan
43 Occupied, as a restroom
44 Blue-pencil
45 Coarse file
46 They're stuck in milk shakes
48 Eject in all directions
50 Bon ___ (witticism)
51 Studio stages
53 Lived
55 Supertough
61 Destiny
63 Become tiresome
64 Throw, as a shot put
65 Dr. Frankenstein's assistant
66 Swedish furniture giant
67 '50s–'60s singing sensation
68 Violinists' needs
69 Golf pegs
70 Fishing rod attachments

DOWN

1 European car
2 Not yet final, at law
3 Completely fill, as a hungry person
4 Tennyson's ___ Arden
5 Attire accompanying a cane
6 Early baby word
7 Prison unrest
8 That is, in Latin
9 Affixes in a scrapbook, say
10 School for which one feels nostalgic
11 Ring
12 "Just a ___!" ("Hold on!")
13 Before, in verse
21 Watching intently
22 Artist Max
25 Calcutta dresses
26 Ten-percenter
27 Tree-dwelling primate
29 Shakespearean shrew
30 Devices getting music downloads
32 It's skimmed off the top
33 Kutcher character on "That '70s Show"
34 Took the World Series in four games
36 Hurricanes, fires, etc.
38 Scissors cut
41 More modern
42 Frets
47 "Quit that!"
49 Laundromat fixture
52 What a charmer may charm
54 Inscribed pillar
55 Put away for later
56 Merriment
57 " 'Tis a shame"
58 Icicle's place
59 Blackhearted
60 Not so much
61 Little lie
62 "Long ___ . . ."

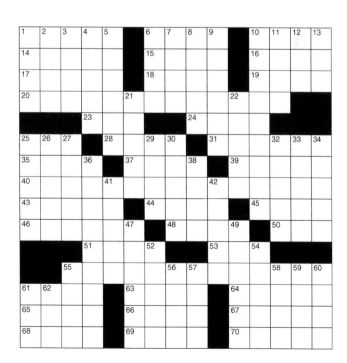

by Mike Torch

104

ACROSS

1 Jellied garnish
6 Prefix with phobia
10 "That was close!"
14 Zachary, for daiquiri, e.g.
15 Island near Lanai
16 Narrow path
17 Atkins diet no-nos
18 Pickpockets' targets
20 Worker with polish and a 23-Across
22 Furthermore
23 Tattered cloth
24 Pitching star
27 Acts like
32 Sprinkle with spices
34 '60s war zone, briefly
35 Her talk is, like, totally . . .
37 Colorado resort
40 ___ Paulo, Brazil
41 "Me, too!"
42 Southern fellow
45 Nav. rank
46 Make certain
47 Reacts angrily toward
50 Chicago-to-Tampa dir.
51 Bumped into
53 Anonymous John
54 Madonna, with "the"
60 Shady, as a street
63 Full of vigor
64 Worker's compensation
65 Ration (out)
66 Glowing coal
67 Run ___ (go crazy)
68 "A Day Without Rain" singer
69 Thick

DOWN

1 Circle segments
2 Former Iranian ruler
3 Fire fancier, for short
4 Comment at the end of a long, hard day
5 Big name in small planes
6 Prefix with dextrous
7 Brother of Abel
8 Sovereign
9 Primer type
10 Clever tactic
11 Computer in "2001"
12 Conclusion
13 "Scream" director Craven
19 Old-fashioned types
21 Modern viewing option, for short
24 Actors' lines to no one in particular
25 Eclipse phenomenon
26 Sign up
27 Since way back when
28 Bricklayers
29 Levy
30 Simplicity
31 Thick chunks
33 In the past
36 Diving bird
38 University Web address suffix
39 Like a body temperature of 98.6°
43 Water current with the wind
44 In triplicate, a Seinfeld catchphrase
48 Wheeled (out)
49 Peanut, for one
52 Mortise insert
54 Submissive
55 Count (on)
56 "You have no ___"
57 Library ID
58 Numbered rds.
59 Greek harp
60 Howard Hughes's airline
61 Hit head-on
62 Psychologist's "I"

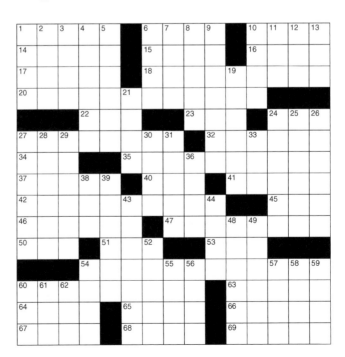

by Norm Guggenbiller

ACROSS

1 Problem with an old record
5 Jalopy
10 Glimpse
14 Jai ___
15 Chill out
16 The Buckeye State
17 Sailor's meteorological concern, in a saying
20 Classic party host Perle ___
21 Bob Marley fan
22 Links org.
23 "Where would ___ without you?"
25 Gerund's end
27 "The Wizard of Oz" route
36 Suffix with pay
37 Frenchman's topper
38 Taste or smell
39 "Steee-rike!" callers
41 Latin dance
43 Labor Day mo.
44 Egg sites
46 Six-stringed instruments
48 Berg composition
49 19th-century U.S. money
52 Letter after sigma
53 Trick winner, often
54 The Trojans of the N.C.A.A.
57 Steamed
61 The British ___
65 Starts of 17-, 27- and 49-Across, collectively
68 "___ on Down the Road"
69 Atlanta's Omni
70 Rewrite
71 Go bananas
72 Tennessee senator Alexander
73 Hankerings

DOWN

1 In the 80's, temperaturewise
2 Sheltered, at sea
3 X-ray units
4 Stamen's counterpart
5 Have a bawl
6 Derrière
7 Ski resort near Snowbird
8 Scottish caps
9 Strange and rare
10 Span longer than an era
11 Use FedEx, say
12 Sonar sound
13 Lotus position discipline
18 Dish on a skewer
19 Major and captain, e.g.
24 Lambs' ma'ams
26 Some college tests, for short
27 Offspring
28 Cartoondom's ___ Fudd
29 Run out, as a subscription
30 Cheer for a diva
31 Archaeologist's find
32 "No problem!"
33 Newsman Roger
34 Pet protection org.
35 Dissuade by threat, maybe
40 Leave in, as text
42 Hawkeye player on "M*A*S*H"
45 Symbol of slowness
47 Prefix with logical
50 Time capsule event
51 Stahl of "60 Minutes"
54 Employs
55 Ollie's partner in comedy
56 ___ Nostra
58 Taj Mahal site
59 Those guys
60 Sicilian volcano
62 Valuable vein
63 Leprechaun's land
64 Jet-setters' jets, once
66 Vim
67 Train unit

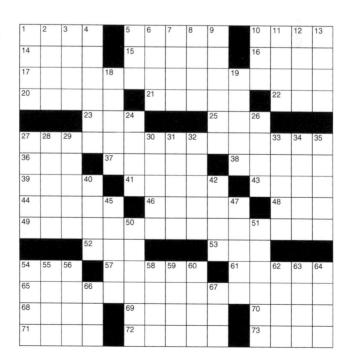

by John R. Conrad

106

ACROSS

1 Early 20th-century art movement
5 Dernier ___ (the latest thing)
8 Turtle cover
13 Designer Christian
14 Decay
15 Gather into a bundle, as wheat
16 Forest unit
17 Flying saucer fliers, for short
18 Awful
19 Island east of Australia
22 Tile art
25 Grasp
26 "Exodus" hero
27 Title for Prince Andrew
32 Dashboard meas.
33 List-ending abbr.
34 Onionlike plant used in cookery
36 Bake, as eggs
38 ___ de France
40 Enlarge
41 Angel topper
42 Org. with an academy near Colo. Springs
44 Western Indian
45 Proselytizer's success
49 Horned animal
50 Diva's delivery
51 Teens' rooms, typically
53 Gary Cooper title role
58 Opus Dei member
59 "___ the land of the free . . ."
60 Tiniest bit
64 Ancient markets, old-style
65 Letter between ex and zee
66 Atomic particle
67 Schlepper
68 Actor Beatty
69 Zebras, for lions

DOWN

1 Banned pesticide
2 A lungful
3 A deer, a female deer
4 Where the action is
5 Soldier's hairstyle
6 Campus mil. program
7 Lyric in the song named by the starts and ends of 19-, 27-, 45- and 53-Across
8 Poorly made
9 Medal recipient
10 Make, as an income
11 Roman 57
12 Helen's mother, in Greek myth
15 Bookcase unit
20 Duck with soft down
21 W.C.
22 Bog
23 Parentless child
24 Cute as a button, for one
28 China's Chiang ___-shek
29 No longer funny
30 Makes over
31 Stovetop vessel
35 Wackos
37 Use an oar
39 180° from WNW
40 Time ___ time
43 Like a Brink's truck
46 "Et tu, Brute?" utterer
47 Speak from a soapbox
48 Diarist Anaïs
52 Cut corners
53 Tiff
54 It then follows that . . .
55 Protest gone bad
56 Actor Richard of "Chicago"
57 Style of 1960s French pop music with a repetitive name
61 Lord's Prayer start
62 Foot's end
63 Whichever

by Edgar R. Fontaine

ACROSS

1 Soccer scores
6 Not go to
10 Crow's call
13 "Kate & ___" of 1980s TV
14 Opera set on the banks of the Nile
15 Pepsi, but not 7-Up
16 Conversation filler #1
18 Tends a garden
19 Rotary telephone part
20 Sale tag words
21 Cowboy's workplace
22 Lively, playful musical piece
24 Rank above maj.
25 Conversation filler #2
31 An arm and a leg
35 Place for an F.D.R. chat
36 Smell
37 ___ Michaels of "S.N.L."
39 Les États-___
40 Lamp fuel
42 Dead tired
43 Conversation filler #3
46 "Obviously!"
47 Lines on weather maps
52 Geek
55 Not just one of the two
57 Basic util.
58 Frees (of)
59 Conversation filler #4
61 Meter or liter
62 Shoe bottom
63 Ouzo flavoring
64 Understand
65 Gorbachev was its last leader: Abbr.
66 Extend the due date of

DOWN

1 "Oh, fer ___ sake!"
2 Kind of acid
3 To whom a Muslim prays
4 City NNE of Paris
5 The Caribbean, e.g.
6 Gives the green light
7 New Zealand bird
8 Mrs. William McKinley and others
9 Salary
10 Masked critter
11 Actor Baldwin
12 Laundry
15 Attributes (to)
17 "The Producers" extra
21 Womanizer
23 "Treasure Island" inits.
24 Very center
26 Violinist Zimbalist
27 Yang's counterpart
28 Full complement of baseball players
29 Valhalla chief
30 Pacific states, with "the"
31 Trickster in Norse myth
32 The same: Lat.
33 Extra
34 Most encompassing
37 Lustful one, informally
38 Yoko, the "fifth Beatle"
41 Treat rudely
42 ___-cone
44 One or the other
45 Worker safety grp.
48 Designer Geoffrey
49 ___ Ailey American Dance Theater
50 Witherspoon of "Walk the Line"
51 Fastener that's twisted in
52 Pharmaceutical
53 Merlot, for one
54 Revise
55 Warner ___
56 Big-eyed birds
59 Sch. in Stillwater
60 Sailor

by Alex Boisvert

ACROSS

1 Padlocked fasteners
6 Diet drink phrase
11 Beaver's work
14 God to a Muslim
15 Ralph's wife on "The Honeymooners"
16 Brazilian hot spot
17 Levy on consumer goods
19 I love: Lat.
20 Rock concert blasters
21 Web address ender
22 Shovel user
24 Chopped liver spread
26 Makes safe
27 "Evita" star Patti
30 ___ Quimby (Beverly Cleary heroine)
31 Dizzying designs
32 Most common throw with two dice
33 "Moo" maker
36 Cut and paste, say
37 Starts of 17- and 55-Across and 11- and 29-Down, impolitely
38 Knotty wood
39 Rockers ___ Jovi
40 Red-tag events
41 Explorer ___ de León
42 Popular candy bar
44 Stuck out
45 Source of a licoricelike flavoring
47 Piece of rodeo gear
48 Fountain treat
49 Have the flu, maybe
50 Was a fink
54 Humorist Shriner
55 Exterminator's work
58 Street crosser: Abbr.
59 Songstress Gorme

60 Striker's demand
61 "So's ___ old man!"
62 Hatchlings' homes
63 Cosmetician Elizabeth

DOWN

1 Mandlikova of tennis
2 Homecoming attendee, for short
3 Woman's undergarment
4 Globetrotter's document
5 Oldies group ___ Na Na
6 Mother-of-pearl
7 Cassini of fashion
8 Op. ___ (footnote abbr.)
9 College professors, e.g.

10 Dictionary
11 Activity on a strip
12 Actress Anouk
13 Othello's people
18 Post-it message
23 Pistol, e.g.
25 Aardvark's morsel
26 Doesn't spend everything
27 Leopold's co-defendant in 1920s crime
28 High hair style
29 Morphine, e.g.
30 Convened anew
32 "Rabbit food"
34 Years back
35 Lawn intruder
37 Unaided sight
38 Guiding light
40 Increase in verticality
41 Young seal
43 Believer's suffix

44 Tie with a clasp
45 Home products seller
46 Artless
47 Reduces to bits
49 Going ___ (bickering)
51 Dry as dust
52 Scent detector
53 Secluded valley
56 '60s protest grp.
57 Pro-Second Amendment grp.

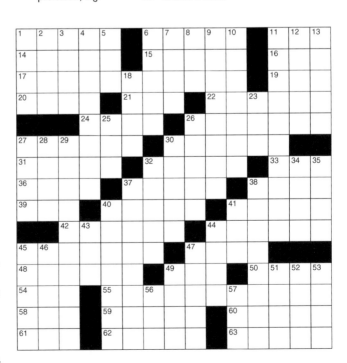

by Fred Piscop

ACROSS

1 Prison division
5 Prevalent
9 Ludicrous comedy
14 Tennis's Nastase
15 Make in income
16 Full of activity
17 Jam-packed with laughs and entertainment
19 Activist Chávez
20 "Sounds good to me!"
21 Yadda yadda yadda
23 Bean counter, for short
24 Remove, as a hat
25 Result of overexercise
28 ___ Paulo, Brazil
30 Checking out, as before a robbery
35 Dude
36 ___ fatale
38 Unusual object
39 Gridiron game with imaginary teams
42 Chilean range
43 Congestion location
44 Proof finale
45 Actor Warren
47 Prime meridian std.
48 Leaning Tower city
49 Porgy and bass
51 By way of
53 "Hurry up!"
57 Available, as a doctor
61 Nintendo's ___ Bros.
62 One way to jump in a pool
64 Turn topsy-turvy
65 Not made up
66 In the vicinity
67 Orals, e.g.
68 Lith. and Ukr., formerly
69 Bagful for Dobbin

DOWN

1 Modern kind of network
2 Homecoming attender
3 Saturn feature
4 Scrawl graffiti on, e.g.
5 Puts out, as a record
6 Suffix with president
7 Some guerrillas
8 Put an ___ (halt)
9 Be realistic
10 Help in a getaway, e.g.
11 Deception
12 Powerful person
13 Book after II Chronicles
18 Little scamp
22 Ozone depleter, for short
25 '90s Brit sitcom
26 See 33-Down
27 Civic maker
29 The Carters' daughter and others
31 Footlong, e.g.
32 Baghdad resident
33 With 26-Down, "Frasier" character
34 Mideast's Meir
36 Fare at KFC, McDonald's, Burger King, etc.
37 Geologic periods
40 Asian holiday
41 Defeats at the ballot box
46 Yang's counterpart
48 Al of "Insomnia," 2002
50 Sorts (through)
52 Like Beethoven's "Pastoral" Symphony
53 Dirty reading
54 Surveillance evidence
55 "You are" in Spain
56 Pub serving
58 Department
59 Future atty.'s exam
60 P.O. items
63 Where Switz. is

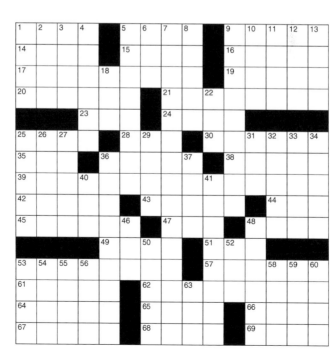

by Curtis Yee

110

ACROSS

1 E-mail from a Nigerian with $10 million to give you, e.g.
5 Average
9 Dwarf planet whose name is a Disney character
14 Loser to the tortoise
15 ___ vera
16 Poe bird
17 Clapton who sang "Layla"
18 ___ Hari (spy)
19 Musical work featuring 3-Down
20 State flower of Maryland
23 Light into
24 Kind of number: Abbr.
25 Flower with large velvety clusters
32 Sweetie
35 Words of comparison
36 Southwest plant
37 Much
39 Request from a doctor with a tongue depressor
42 Pagoda instrument
43 Late princess
45 Said aloud
47 Born: Fr.
48 Flower in the violet family often seen on roadsides
52 Prefix with thermal
53 Grand and baby grand
57 Frilly white flower also called wild carrot
62 It makes scents
63 "Open late" sign, maybe
64 Old balladeer's instrument
65 Wash off
66 "Otello" baritone
67 City east of Utah Lake
68 Quickness
69 Historic school on the Thames
70 Deep grooves

DOWN

1 Biblical land with a queen
2 Olympic track gold medalist Lewis et al.
3 Songs in a 19-Across
4 Places people are drawn to
5 Anonymous
6 Oil of ___
7 Repetitive process
8 Pasture
9 How a peacock struts?
10 Trips around the track
11 Eye part
12 Bird with a forked tail
13 Put ___ show
21 Fuzzy green fruit
22 ___ Lanka
26 Greek "H"
27 "Happy birthday ___"
28 Haul
29 Much-respected person
30 Clearasil target
31 Sorcerer
32 Muslim pilgrimage
33 Mishmash
34 He released a dove in Genesis
38 Old cable inits.
40 Sling's contents
41 Discover accidentally
44 Irate
46 San ___ Obispo, Calif.
49 Tokyo money
50 "Happy Days" character
51 Wanness
54 Pacific nation once known as Pleasant Island
55 Group of eight
56 Appears
57 Common cosmetics applicator
58 Eclectic magazine
59 Lighten, as a burden
60 In apple-pie order
61 Aborted
62 "___ Poetica"

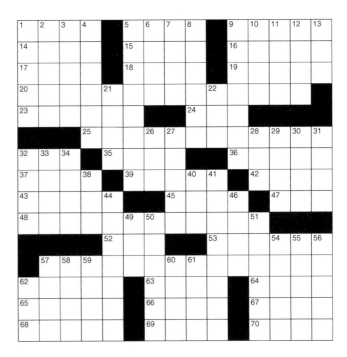

by Raymond Hamel

ACROSS

1 Untidiness
5 Gillette razor
9 Felt good about
14 Border on
15 Karate blow
16 ___ Pendragon, King Arthur's father
17 Crime bigwig
18 Genuine
19 Beauty queen's headgear
20 "The Man Who . . ." (1956)
23 Basinger of "Batman"
24 Cincinnati team
25 Homo sapiens, for man
27 Jogged
29 Ladder rung
32 Jackie's second spouse
33 Sightings the U.S.A.F. may investigate
35 Notion
37 Debate
41 "The Man Who . . ." (1973)
44 Muse of love poetry
45 Cruel
46 Time ___ half
47 Bird that hoots
49 Actress Meg
51 Deity
52 England/France connection
56 Give up, as territory
58 ___ Tin Tin
59 "The Man Who . . ." (1976)
64 Musical with the song "Don't Cry for Me, Argentina"
66 Long, long time
67 Seldom seen
68 Bit in a bed of roses
69 Repair
70 Hip bones
71 '50s Ford flop
72 Neighborhood
73 Boy ___ door

DOWN

1 Ted with TV's old "Original Amateur Hour"
2 Abba of Israel
3 Exploding star
4 Vermont ski resort
5 Verse with a hidden message
6 Lt. Kojak on "Kojak"
7 Wander
8 Great grade
9 Protestant who believes in the Book of Concord
10 "Lord, is ___?"
11 Park ranger's uniform color
12 Spine-tingling
13 Apothecaries' units
21 N.F.L. scores
22 Asst. on taxes
26 About
27 Reign
28 Get an ___ effort
30 Dutch cheese
31 Paul and Mary's partner in folk music
34 ___ Hall University
36 "An apple ___ keeps . . ."
38 Canada Dry product
39 Destroy
40 Old oath
42 Waterloo
43 Amazon menace
48 Harper who wrote "To Kill a Mockingbird"
50 Jacqueline Kennedy ___ Bouvier
52 Breakfast item with syrup
53 Made a home, as bees
54 The U's in B.T.U.'s
55 Andean animal
57 Bobby who sang "Beyond the Sea"
60 Sideways glance
61 Musical signal
62 Cereal with a rabbit mascot
63 Oven setting
65 Menlo Park inits.

by Randy Sowell

112

ACROSS

1 "___ Las Vegas" (1964 Elvis movie)
5 Armageddon
9 Snapshot
14 Gulf of ___, off the coast of Yemen
15 River of Spain
16 Pavarotti, notably
17 First digit in a California ZIP code
18 Hammer's end
19 ___-Seltzer
20 Those seeking attention?
23 Had a bite
24 Obstinate one
25 Convoy's front
29 Rapper Dr. ___
30 Waterfall effect
31 Cheer for a torero
32 Hearth contents
35 Dobbin's dinner
36 Skin cream ingredient
37 Mark on a Russian author's to-do list?
40 Gen. Patton, to George C. Scott
41 Pod contents
42 Subtle reminders
43 First lady?
44 Casino card game
45 Five-spot
46 Graduates-to-be
48 Chaney of horror films
49 U-turn from NNW
52 A Bangkok drink I had?
55 Clean in a tub
58 Go beyond a once-over
59 Make yawn
60 TV studio sign
61 Algerian seaport
62 Jai ___
63 Twists out of shape

64 What it may take to answer the question "Does this make me look fat?"
65 City near Carson City

DOWN

1 Title uncle in a classic Russian play
2 Doofus
3 Show's place
4 Once more
5 Topple, as a ruler
6 Follows directions
7 Splittable cookie
8 Single-slab stone monuments
9 J.F.K. commanded one in W.W. II
10 He ordered the execution of John the Baptist
11 Lennon's Yoko
12 Mr. Turkey
13 El Dorado's treasure
21 Like an arctic winter
22 Hermann who wrote "Siddhartha"
26 :
27 In the air
28 Snorkeling destinations
29 Hockey player's deceptive move
30 Former Portuguese territory in 39-Down
32 1960s TV's "Green ___"
33 Subway rider's move
34 Hunt of "As Good as It Gets"
35 Go too far
36 Related (to)
38 Dizzying museum display
39 Home to 1.3 billion people
44 Gathering spots at intermission
45 Instigate
47 "Gotcha, bro"
48 Shade of purple
49 Ripped off
50 Food wrap
51 Old MacDonald refrain
53 Taj Mahal site
54 Letter-shaped girder
55 Arrow's shooter
56 Santa ___, Calif.
57 Road goo

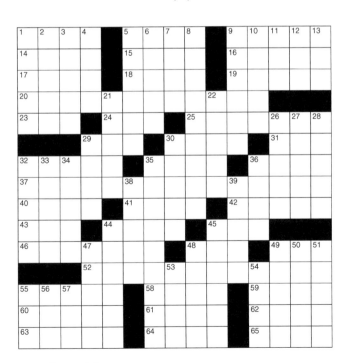

by Randall J. Hartman

ACROSS

1 President pro ___
4 Back biter?
9 ___ Polo, visitor to Cathay
14 Manipulate
15 Bad treatment
16 Flip one's lid?
17 Record label with a dog in its logo
18 Prove false
19 Movers and shakers
20 Outlaw William + actor Alan= Scottish boy?
23 Neither's go-with
24 Bay window
25 ___ the pants off
27 ___-mo replay
29 Pittsburgh team
33 Loud speaker
35 New Mexico art community
37 Hopping mad
38 Archaeologist Louis + actress Farrah = job for a plumber?
43 Huge mistake
44 Plummet
45 Lives
47 Declared
53 Minister, slangily
54 Sushi fish
56 Skedaddle
57 Guy's date
59 Wit Oscar + writer Joyce Carol = things to sow?
63 "Dig?"
65 Supermodel Campbell
66 Suffix with differ
67 Perfume
68 ___ Island, immigrants' arrival point
69 Karel Čapek drama
70 The Evita of "Evita"
71 Nick of "Lorenzo's Oil"
72 Hush-hush job

DOWN

1 Supercharged engines
2 Accompany to a party
3 No Mr. Nice Guy
4 Onetime phone company nickname
5 Toe the line
6 Break in the action
7 Continent explored by 9-Across
8 Oboe and bassoon
9 Wet dirt
10 Ever and ___
11 Brightness regulator
12 Singer Vikki + senator Trent = auto site?
13 Extra play periods, for short
21 Maiden name preceder
22 Twosome
26 Clapton who sang "Layla"
28 Lode load
30 Summer on the Riviera
31 They're soaked up at the beach
32 Capital of Bulgaria
34 "___ you nuts?"
36 Without: Fr.
38 Actor Rob + actor Richard = something to put a truck in?
39 One way to get up in the world?
40 Everything
41 MacLachlan of "Twin Peaks"
42 Divs. of a year
43 New Deal pres.
46 Stitch (up)
48 Plaza Hotel girl of fiction
49 Stephen of "Michael Collins"
50 Spuds
51 Align the edges of
52 "___ Rides Again" (1939 western)
55 Tablecloths
58 Chauffeur-driven vehicle
60 Film composer Schifrin
61 Barbie, e.g.
62 Give off
63 Opening
64 Beachgoer's shade

by Randall J. Hartman

114

ACROSS

1 Rollick or frolic
5 Singer Seeger
9 It's a no-no
14 Cleveland's lake
15 "Roots" writer Haley
16 Summer TV fare
17 Eat
18 Crossworder's crutch: Abbr.
19 Hopping mad
20 Did accounting hanky-panky, to a housekeeper?
23 Chicken ___ king
24 Loaf with seeds
25 Free (of)
26 Letters after els
28 Prefix with -gon
30 Variety, in life, so it's said
32 Visage overlooking Tiananmen Square
33 Made in the ___
35 ___ v. Wade
36 Belgrade resident
37 Did crime scene work, to a housekeeper?
42 Popular pizza/grill chain, informally
43 Newsman Rather
44 Speaks, informally
45 Thirsty
46 Hägar the Horrible's wife
48 Greek moralist
52 ... --- ...
53 &
54 W–Z, e.g., in an encyc.
56 "Able was I ___ . . ."
57 Handled Mob finances, to a housekeeper?
61 Threw
62 Cape Town currency
63 Cartoon opossum
64 Right-hand page

65 Chills and fever
66 Jog
67 Classic theater
68 Immodest look
69 Right-minded

DOWN

1 Baggage porter
2 Camden Yards player
3 Dweller on ancient Crete
4 What not to do before December 25?
5 Rice field
6 Upper crusts
7 Kind of support
8 Outside
9 Certain vacuum tube
10 Prefix with nautical
11 Some railroaders
12 Defeat with cunning
13 Air Force ___
21 Rub out
22 Muscle that's often shown off
27 Blubbers
29 Sounds of reproof
31 Part of a fork
34 Part of a sum
36 Petite or jumbo
37 Bombs without bangs
38 Opened, as a carpet
39 Chow mein flavorer
40 Nonsense: Var.
41 Domain
46 "Not so fast!"
47 Madison in New York or New York in Washington
49 Title in Tijuana
50 The Beaver State
51 Mescaline source
55 Weirder
58 Golden rule preposition
59 Fury
60 Chooses (to)
61 Bushy do, for short

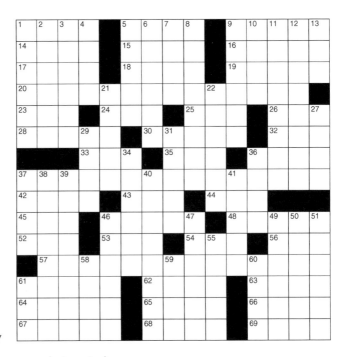

by Larry Paul

ACROSS

1 Lacking face value, as stock
6 For fear that
10 "The doctor ___"
14 Speechify
15 Blues singer James
16 ___ extra cost
17 Discotheque performer
19 The "N" of N.B.A.: Abbr.
20 ___ Gay (W.W. II plane)
21 Get sleepy-eyed
23 "Norma ___" (Sally Field film)
24 Extinct bird
26 Walking the dog and others
29 Up in the air
31 Schlep
32 Lenten symbol
33 Never-before-seen
34 Hockey star Lindros
36 Nine-digit ID
37 1920s musical with the sequel "Yes, Yes, Yvette"
41 Sombrero, e.g.
42 "Beloved" author Morrison
43 Mover's vehicle
46 One more time
49 Prosecutors, for short
50 Cream cheese flavoring
52 Haute couture icon with her own perfume
55 Dairy case item
56 Hanoi holiday
57 Chatter
58 PC storage medium
60 Brezhnev's land, in brief
62 It might have two stars
66 Slightly
67 "Bring ___!"

68 Bright bunch
69 Red ink entry
70 London gallery
71 "A burger, fries and a large Coke," e.g.

DOWN

1 Yuletide beverage
2 Conquistador's treasure
3 Scroll key on a computer
4 Many, many
5 Make over
6 "Chocolat" actress
7 And so on: Abbr.
8 Shorthand specialist, for short
9 Fortuneteller's card
10 Fleming who created 007
11 Shirt stiffener

12 Amount eaten
13 At a minimum
18 Prince ___ Khan
22 Severe
24 Former CBS anchor Rather
25 Corrida call
27 Mexican peninsula
28 Stevie Wonder's "___ She Lovely"
30 Period of a renter's lease
35 Balderdash
36 One of 100 on Capitol Hill: Abbr.
38 Birthplace of seven U.S. presidents
39 Front section of a rocket
40 Lex Luthor, for one
44 St. crossing
45 Prefix with classical
46 Genuine

47 Attends
48 Pretends to be
49 End of two state names
51 Loser to Roosevelt in 1932
53 ___ coming (warrants punishment)
54 King or emir: Abbr.
59 San ___ (Riviera resort)
61 Hwys.
63 Tippler
64 Language suffix
65 1970 #1 hit with the lyric "huh, yeah, What is it good for?"

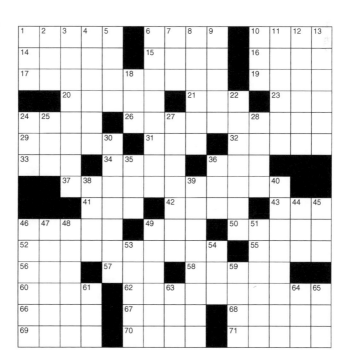

by Richard Chisholm

116

ACROSS

1 House in Spain
5 Keach of the small screen
10 Peter the Great, for one
14 European auto
15 Machine shop tool
16 River to the Seine
17 Little ___, Dickens girl
18 Place for sketches
20 Introduction in a Dr. Seuss book
22 Go on all fours
23 Coffee dispenser
24 Computer data holders
28 Order that may be scrambled or sunny-side up
30 Passed, as laws
32 Onetime Illinois governor Stevenson
34 "See ya!"
35 Golfer Ernie
36 Introduction in "Moby-Dick"
40 U.S./Gr. Brit. separator
41 6 on a phone pad
42 Answer
43 Like Marcel Duchamp's "Mona Lisa"
46 Jolt provider in a car
47 Typical Court TV programming
48 Berlin's land: Abbr.
50 Showbiz twin Mary-Kate or Ashley
54 Introduction in an NBC sitcom
57 Cleans up financially
60 100%
61 Line of rotation
62 Dweebs
63 Like ___ not

64 ___ messaging (modern communication)
65 Judge the value of, as ore
66 Congers

DOWN

1 Shaped like a dunce cap
2 ". . . partridge in ___ tree"
3 1965 Alabama march site
4 "Things are fine . . ."
5 Door-closing sound
6 Set of foot bones
7 Perfume from petals
8 Passageways for Santa
9 "Can" opener?
10 "Like wow, man"
11 Five-digit number on an envelope
12 Happy ___ lark
13 Ketchup-colored
19 "Look, I did it!"
21 Like pond scum
25 Stainless ___
26 Clarkson who won the first "American Idol"
27 Radical '60s grp.
29 "Hand it over, buster!"
31 First P.M. of modern India
32 Thespian
33 ___ Lama
34 Life story
37 Chess finales
38 Office messages
39 With mom, symbol of Americanism
40 15-percenter: Abbr.

44 Least wild
45 Tarzan player Ron and others
46 Starr of the comics
49 Mideast leaders
51 Cook, as onions
52 Swashbuckler Flynn
53 Mets and Cubs, for short
55 "Peter Pan" dog
56 ___-bitsy
57 Small rug
58 Logger's tool
59 General Mills cereal

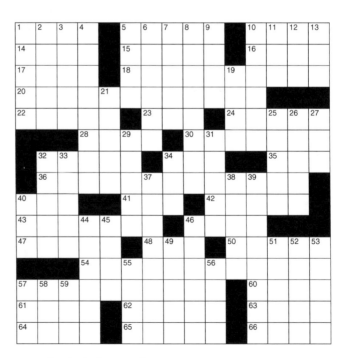

by Elizabeth C. Gorski

ACROSS

1 Jewel
4 Accumulate
9 One making a point at church?
14 Mine find
15 Money in India
16 Hearing-related
17 Top-ranked player in a tournament
19 Little old man in a fairy tale
20 Supernatural
21 Confucian path
23 Network that covers the N.Y.S.E.
24 Reward from a boss
25 Holdup victim's plea
27 Kids' guessing game
29 Cereal that's "for kids"
30 Smoker's mouthpiece
34 Shoot using a scope, say
37 Ripken who played 2,632 straight games
38 Dutch island in the Caribbean
41 Playa __ Rey, Calif.
42 Trap
45 Decorative foil
48 Cheap laughs
50 Patricia __, Best Actress for "Hud"
51 Beer drinker's bar request
55 "Of course," slangily
59 See 60-Across
60 With 59-Across, battle planning site
61 Pay no heed
62 Kofi of the U.N.
64 Pilgrims' carrier
66 Long, drawn-out attack
67 Indifferent
68 Dig into, as dinner
69 Check recipient

70 Furrier John Jacob __
71 Area between N. and S. Korea

DOWN

1 Try to attain
2 "Fear of Fifty" writer Jong
3 Parisian thanks
4 Lacking guile
5 Be compelled to
6 Cousin of a human
7 Look after
8 Alternative to a convertible
9 Slump
10 Hit the time clock
11 Rust
12 Classic Stallone role
13 Send to the Capitol
18 "Wake Up Little __"
22 Hall-of-Famer Mel

25 Easter egg decorator
26 Sophs., two years later
28 Mom-and-pop grp.
30 Dell products
31 Singer Janis
32 Monopoly game equipment
33 Face on a "wanted" poster
35 Vegetable on a vine
36 North Pole helper
39 School funder, often
40 Drink with a head on it
43 Search (through)
44 Squeeze (out)
46 Tassel on a cap, e.g.
47 Grassy plain of South America
49 Logging tool
51 Understanding

52 Ancient region with an architectural style named after it
53 "La __" ('59 hit)
54 European/Asian range
56 Dragged behind
57 Cat's saucerful
58 Avis rival
61 In that case . . .
63 Born: Fr.
65 China's Sun __-sen

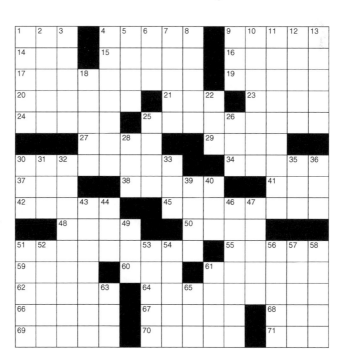

by Lynn Lempel

118

ACROSS
1 High-I.Q. group
6 Pennsylvania university, for short
10 Change, as the décor
14 Island with a reef
15 Sound in a cave
16 Allege
17 Got fit, with "up"
18 23-Across's representative in the 38-Across
20 Battery terminal
21 The New World: Abbr.
22 Howe'er
23 One of two parties to 38-Across
27 He can go to blazes
30 Cries convulsively
31 W.C. in London
32 "Cómo ___?"
34 Dog in "The Thin Man"
38 Declaration of August 14, 1941, regarding peace aims after W.W. II
43 Island east of Java
44 "Little piggies"
45 "Exodus" hero
46 Scholastic sports grp.
50 Common entree at a potluck dinner
52 One of two parties to 38-Across
56 Silent assent
57 Arnaz of 1950s TV
58 Biblical land with a queen
62 52-Across's representative in the 38-Across
65 Spreader of seeds
66 ___ of Wight
67 Plenty mad
68 Build
69 Mole, to a gardener

70 Bygone Fords
71 Library stations

DOWN
1 ___ Hari (W.W. I spy)
2 School for Prince William
3 Taboo
4 Heavy hitter
5 Municipal lawmakers
6 Chest muscle, for short
7 Popular Apple communication software
8 Hitchhikers' digits
9 Caped fighter
10 Word of cheer
11 The second Mrs. Perón
12 Indian city of 12+ million

13 Acrylic fiber
19 Place for a mobile
24 90° from north
25 One who hasn't turned pro?
26 Old Russian monarch
27 Spare tire
28 Not one ___
29 Somersault
33 Do something
35 Antlered animal
36 Seabird with a forked tail
37 Opera solo
39 Fats Waller's "___ Misbehavin'"
40 Pepsi, e.g.
41 Summer woe
42 Evaluated
47 Give up
48 Have ___ of a time
49 Declare

51 On the beach
52 Tear open, as seams
53 Loop with a slipknot
54 Hero types
55 Like most bathroom floors
59 Wool coat wearers
60 Call's partner
61 Word with liberal or martial
63 Call between ready and go
64 Six-pointers, for short

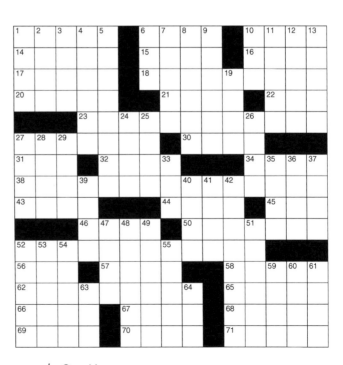

by Gene Newman

ACROSS

1 Capital of Tibet
6 [Oh, my heavens!]
10 "Get lost, kitty!"
14 String ties
15 Sharif of film
16 Tiny bit
17 Sound after a tear is shed
18 Shoestring
19 Unappetizing food
20 Parental demand #1
23 Major leaguer
24 British rocker Brian
25 Actor Beatty
26 Sheet of ice
29 Putin's rejection
32 Sets (down)
34 Parachute part
35 Grooved on
36 Lobbying grp.
37 Parental demand #2
43 General at Appomattox
44 ___ favor (please, in Spanish)
45 Gumbo vegetable
46 "Gee willikers!"
48 Surmounting
49 "Hey . . . you!"
50 Cousin of "ruff!"
51 Column's counterpart
53 "Well, ___-di-dah!"
55 Parental demand #3
61 Supply-and-demand subj.
62 Long car, for short
63 Construction piece
65 Salon job
66 Mishmash
67 Fine thread
68 Sequoia, for one
69 Barclays Center hoopsters
70 Kid's response to 20-, 37- and 55-Across

DOWN

1 Abbr. on a dumbbell
2 ___ Kong
3 "That's ___!" (debate retort)
4 Plays down, as an issue
5 In reference to
6 Sport with woods and Woods
7 Part of a Latin 101 conjugation
8 Scented pouch
9 Fuss over oneself
10 [Isn't he dreamy?!]
11 Massachusetts, e.g., before 1776
12 Makes amends
13 Not live
21 Dipping dish
22 Like Peary's explorations
26 Govt. media watchdog
27 Chat room joke response
28 Miner's load
30 Nope's counterpart
31 Pharaoh's land
33 Woe on an observation deck
36 Lilac or violet
38 India's first P.M.
39 Tic-tac-toe win
40 Green-lights
41 Surgery sites, for short
42 "Welcome" site
46 Worker with an apron
47 From way back when
48 For some time
50 Skillful
52 Synthetic fiber
54 "Where there's ___ . . ."
56 "This one's ___!"
57 Fail to mention
58 Dairy farm sounds
59 Take a break
60 Cabbagelike vegetable
64 Mal de ___

by Elayne Cantor

120

ACROSS

1 Bullets and such
5 High-tech appt. books
9 Duo times four
14 Gather, as grain
15 The New Yorker cartoonist Peter
16 Plant life
17 "It's true!" (#1)
20 Shorthand pro, for short
21 Cousin of contra-
22 "The King and I" heroine
23 Emcee
25 "I get it, stop nagging me!"
27 Chinese temples
30 Leap day's mo.
31 Astern
34 Rights org.
35 Hooey
37 Prefix with continental
39 "It's true!" (#2)
43 Places to build on
44 Crew member's implement
45 Ends up with
46 Abbr. on a golf scorecard
47 __ green
50 Palestine's locale
52 U.N. member through 1991
53 Leave port
54 Verdon of Broadway
57 Hemingway nickname
59 Greedy king of myth
63 "It's true!" (#3)
66 Fable's end
67 Where the Euphrates flows
68 Give off
69 Skiing locale
70 Cows chew them
71 Installs, as an outfield

DOWN

1 Sciences' partner
2 Beef or bacon
3 Cobble together
4 Realtor's event
5 Be worthwhile
6 Baker St. assistant
7 Poetic adverb
8 In a way
9 Not quite oneself
10 Part of a Dracula costume
11 Unable to decide
12 Nickname for Ireland
13 Informal farewell
18 Frame of mind
19 Flood protector
24 Calcutta attire
26 Newspaper notice
27 Unwitting victim
28 Sharply stinging
29 Overstuffs
31 Between ports
32 Outstanding accomplishments
33 Secret meeting
36 A wee hour
38 Cat's asset, it's said
40 Recipe amts.
41 Post-Easter sandwich content
42 Puccini piece
48 Fox Sports alternative
49 Official language of Libya
51 Thin coin
52 Open, as a toothpaste tube
54 Workout centers
55 Scarf material
56 Money in Madrid
58 Cuzco's country
60 Floor model
61 In the thick of
62 Collect-'em-all collections
64 Drink on draught
65 Mental measures, for short

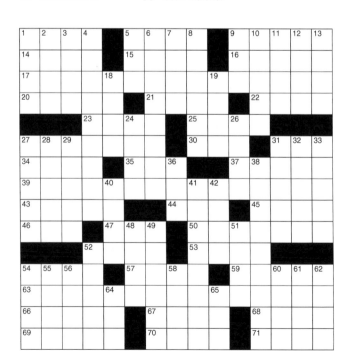

by Stanley Newman

ACROSS

1 Part of a flower or wineglass
5 "Exodus" author Leon
9 "Aladdin" villain
14 Volcano output
15 Quarter of a bushel
16 Had dinner at home
17 Jai ___
18 Sycamore or cypress
19 Diploma receivers, for short
20 The best place to sleep
23 Drought relief
24 This-and-that dish
25 Most strange
28 They may be tapped for fraternities
32 Singer in ABBA
33 Give up a poker hand
34 "Vive le ___!"
35 The best place to sit
39 Vietnamese New Year
40 Abhor
41 Make up (for)
42 Long journeys
45 Name holders
46 "Little piggies"
47 About, on a memo
48 The best place to see
54 Narrow openings
55 Ending with peek or bug
56 Place to order a ham on rye
57 Secret stash
58 Take care of, as a store
59 Prez, e.g.
60 Like a stamp pad
61 Guitarist Townshend
62 Carve in stone

DOWN

1 Response to a rude remark
2 A fisherman might bring back a big one
3 Bayh of Indiana
4 They show you to your table
5 Ready for a challenge
6 Second airing
7 Summer coolers in tiny cups
8 ___-Ball (arcade game)
9 Alternative to a Mercedes or BMW
10 In jeopardy
11 Burlesque show accessory
12 Capitol Hill worker
13 E.R. workers
21 Attacks
22 Loses hair, as a dog
25 "We're ___ See the Wizard"
26 Hung on the clothesline
27 Prank that's not nice
28 Yachts, e.g.
29 Otherwise
30 On one's way
31 Trig functions
33 Whip
36 Where VapoRub may be rubbed
37 Training group
38 Conference-goer
43 Relieve
44 Felt
45 Like secret messages
47 "Not gonna do it"
48 Custard dessert
49 Highway exit
50 Theater award
51 Student's book
52 Monthly util. bill
53 Having megamillions
54 Chem. or biol.

by Mike Nothnagel

ACROSS

1 Blind trio in a children's rhyme
5 Cripples
10 Hindu prince
14 On the ocean
15 Eve of "Our Miss Brooks"
16 "Be it ___ so humble . . ."
17 Tenant's monthly check
18 Embroidery, e.g.
20 Crosses (out)
21 Wrote fraudulently, as a check
22 Armored vehicles
23 Chicago-based TV talk show
25 Actor Bert in a lion's suit
27 Lantern usable during storms
31 Snaky curves
32 Activist Brockovich
33 Mauna ___ (Hawaiian volcano)
36 Like arson evidence
37 Bread for breakfast
39 Bucket
40 Prefix with cycle
41 Closed
42 Refuse a request
43 Hanukkah food
47 Dramatist Simon who wrote "Plaza Suite"
48 Rewords
49 Tolerate
52 Fable writer
54 Olympic gold-medal runner Sebastian
57 Some makeup
59 Alluring
60 Actor Baldwin
61 Hackneyed
62 Leg's midpoint
63 Hazard
64 Without the help of written music
65 Hankerings

DOWN

1 Karl who philosophized about class struggle
2 "Aha!"
3 Government suppression of the press
4 Have dinner
5 Nutcase
6 Franklin known as the Queen of Soul
7 ___ fixe (obsession)
8 Busybodies
9 Weekend NBC hit, for short
10 Put on the stove again
11 The Bard's river
12 Bozo
13 Torah holders
19 Wharton's "___ Frome"
21 ___ Kringle
24 Hunter's target
26 Landed (on)
27 Summer oppressiveness
28 SALT I signer
29 "Cool!"
30 Do some acting
34 Sty sound
35 ___ vera
37 Spicy Asian cuisine
38 Criminal activity
39 Treaty
41 Precipitous
42 Small scissor cut
44 Next up
45 Pre-euro Spanish coin
46 Worshipful one
49 Way, way off
50 "___ Ha'i" ("South Pacific" song)
51 Frosty desserts
53 ___ Britt on "Desperate Housewives"
55 Yoked beasts
56 What the starts of 18-, 27-, 43- and 57-Across all have
58 Wagering loc.
59 Heavens

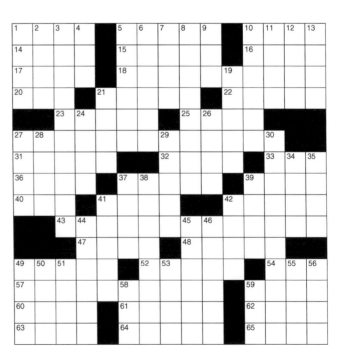

by Lynn Lempel

ACROSS

1 Comedian Foxworthy
5 Tiff
9 Manhandle
14 Early TV role for Ron Howard
15 Author Victor
16 Comment to the audience
17 1960s series about a boy and his bear
19 Outsides of lemons and limes
20 12th-grader
21 Swiss-based relief group
23 Johnny of "Pirates of the Caribbean"
25 Itsy-bitsy
26 Choose
29 Greeting with a hug and a kiss, say
35 Cawing birds
37 Go bankrupt
38 Ever and ___
39 Kind of lamp at a luau
40 Composer Franz
41 Give temporarily
42 Genesis garden
43 ___ Major
44 Popeye's burly foe
45 Feature of the Christian God
48 Cathedral seat
49 Dernier ___ (the latest thing)
50 Cold and damp, as a basement
52 Home of a hypothetical monster
57 "I haven't the foggiest"
61 Miss ___ of TV's "Dallas"
62 Compliment
64 Grabs (onto)
65 Object of devotion
66 Mailed

67 "Full House" actor Bob
68 Being nothing more than
69 "The Bridge on the River ___"

DOWN

1 Runs for exercise
2 Sporting sword
3 Huckleberry ___
4 Offensive-smelling
5 Mountain climber's guide
6 Place to play darts
7 Chemical used by document forgers
8 Dial ___
9 Package
10 "If memory serves . . ."
11 Overindulger of the grape
12 Throws in
13 ___ Trueheart of "Dick Tracy"
18 Big name in movie theaters
22 Lived (in)
24 Employer of flacks
26 Santa's reindeer, minus Rudolph
27 Egotist's sin
28 Subway coin
30 En ___ (as a group)
31 Harry Potter, for one
32 Outdo by a little
33 Three-card scam
34 Furnish with a fund
36 Porch music maker
40 Alison who won a Pulitzer for "Foreign Affairs"
44 Previously, up to this point
46 Polar explorer Shackleton
47 Wick holder
51 Newsstand
52 Chicken drumsticks
53 Earthenware pot
54 Job for a drain cleaner
55 Read over hurriedly
56 Pro or con
58 Provoked, as enemy fire
59 Poet ___ St. Vincent Millay
60 Wine-producing region of Italy
63 Neither hide ___ hair

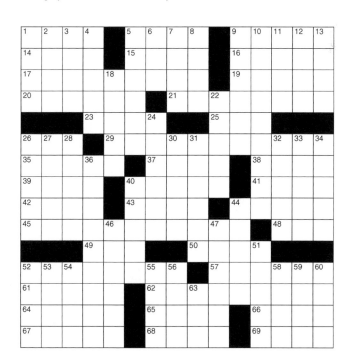

by Dave Tuller

124

ACROSS

1 Word repeated before "black sheep, have you any wool?"
4 Semester
8 Seizes (from)
14 Building add-on
15 Downwind, on a ship
16 Kitt who played Catwoman on "Batman"
17 Avg., sizewise
18 Aromatherapy liquid
20 Cereal named for two ingredients it doesn't have
22 ___ of Cleves, English queen
23 Back of a boat
24 Emergency PC key
25 SSW's reverse
26 The "I" in T.G.I.F.
28 Jacuzzi
31 Jacuzzis
34 Maxima maker
38 "Put ___ Happy Face"
39 Really tired
42 Small bed
43 Followed the leader
44 Shady giants
45 Becomes a parent not by childbirth
47 Slangy assent
49 "Once upon a midnight dreary" writer
50 Veneration
53 Numbskull
57 No. on a baseball card
59 Gary Cooper film of 1928
61 Overwrought writing
64 Architect I. M. ___
65 Removes, as a knot
66 Sporting sword
67 Nest item
68 Turns back to zero
69 Lifeless
70 "Nope"

DOWN

1 Floaters in northern seas
2 Vigilant
3 Tiny pond plants
4 Aptitude
5 Pizazz
6 Variety show
7 Swim competitions
8 Said "I do" together
9 Norma ___, Sally Field role
10 On the wrong course
11 Paleolithic hammer or ax
12 Skinny
13 Realtor's aim
19 President's foreign policy grp.
21 Light refractor
25 All's opposite
27 Rebuffs rudely
28 Robust
29 E pluribus ___
30 Upside-down sleepers
31 Org. offering creature comforts?
32 Trudge
33 Fenders, taillights, etc.
35 Swelling reducer
36 Where a telescope is aimed
37 "Get it?"
40 Lug
41 Train stop
46 Baked entree with a crust
48 Controlled the mike
50 Austrian peak
51 Sent by bank transfer
52 Get hitched hastily
54 Turn red, as an apple
55 End of the Greek alphabet
56 Whinny
57 Cowboy boot part
58 Ditty
60 Between ports
62 Permit
63 Twisty turn

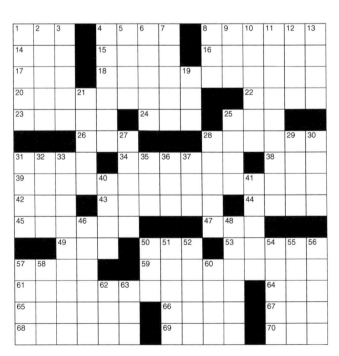

by Lynn Lempel

ACROSS

1 "Mutiny on the Bounty" captain
6 Half a McDonald's logo
10 Blend
14 Anouk of "La Dolce Vita"
15 Mineral in transparent sheets
16 "Told you I could do it!"
17 1944 Judy Garland movie
20 Feathery scarves
21 Magazine revenue source
22 Soda can opener
23 Gets on the nerves of
25 Mideast leaders
27 Marsh plant
29 Facing trouble
33 With 45-Across, 1993 Tom Hanks/Meg Ryan movie
37 Aerosol
38 Krazy ___ of the comics
39 Jamboree participant
41 Going way back, as friends
42 Dog collar attachment
45 See 33-Across
48 Hits the roof
50 Morales of "NYPD Blue"
51 Pointed, as a gun
53 Mild aftershock
57 "Oh my heavens!"
60 Luau instrument, informally
62 Nickelodeon's ___ the Explorer
63 2000 Richard Gere/Winona Ryder movie
66 Russia's ___ Mountains

67 Early Bond foe
68 Spine-chilling
69 Portend
70 Twist, as findings
71 Utopias

DOWN

1 "La ___," 1959 hit
2 Rest atop
3 "To put it another way . . ."
4 Become peeved
5 Skirt edge
6 Surrounded by
7 Step after shampooing
8 Syringe amts.
9 Millinery accessory
10 Clogs, as a drain
11 Drawn tight
12 Prefix with -syncratic
13 Hoarse voice
18 Flip chart holders

19 The ___ Prayer
24 "You betcha!"
26 Apply incorrectly
28 Make up one's mind
30 Gait between walk and canter
31 Ring up
32 Jekyll's bad side
33 Slaloms
34 Stow, as cargo
35 Suffix with cigar
36 Prince, to a king
40 Exam taker
43 Generally speaking
44 Brother with a fairy tale
46 Swiss river to the Rhine
47 Like some Grateful Dead fans' attire
49 Corrects
52 Irene of "I Remember Mama"

54 Poet Clement C. ___
55 Sen. Hatch
56 Does fall yard work
57 Apply carelessly, as paint
58 Continental coin
59 Not much
61 Have down pat
64 Vex
65 Minuscule

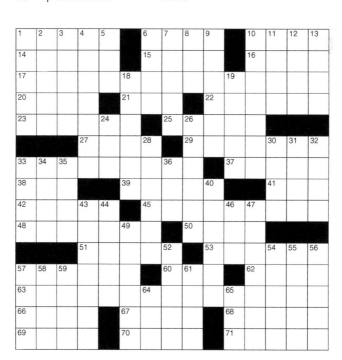

by Harvey Estes

126

ACROSS

1 The life of Riley
5 Blessings
10 "How about ___?!"
14 Voting group
15 AM/FM device
16 Rabbit moves
17 When one might wear a hat
19 Singer India.___
20 Binary code digit
21 Presidential advisers
23 Done permanently, as writing
26 The first "T" of TNT
28 Smart ___ (wiseacres)
29 Neighbor of Vietnam
30 Gidget player in "Gidget"
32 "___ Abner"
33 Popular soap
35 Son of, in Arabic names
36 Motto of New Hampshire
41 Western treaty grp.
42 Rick's love in "Casablanca"
43 Bit of hair cream, say
45 Generic modeling "clay" for tots
49 Bull in a bullfight
50 Airs, in Latin
51 ___ Beta Kappa
52 "A right ___ old elf" (Santa)
53 Three-letter combo
55 Mooer
56 Ascent
57 Stamp on an envelope without enough stamps
63 Verb type: Abbr.
64 ___ Park, Colo.
65 Late civil rights activist Parks
66 "What ___!" ("How cool!")
67 Fashion
68 Headliner

DOWN

1 Flow's partner
2 Chicken ___ king
3 Lawn makeup
4 Sounds in an empty hall
5 Cheese from France
6 Boater's blade
7 Like 1, 3, 5, 7 . . .
8 An essential vitamin
9 Kind of bean
10 It was once Siam
11 Like bulls' heads
12 Each
13 Sleeping sickness carrier
18 Raggedy ___
22 Singer Streisand
23 Running a temperature, say
24 Hammer's target
25 ___ sci (college major, informally)
26 Pre-1917 Russian ruler
27 North Carolina's capital
31 "Vaya con ___" ("Go with God")
33 More tired
34 Assuming that's true
37 Travelers
38 Relating to grades 1–12
39 British rocker Billy
40 Countess's husband
44 "Whew!"
45 Homeland, to Horace
46 Tempting
47 Record label for many rappers
48 Highest
49 TV transmission sites
52 Morning run, perhaps
54 "Planet of the ___"
55 24 cans of beer
58 Hog haven
59 No. with an area code
60 Period
61 Land north of Mex.
62 End point for an iPod cord

by Sarah Keller

ACROSS

1 With: Fr.
5 Milkshake item
10 In ___ (together)
14 Hawaiian port
15 "The Devil Wears ___"
16 Get better, as a cut
17 State with conviction
18 Drive away
19 Artist Bonheur
20 Historic Boston neighborhood
22 Wiggle room
24 Loads and loads
25 Gush
26 Totaling
29 Comedian who created the character Jose Jimenez
33 Manipulate
34 Burden of proof
35 Half a sch. year
36 Toll unit on a toll road
37 What "yo mama" is
39 Cover for a wound
40 Plop oneself down
41 "Are you ___ out?"
42 Gem of an oyster
43 Ailment that may cause sneezing
45 Go by, as time
46 Wolf's sound
47 Jump named for a skater
48 Empty, as a lot
51 Auxiliary wager
55 Composer Stravinsky
56 Some Apples
59 Say yea or nay
60 Line of stitches
61 Modern assembly line worker
62 Love god
63 "The Thin Man" dog
64 Les ___-Unis
65 Mardi Gras follower

DOWN

1 Melville captain
2 Start of a Spanish cheer
3 Util. bill
4 Sound-absorbing flooring
5 Helped bust out, as from prison
6 Cards above deuces
7 Séance sound
8 Juice drink
9 Where to get juice for a household appliance
10 Astute
11 "Man, that hurts!"
12 Astronaut's insignia
13 Potter's medium
21 007
23 Slithery fishes
25 Ireland's ___ Fein
26 Covered with water
27 The South
28 River mouth feature
29 Word that can follow the first words of 20-, 29-, 43- and 51-Across and 4-, 9-, 37- and 39-Down
30 BMI rival
31 Draws nigh
32 Mosey (along)
37 Winter traction provider
38 Lounge
39 Death Valley is below it
41 Computer image
42 Appealed earnestly
44 Greg's sitcom partner
45 Is
47 English race place
48 Document checked at a border
49 Matures
50 Jacket
52 Bloviator, often
53 Princely prep school
54 Exam
57 Bon ___ (witticism)
58 Lawyer's org.

by Paula Gamache

128

ACROSS

1 End place for many a car accident
6 Mire
9 "Shhh!"
14 Novelist Calvino
15 Bother
16 The "U" of UHF
17 Astronaut's attire
18 Fluffy scarf
19 Go into
20 Not the real Charlie of Star-Kist ads?
23 Born: Fr.
24 Big part of an elephant
25 Ambulance worker, for short
26 Tetley product
29 Vintage French wines?
32 Rabble-rouse
34 Inexperienced in
35 Italian volcano
36 Assistant in a con game
39 Nix by Nixon, e.g.
40 Mire
42 Peanuts
44 1960s sitcom ghoul on the terrace?
47 1976 and 2001, e.g.: Abbr.
48 Sunbather's shade
49 Founded: Abbr.
50 Korean automaker
53 What 20-, 29-, 44- and 53-Across are of each other
56 Actress Sarandon
59 "Exodus" hero
60 Muscat native
61 Prank
62 Lower, as the lights
63 Stirred up
64 With feigned shyness
65 Reverse of WNW
66 Trap

DOWN

1 "Start eating!"
2 Reply to "Who's there?"
3 Brownish gray
4 Annual award named for a Muse
5 Stressful spot
6 The Sultan of Swat
7 Smell
8 Uncle Sam facial feature
9 Director Tarantino
10 Arm bone
11 Major defense contractor
12 "But I heard him exclaim, ___ he . . ."
13 Driveway surface
21 Bye-byes
22 Referee
26 Pisa landmark
27 French political divisions
28 Regarding
29 City on Biscayne Bay
30 Have the throne
31 Emphatic no
32 In armed conflict
33 Pesky swarm
35 Catch sight of
37 Lollygag
38 "___ luck!"
41 Effectiveness
43 Racetrack habitués
45 Deface
46 Like beds before housekeeping
50 Australian "bear"
51 Word before tube or circle
52 Off the direct course
53 Bucket
54 "Exodus" author
55 Poker player's declaration
56 Anatomical pouch
57 Tres – dos
58 Muddy enclosure

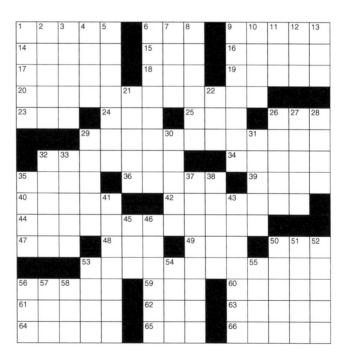

by John Calvin Williams

ACROSS

1 Soaking site
5 Cry like a baby
9 Early Peruvian
13 Jai ___
14 Category
15 Sweetheart
16 Window ledge
17 Jason's sorceress wife
18 Long and lean
19 Comment upon bumping into an old friend, #1
22 Russian refusal
23 Soul singer James
24 San Francisco/ Oakland separator
27 Comment #2
31 John, Paul and George: Abbr.
34 Hi-___ monitor
35 Wordsworth works
36 Pistol, e.g.
39 "Forget about it!"
41 Bubbling on the stove
42 Like sushi
43 Militant '60s campus org.
44 Comment #3
49 Absorb, with "up"
50 Word that's an example of itself
51 Klutz's cry
54 Comment #4
59 "Let's get crackin'!"
61 Forearm bones
62 "Agreed!"
63 Wolf's cry
64 ___ Rizzo of "Midnight Cowboy"
65 Peaceful period
66 ___-bitsy
67 Deuces
68 Häagen-Dazs alternative

DOWN

1 Wingding
2 Visitor from another planet
3 Running total
4 Jewish campus group
5 Borscht ingredient
6 Julie who played Mary Poppins
7 Christmas garland
8 Makeshift shelter
9 Run in place
10 Not-so-potent potables
11 Campbell's container
12 Biblical boat
14 Baseball bigwigs: Abbr.
20 Plains Indian
21 Responses of shock
25 Carrying a weapon
26 Go-aheads
28 Sch. named for a televangelist
29 Author Kesey
30 ___ polloi
31 Persian potentates
32 Just not done
33 Blizzard battlers
37 Opposite of multiplication: Abbr.
38 First American to orbit Earth
39 Arrest
40 Have bills
42 Meet unexpectedly
45 Dannon product
46 Wanted felon
47 Ages and ages
48 Pasta bit
52 Nom de plume: Abbr.
53 Serta competitor
55 Nothing but
56 The "m" of E = mc^2
57 "___ Beso" (Paul Anka song)
58 Building additions
59 "The Sweetheart of Sigma ___"
60 Bon ___ (witticism)

by Nanoy Salomon

130

ACROSS

1 PC alternatives
5 Big name in pest control
10 Resident of 29-Down
14 "Shake ___" (1981 song by the Cars)
15 "Me, too!"
16 Get the wrinkles out of
17 Dickens's "little" girl
18 Showed interest in, as at a bar
19 This, in Madrid
20 Jakarta
23 Poet's Muse
24 Common Web site section, for short
25 O, Us or GQ
28 Cats' prey
32 TWA competitor
34 "___ Poetica"
37 Nickname for Namath
40 Certain carpet or hairdo
42 Skylit courts
43 What a casting director tries to fill
44 Employee benefit
47 Free from, with "of"
48 Madison Avenue worker
49 Japanese wrestling
50 Take care of a bill
51 Helpers for profs
54 Singer ___ Khan
59 Fuddy-duddy
64 Sites of monkey business?
66 Closet wood
67 Calf-length skirt
68 Rick's love in "Casablanca"
69 Squiggly mark in "señor"
70 Nuclear energy source
71 Peelable fruit
72 Proceed on tiptoe
73 Nasdaq alternative

DOWN

1 Cut into tiny bits
2 "Don't shed ___"
3 Mea ___
4 Challenging bowling pin arrangement
5 Agency with workplace regs.
6 Agitate
7 The Green Hornet's valet
8 Cry at a leave-taking
9 "Teenage Mutant ___ Turtles"
10 Chicken ___
11 Big Dipper's locale
12 Decompose
13 Genetic stuff
21 ___ of the Unknowns
22 Blue hue
26 Garlicky mayonnaise
27 King Midas's downfall
29 Mideast land
30 Big maker of perfumes
31 Famous family of Western lawmen
33 Damascus's land: Abbr.
34 BMI rival
35 "The Mary Tyler Moore Show" spinoff
36 1998 National League M.V.P.
38 God, in Paris
39 In the 70s or so
41 3.5, e.g., for a student
45 Prefix with lock
46 1970s–'80s Big Apple mayor
52 Bank holdings: Abbr.
53 Coil of yarn
55 Muscly fellow
56 Friendship
57 Praise
58 Stop on ___
60 Ivan the Terrible, e.g.
61 Not in use
62 It means nothing to Juan
63 Long, long walk
64 12345, in Schenectady, N.Y.
65 Corrida shout

by Christina Houlihan Kelly

ACROSS

1 Practice boxing
5 Setting for "Hansel and Gretel"
10 Like very early education, for short
14 Brand of blocks
15 ___ Hoffman of the Chicago Seven
16 Education by memorization
17 Region
18 Religious belief
19 Super-duper
20 One-L lama
23 Rational
24 "___ Misérables"
25 Cutting up, as logs
28 Housekeeper
30 Crow's call
33 "___ goeth before a fall"
34 Building with a loft
35 Sulk
36 Two-L llama
39 Architect ___ van der Rohe
40 Some Keats poems
41 Put into law
42 Upper chamber member: Abbr.
43 War god on Olympus
44 Speakers' spots
45 No. of ft. above sea level
46 . . . .
47 Three-L Illama?
55 Toward the rising sun
56 Ricochet
57 4, on a sundial
58 Nick at ___
59 Express a thought
60 Lease
61 ___ the Red
62 Stuffed
63 Actions on heartstrings and pant legs

DOWN

1 Hunk of marble, e.g.
2 Where Lima is
3 Elderly
4 Locales for rest stops
5 Using the kiddie pool, say
6 More than fat
7 Sad news item
8 Gossip, slangily
9 Wheat product used in making pasta
10 Bows one's head in church
11 Kitchen or bath
12 Sicilian spouter
13 Eager
21 Fruit of the Loom competitor
22 Conducted
25 Bombards with unwanted e-mail
26 Golfer Palmer, to pals
27 Expand, as a highway
28 Old battle clubs
29 Torah holders
30 Unconscious states
31 Quickly
32 Whip marks
34 Wished
35 Attire covering little of the legs
37 Temple entrances
38 "Groovy!"
43 Drink often labeled XXX in the comics
44 Heading to a bad end
45 Indian conquered by the conquistadors
46 Hum
47 The "B" of N.B.
48 Hideout
49 ___ Spumante (wine)
50 Auto parts giant
51 Londoner, e.g., informally
52 In ___ of (replacing)
53 ___ Yang Twins (rap duo)
54 Things to pick

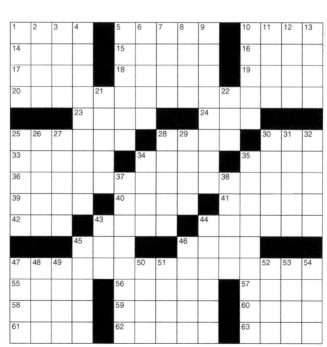

by Peter A. Collins

132

ACROSS

1 Rock outcropping
5 Dive among coral reefs, say
10 Sheep cries
14 Gossipy Barrett
15 Artist's stand
16 Break in the action
17 Wading bird
18 Tear away (from)
19 Airport for Air France
20 FLOP
23 Power for Robert Fulton
24 Razor sharpener
25 Stare (at)
28 Smother
32 Serving of corn
35 Civil rights org.
38 Game move
39 FLAP
43 Kind of lily
44 Royal headpiece
45 Tues. follower
46 Texas city named for a city in Ukraine
49 Keep ___ on (watch)
51 Continental money
54 Marina sights
58 FLIP
62 Pseudonym of H. H. Munro
63 Borden cow
64 Ivy, for one
65 Landed (on)
66 Wasps' homes
67 Part that's sharp
68 ___ club (singers' group)
69 Lovers' get-together
70 Burn the outside of

DOWN

1 Baby holders
2 Mechanical man
3 Japanese cartoon art
4 One who talks, talks, talks
5 In stitches
6 Low-___ diet
7 People before rehab
8 Intoxicate
9 Places for wedding vows
10 Tube on a welding tool
11 Special glow
12 Friend in war
13 Foxlike
21 Native of Muscat
22 "i" topper
26 Washed-out in complexion
27 Actor William of "The Greatest American Hero"
29 Piloted
30 Spend half the afternoon in a hammock, e.g.
31 Got a good look at

32 Exxon, formerly
33 Wowed
34 Fury
36 Greek X
37 Fuel from a bog
40 California national park
41 Victoria's Secret item
42 Jewish leader
47 Take to court
48 Hot-blooded
50 Does crosswords, say
52 Ship from the Mideast
53 Impudent
55 Off the direct path
56 South Seas kingdom
57 Look with a twisted lip
58 Ring up

59 Dust Bowl refugee
60 Tiny complaints
61 Toward sunset
62 Droop

by Bernice Gordon

ACROSS

1 Family
5 Winter neckwear
10 Conclusions
14 Harvard rival
15 ___ Slobbovia (remote locale)
16 Vista
17 Store safely
18 Cockamamie
19 Ancient Peruvian
20 Start of a quote by Bertrand Russell relevant to crossword solvers
23 Roy Orbison's "___ the Lonely"
24 Rots
25 How to divide things to be fair
28 Revolutionary pamphleteer Thomas
30 Supersmart grp.
31 Atmosphere
32 Back talk
36 Ltd.
37 Middle of the quote
40 Chairman with a Little Red Book
41 In ___ of (standing in for)
43 Actor Tim of "WKRP in Cincinnati"
44 Adhesive
46 Pie nut
48 Quenches
49 Simoleons
52 Swizzle
53 Conclusion of the quote
59 Mission-to-Mars org.
60 Cognizant
61 One with adoring fans
62 Squeezed (out)
63 Hayseed
64 Capone fighter Eliot ___

65 Cry from Charlie Brown
66 Pivots
67 Way to get out of a field

DOWN

1 Anatomical sac
2 Strip of wood in homebuilding
3 ___ vera
4 Eponymous units of force
5 By a narrow margin
6 Brooklyn's ___ Island
7 Not at home
8 Gambling mecca
9 Revealing kind of slip
10 Demonstrates clearly
11 Old Japanese assassin
12 Wooden duck, say
13 Persuades
21 Member of an extended family
22 Poetic time after dusk
25 Disney's "___ and the Detectives"
26 "___, vidi, vici" (Caesar's boast)
27 Suffix with differ
28 Vladimir of the Kremlin
29 Like most of west Texas
31 Between ports
33 One way to run
34 ___-Coburg (part of historic Germany)
35 High-protein beans
38 Sites for grand entrances
39 Icy cold
42 Transfers files to a computer, maybe
45 It's "such sweet sorrow"
47 Have supper
48 Braces (oneself)
49 Worker with a light and a pick
50 Japanese port
51 Beginning
52 Spread, as seed
54 Dicey G.I. status
55 Drink with sushi
56 Notion
57 Maximum
58 ". . . or ___!" (threat)

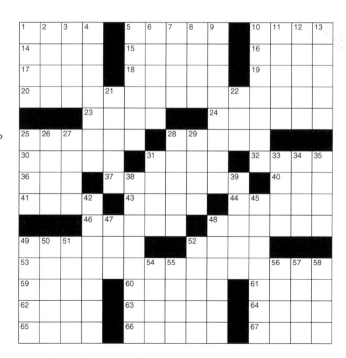

by Marlon R. Howell

134

ACROSS

1 Variety of poker
5 Actress Rowlands
9 Vice president Spiro
14 Prefix with glycemic
15 Patron saint of Norway
16 Dog's restraint
17 Unlock
18 Not all
19 "Heavens to ___!"
20 "Sahara" co-star, 2005
23 Capital of New Mexico
24 Lagasse once of the Food Network
28 Shack
29 Up to, briefly
31 Prefix with tiller
32 Luggage attachment
35 Theme
37 Ukraine, e.g., once: Abbr.
38 Trip to Tahiti, for example
41 What andirons support
42 Blocked from sunlight
43 Result of a hit by a leadoff batter
44 Med. school subject
46 "Pick a card, ___ card"
47 Getting on in years
48 Shooting star
50 Italian city on the Adriatic
54 Groups collecting litter
57 Ones attracted to flames
60 ___ Hashanah
61 Landed (on)
62 Sharpshooter Oakley
63 "Puppy Love" singer Paul
64 Heredity unit
65 All gone, as food
66 Ship's petty officer, informally
67 To be: Lat.

DOWN

1 Mall units
2 Aggressive, as a personality
3 Ivy League school in Phila.
4 Words after "been there"
5 Become lenient (on)
6 Act on a sudden itching for a hitching
7 Title
8 With: Fr.
9 Photo book
10 Codger
11 Singer ___ King Cole
12 Letter before tee
13 Philosopher's question
21 Guffaws
22 Archaeological find
25 O'Donnell of "The View"
26 "___ easy to fall in love" (1977 lyric)
27 Sophia of "Two Women"
29 Fawner
30 ___-bitsy
32 Muhammad's religion
33 "Lorna ___"
34 Gently pull on
35 Average
36 Merry play
39 Stock unit
40 20 or less, at a bar
45 Computer whiz
47 Parentless child
49 With 52-Down, showbiz's Mary-Kate and Ashley
50 Walrus features
51 Tennis's Monica
52 See 49-Down
53 Cosmetician Lauder
55 Syrian or Yemeni
56 Taboo
57 Sex kitten West
58 Go ___ rampage
59 Explosive letters

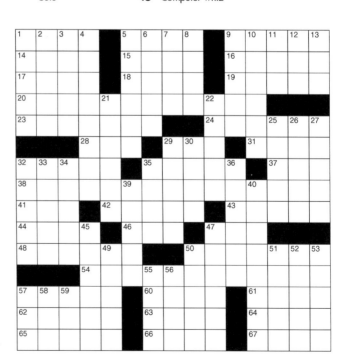

by Richard Chisholm

ACROSS

1 Network to keep an "eye" on
4 Singer's sound
9 Provide for free, informally
13 Sedan or wagon
15 Ancient Peruvians
16 W.W. II general Bradley
17 "___, crackle, pop"
18 Birthplace of 59-Across
20 59-Across, e.g.
22 Having a ghost
23 Cut, as sheep's wool
24 Drunkards
25 TV program for which 59-Across won an Emmy, 1977
32 Debussy's "La ___"
34 Bullfighter's cloth
35 Melodic subject, in music
36 Album for which 59-Across won a Grammy, 1972, with "The"
41 It's a butter alternative
42 "The Wizard of Oz" pooch
43 French word before and after "à"
44 Movie for which 59-Across won an Oscar, 1961
49 The "E" in E.R.: Abbr.
50 Spicy sauce . . . or dance
53 Milan opera house
57 Play for which 59-Across won a Tony, 1975
59 Star born on 12/11/1931
61 ___ the kill
62 Lyric poems
63 Part of the head that may be congested

64 Campbell of the "Scream" movies
65 Snoozes
66 Exams
67 Jiffy

DOWN

1 Spanish houses
2 Cluster
3 Ohio's buckeye, California's redwood, etc.
4 Big shots, for short
5 Burden
6 Freezer trayful
7 Server at a drive-in
8 Aristocrat's home
9 ___ flakes
10 Forget to mention
11 Protective spray
12 Motivate
14 TV host with a book club

19 Get rid of
21 Straight up
24 Phantom
26 Scratch
27 Reuters competitor
28 Engine additive brand
29 Map borders, usually
30 Prefix with potent
31 ___ and Means Committee
32 Tabby's cry
33 French "she"
37 Foldaway bed
38 Comedian Bill, informally
39 Giant slugger Mel
40 Antlered animal
45 Tailor's line
46 "This is not making sense to me"
47 Little loved one

48 ___ to go (eager)
51 Ward (off)
52 Pre-Columbus Mexican
53 Scientologist ___ Hubbard
54 Opera set in the age of pharaohs
55 Stair part
56 Mama ___ of the Mamas and the Papas
57 Carpenter's metal piece
58 "Bonanza" brother
60 Lt.'s inferior, in the Navy

by David J. Kahn

136

ACROSS

1 Cry after "Forward!"
6 Solder
10 Belgrade native
14 Central Florida city
15 Words of understanding
16 Peter, Paul and Mary, e.g.
17 Holiday decoration
20 Retain
21 Numbered work of a composer
22 "Come in!"
23 Preservers of preserves
25 "This looks bad!"
27 Cleopatra's lover
30 Hissy fit
31 Air blower
34 Like a pitcher's perfect game
35 Flub
36 Look into a crystal ball
37 Holiday decoration
40 Fabric fuzz
41 Memo opener
42 Plural of 21-Across
43 U-turn from WSW
44 Assns.
45 Frigate or ferry
46 Fleeting trace
47 Neat
48 Offspring
51 Butcher's cut
53 Shopping place
57 Holiday decoration
60 Abbr. before a colon
61 Feed the kitty
62 Make amends
63 General emotional state
64 Some boxing decisions, briefly
65 Snapshot

DOWN

1 Make fun of
2 Liniment target
3 Like one in a million
4 Business that routinely overcharges
5 Possesses
6 Ones likely to chicken out
7 Biblical pottage purchaser
8 First chapter in a primer
9 Morning moisture
10 Shorthand pro
11 The "E" in Q.E.D.
12 Baptism or bar mitzvah
13 Danish Nobelist Niels
18 British Conservative
19 What homeowners don't have to pay
24 1998 animated bug film
26 Player of 45s
27 Site for a monitoring bracelet, maybe
28 Hopeless, as a situation
29 Feudal landholder
30 Whiskey drinks
31 Confronts
32 Sky-blue
33 View from Mount Everest
35 Ship-to-shore accessway
36 Insect whose larvae destroy foliage
38 Broadcasts
39 ___ the line (behaved)
44 Pig's sound
45 Handful for Tarzan
46 Coiled
47 Multiplied by
48 Pillow cover
49 Famed Roman censor
50 Diggin'
52 "___ be in England": Browning
54 Suffix with buck
55 Long, angry discourse
56 Lt. Kojak
58 Krazy ___ of the comics
59 Doze

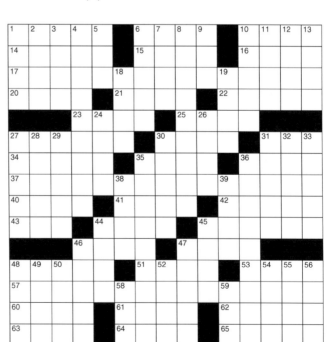

by Donna S. Levin

ACROSS

1 Up to the task
5 Machinist's tool
10 Study all night, say
14 Common cause of postponement
15 Rural units
16 Olympic swimmer's assignment
17 Kelly Ripa and others
20 Hive occupant
21 Ariz. neighbor
22 Actor Milo
23 Actress Farrow
24 Foal's mother
26 Motion picture academy honor
33 Tureen accessory
34 Hands (out)
35 Wall St. deal
36 Mystery writer __ Stanley Gardner
37 "See? . . . huh, huh?"
38 Emptiness
39 Get older
40 Gift recipient
41 Lemon peels, e.g.
42 Alumni
45 Toward shelter
46 Passé
47 Beauty's counterpart
50 The Beatles, e.g.
52 __ Na Na
55 There's one in 17-, 26- and 42-Across
59 Gen. Robert __
60 Alaskan native
61 Transnational currency
62 Wines to serve with beef
63 Singer Turner and others
64 Comic Sandler

DOWN

1 __-Israeli relations
2 Sweetie pie
3 Head case?
4 Finale
5 Nonprofessional
6 Part of a French play
7 Cereal "for kids"
8 Haw's partner
9 Language suffix
10 Place for hangers
11 Impetuous
12 A few chips, say, in poker
13 Tableland
18 Japanese cartoon style
19 Jewish circle dances
23 French miss: Abbr.
24 Setting
25 Working without __
26 North Dakota's largest city
27 Slacker
28 Danish birthplace of Hans Christian Andersen
29 Sacred choral work
30 Irving Berlin's "When __ You"
31 Back-of-newspaper section
32 Nonverbal O.K.'s
33 Bit of foliage
37 Reason for an R rating
38 Sell
40 Airline once said to be "ready when you are"
41 Nintendo's The Legend of __
43 Pulverizes
44 Dunkable treats
47 1930s boxing champ Max
48 Vogue competitor
49 Mimicked
50 Square in the first column of bingo
51 Water
52 Simple earring
53 Zeus' wife
54 Molecule part
56 Flier in a cave
57 __ Lilly, maker of Prozac
58 Actor Stephen of "The Crying Game"

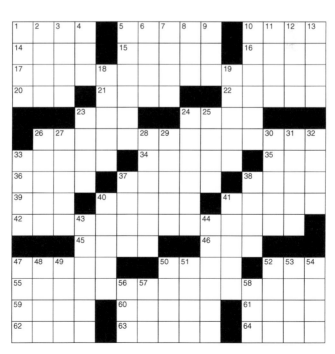

by Adam G. Perl

138

ACROSS

1 Mrs. Dithers of the comics
5 Holder of billiard balls
9 County, in Britain
14 Breakfast chain
15 Jazz's Fitzgerald
16 Blender setting
17 Huge
18 Numbskull
19 Modern missive
20 Anger
21 Carnival treat
23 More shrewd
25 "It's not easy ___ green"
26 Like some modern music
29 ___ Pieces
33 Lindbergh's trans-Atlantic destination
35 Farm billies
37 Charlottesville sch.
38 Cutlass, e.g., informally
39 Starts of 21- and 53-Across and 3- and 30-Down
40 Gets older
41 Golf ball position
42 Storms
43 Eurasian mountains
44 The Jayhawks of the Big 12
46 Groove-making tool
48 Tiny hill dwellers
50 Skip
53 Carbonated citrus-flavored drink
58 Medical care grp.
59 Cape ___ Islands
60 Diaper problem
61 Keep ___ on (watch)
62 ___ tube
63 Nabisco best-seller
64 160 square rods
65 Jim Morrison's group, with "the"
66 Feathered missile
67 "Sure, go ahead"

DOWN

1 ___ center
2 "Gone With the Wind" surname
3 White House setting
4 Likely
5 Like many evangelicals
6 Loads
7 Arterial blockage
8 Shish ___
9 Canis lupus familiaris, for dogs
10 Compassionate
11 Neighbor of Pakistan
12 Actor/director Tim
13 Slithery
21 Corporate V.I.P.'s
22 "Phooey!"
24 "How sweet ___!"
27 Wide-eyed
28 Toward the bottom
30 1963 #1 hit for the Fireballs
31 Daredevil Knievel
32 Impudent talk
33 President before Taylor
34 Inter ___
36 Too
39 Moisten, as poultry
40 Mars' Greek counterpart
42 New York N.H.L.'ers
43 Great Salt Lake's state
45 Wood-smoothing tool
47 Result
49 Atlantic food fish
51 Shadow
52 Actress Parker ___
53 "Metamorphoses" poet
54 Nevada city
55 River through Florence
56 ___ avis
57 One getting a manual
61 Confucian path

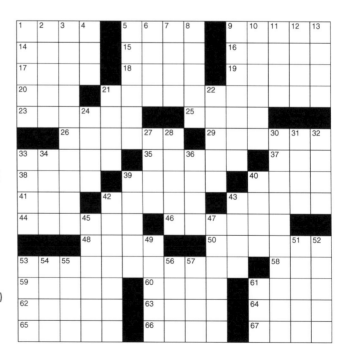

by Randy Sowell

ACROSS

1 Heartbeat
6 Impersonator in "Little Red Riding Hood"
10 Heavy, durable furniture wood
14 Santa ___ racetrack
15 Jai ___
16 Folkie Guthrie
17 Think tank products
18 Not so much
19 Dec. 25
20 Skeptic
23 Web address ender
24 "Little" girl of "Uncle Tom's Cabin"
25 What a 20-Across might say
32 Washed (down), as a sidewalk
34 Just managed, with "out"
35 Historic time
36 Cut ___ (dance)
37 Ways
39 Nose-in-the-air type
40 Snoring sound
41 Plain crazy
42 Scalds, e.g.
43 What a 20-Across might say
47 Baseball stat
48 Hoopsters' org.
49 What a 20-Across might say, ignoring grammar
57 Tobacco plug
58 Jacob's twin
59 Designer Donna
60 Wintry
61 Angry outburst
62 Turn inside out
63 Meowers
64 Bend in the wind
65 50 minutes after the hour

DOWN

1 Settled up
2 Nullify
3 Stead
4 Knife
5 Where Cockney is spoken in London
6 Heavy, durable furniture wood
7 Designer Cassini
8 Bringing up the rear
9 Unfriendly looks
10 I.R.S. worker
11 Humorist Bombeck
12 "Oh, woe!"
13 Some boxing wins, briefly
21 Wedding words
22 "Ars Amatoria" poet
25 Maker of the Rodeo
26 Computer storage unit, informally
27 Words before roses or lettuce
28 Instrument making HI notes?
29 Variety
30 Do post-laundry work
31 Setters of indents
32 Having a bit of smog
33 Ricelike pasta
37 Nicknames
38 Columbus Day's mo.
39 1 + 2 + 3, e.g.
41 Pharmaceutical workplaces
42 Relative of a quilt
44 After-Christmas shopping scenes
45 Working, as a police officer
46 Sash in Sapporo
49 "Stop!"
50 "Stop!"
51 "The Last Time ___ Paris"
52 Comic Carvey
53 "I ___ at the office"
54 Wee warbler
55 Male deer
56 Not duped by
57 Roman 300

by Harriet Clifton

140

ACROSS

1 Church recess
5 Wallop in the boxing ring
9 Catcher's position
14 Deception
15 "Movin' ___" ("The Jeffersons" theme song)
16 What marks and francs have been replaced with
17 Singer Braxton
18 Cunningness
19 German word of appreciation
20 Special occasion
23 Atty.'s org.
24 ___ constrictor
25 Arctic bird
26 Oz musical, with "The"
29 Beatles movie
33 State Farm's business: Abbr.
34 Cry loudly
35 ET transporters
36 Bank contents
39 Unilever soap brand
40 Film critic Roger
41 Wide-eyed
42 ___ Lingus
43 Roman 111
44 Winner of the first Super Bowl
50 Sushi fish
51 Dadaist Jean
52 Motorist's way: Abbr.
53 "Shucks!"
54 Where to find the colors in this puzzle
57 Gather, logically
60 Home of Città del Vaticano
61 Fit of temper
62 Capital of Ecuador
63 Spoken
64 Raced (through)
65 Cast about
66 Nerve
67 S-shaped molding

DOWN

1 Off course
2 One of the friends on "Friends"
3 Beach footwear
4 1928 Oscar winner Jannings
5 Acts obsequiously
6 Singer Bryant and others
7 Christmastime
8 Area from which to hear an aria
9 Pop crooner Neil
10 Waterfront site
11 Vase
12 "Thumbs up"
13 Mao ___-tung
21 Piano key wood
22 Boneheaded
26 Bride, after the vows
27 "Are you ___ out?"
28 Spiciness
30 Feudal lord
31 Unconscionably high interest
32 Hungarian cube maker
36 Caster of spells
37 Fairy-tale meanie
38 Christmas song
39 Spring game?
40 Do well (at)
42 Start of a magician's cry
43 Raspberry
45 Not wide
46 First
47 Holiday quaff
48 Put on the payroll again
49 Parlor piece
54 French head
55 "___ good time, call . . ."
56 "That's all there ___ it!"
57 Figs. averaging 100
58 Macadamia, e.g.
59 Spruce relative

by David Pringle

ACROSS

1 Poppycock
4 Explorer ___ Polo
9 God of love
13 Daredevil Knievel
15 Reside
16 Himalayan priest
17 Road sign #1
19 Genesis garden
20 Actress Verdugo of "Marcus Welby, M.D."
21 Renter's agreement
23 Item scrambled or poached
24 Will's subject
26 Road sign #2
28 Santa's helper
30 "___ harm" (medical maxim)
31 Road sign #3
37 M-1s and AK-47s
40 Slender nails
41 Life story, in brief
42 "The stage ___"
43 Child's request
44 Road sign #4
46 Oolong and others
49 Racehorse, to a bettor
50 Road sign #5
54 Wood nymphs, in myth
59 Stately tree
60 Bogged down
62 Really love something, with "up"
63 Willowy
65 Road sign #6
67 Proctor's call
68 Snakes in the road?
69 Prefix with byte
70 Observed
71 Songstress Della
72 Whom you might see in your rearview mirror if you ignore the above signs

DOWN

1 Gen. in the Confederacy
2 Flattened circles
3 Doctrine
4 Roman 1,550
5 Wanted soldier
6 Stitch again
7 Cloudless
8 Fatherland, affectionately
9 Hearty brew
10 Degraded
11 Alpha's opposite
12 Slender and long-limbed
14 Horne of "The Lady and Her Music"
18 Takes care of the food for the party
22 Musician Brian
25 Lodge member
27 Grind, as teeth
29 Little lies
31 "Peacock" network
32 ". . . man ___ mouse?"
33 Show silently
34 Fancy goodbye
35 Tiny criticism
36 Thug
38 ___ culpa
39 Regulation: Abbr.
42 "Amen!"
45 Cushion
47 Supplier of PIN money?
48 Fast pitch with a curve
50 Homes in trees
51 Kukla, Fran and ___
52 Jagged, as a leaf's edge
53 All keyed up
55 Yin's opposite
56 Cellar's opposite
57 San ___, Calif.
58 Rein, e.g.
61 Fawns' mothers
64 Fraternity members
66 Mao ___-tung

by C. W. Stewart

142

ACROSS

1 Member of a pesky swarm
5 Brighton baby buggies
10 Blighted urban area
14 Change the décor of
15 Wash gently against, as the shore
16 Camp shelter
17 Popular grilled fish
19 ___ Elevator Company
20 Not half bad
21 Concerning
23 Jordanian cash
24 Soft drink since 1885
27 Brit. reference work
28 China, Japan, etc.
31 "... man ___ mouse?"
32 Pâté de foie ___
34 Guns, as an engine
35 All wound up
37 1940 Ronald Reagan role
40 "Cheers" waitress
43 On the bounding main
44 "National Velvet" author Bagnold
48 Golf rarity
49 Sicilian seaport
52 Language suffix
53 Charlie Parker or Dizzy Gillespie
55 Car antitheft device
57 City trashed by Rodan
58 African desert
60 Big bash
61 Da Vinci masterpiece, with "The"
65 A.B.A. member: Abbr.
66 Started a cigarette
67 Clearance event
68 Soldiers' meal
69 Signs of things to come
70 ___ the Red

DOWN

1 Cur's warning
2 More impoverished
3 Tack-ons
4 Puccini opera
5 Course of action
6 Totally absorbed
7 PC program, briefly
8 Al Capp's Daisy ___
9 Harness parts
10 Place to sit streetside
11 Take some pressure off
12 Opposite of dividers
13 Appalachians, e.g.: Abbr.
18 Soft ball material
22 Midler of "The Rose"
23 Husky or hound
24 Inventor
25 Speaker with a sore throat, say
26 Actress ___ Dawn Chong
29 "___ we there yet?"
30 Amuse, as with anecdotes
33 Cardinal's insignia
36 Poet's before
38 All smiles
39 Antistick cooking spray
40 Part of a semi
41 Overlay material
42 Makes tighter, in a way
45 Close to its face value, as a bond
46 Ehud Barak or Ehud Olmert
47 Nancy Pelosi, e.g.: Abbr.
50 Moon-landing program
51 Pearl Harbor's site
54 Gives the go-ahead
56 Run out, as a subscription
58 Zap with a Taser
59 Nile slitherers
60 Pinup's leg
62 Align the cross hairs
63 Sault ___ Marie
64 ___ room (play area)

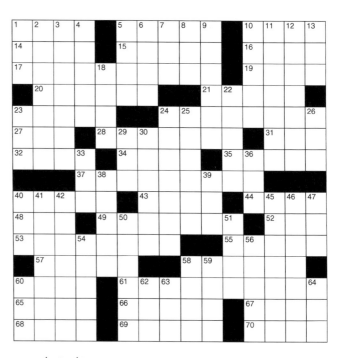

by Fred Piscop

ACROSS

1 1960s–'70s draft org.
4 Purse feature
9 Where hair roots grow
14 Photo
15 Singers Ochs and Collins
16 Causing goosebumps
17 Excitement
18 Pulitzer-winning biography of a Civil War general
19 Take in or let out
20 Modern fashion-conscious guys
23 Didn't participate in
24 Circular staples
25 Appropriate
28 Use a swizzle stick
30 Reception amenity
33 Clubs or hearts
36 Central point
38 Shinbone
39 Unlikely showing at a multiplex
43 Germ cell
44 Day-___ paint
45 "___ of the D'Urbervilles"
46 Item on a gunslinger's hip
49 Bangkok native
51 Perry Como's "___ Impossible"
52 Nectar collector
54 List at a meeting
58 Yanks vs. Mets matchup, e.g.
61 Olympics craft
64 "You ___ right!"
65 ___ Lilly and Company
66 Delight
67 Suddenly cut out, as an engine
68 Rogue
69 Nintendo products
70 Sprayed, as a sidewalk
71 Iris's place

DOWN

1 Sends unwanted e-mails
2 Most-played half of a 45
3 Willard of "Today"
4 Bamboo beginning
5 1973 Newman/ Redford movie
6 Annoy
7 Billy Joel's musical daughter
8 Prefix with intellectual
9 Circus performer with a ball
10 Disney collectibles
11 Paintings
12 Fail a polygraph
13 The "p" in r.p.m.
21 Lists
22 Dangerous hisser
25 Hoffman of 1960s–'70s radicalism
26 Buckets
27 Mine transports
29 Karel Capek classic
31 LAX posting
32 Cooler
33 Some Japanese cuisine
34 Prepare to transplant
35 Fan mail recipients
37 Morass
40 No longer working: Abbr.
41 Final: Abbr.
42 Easy, as a loan
47 Recede
48 Clean again
50 Ancient
53 Keep an ___ the ground
55 Nephew's sister
56 Holdup
57 In reserve
58 Fill up
59 Hawaiian strings, informally
60 "Pro" votes
61 Beer bust purchase
62 Like
63 Thanksgiving side dish

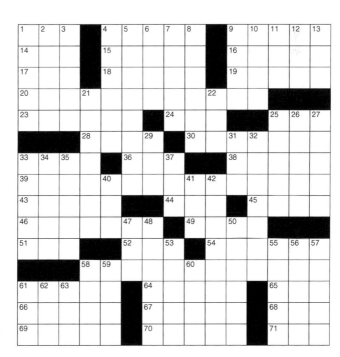

by Joy C. Frank

144

ACROSS

1 "My Fair Lady" horse race
6 Wrigley Field team
10 Hinged fastener
14 Tiresome task
15 "Got it"
16 Germany's von Bismarck
17 Film director Frank
18 Sharp-toothed Atlantic swimmer
20 Ron of Tarzan fame
21 Record-setting miler Sebastian
23 Diner's bill
24 Actress Gardner
25 Overabundance
28 Washing site
30 Fuss
31 Toyota rival
34 Must-have
35 Holey cheese
37 Entice
39 Doohickey
43 Sir __ Newton
44 Skin woes
47 Total flop
50 Evening up, as a score
53 Ice cream purchase
54 About 71% of the earth's surface
56 All-time winningest N.F.L. coach
58 The "I" in T.G.I.F.
59 Acorn producer
62 __ and Coke
63 Seize
64 1978 Donna Summer hit . . . or a hint to 18-, 25-, 39- and 56-Across
67 Tennis's Agassi
69 Nights before holidays
70 Wines like Merlot
71 Prolonged attack
72 Office furniture
73 Annoyer
74 Jackrabbits, actually

DOWN

1 Takes, as an offer
2 Not deep
3 Tweak, as magazine text
4 Hockey legend Bobby
5 Class instructor, informally
6 Roman orator
7 Grp. putting on shows for troops
8 Not straight
9 Big video game maker
10 Opposite of vert.
11 Relaxed
12 Musical Wonder
13 Pope John Paul II's homeland
19 Diminish
22 Cry of wonder
26 Tokyo electronics giant

27 Heartburn reliever
29 Ohio college named for a biblical city
32 Rep.'s foe
33 Dr.'s advocate
36 Lisa, to Bart Simpson
38 Bedwear, briefly
40 __ King Cole
41 Not straight
42 Alternative to a fly ball
45 Expand
46 Navy building crew
47 Heated, as water
48 "Do, re, mi, fa, sol, la, ti, do" range
49 Slobs' creations
51 What the weary get, in a saying
52 Horned beast
55 Silent O.K.
57 Huge hit
60 Org. for those 50+

61 Thigh/shin separator
65 "For shame!"
66 PC inserts
68 Vardalos of "My Big Fat Greek Wedding"

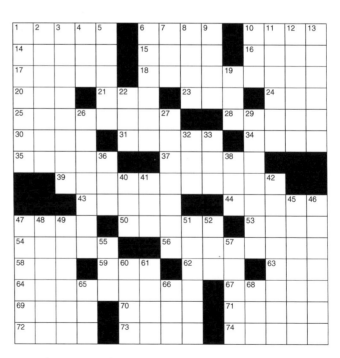

by Lynn Lempel

ACROSS

1 "Survivor" shelter
4 $$$ dispenser
7 Circumference
12 October birthstone
14 ___ Fox of Uncle Remus tales
16 "I love you," in Spanish
17 The year 1052
18 Be an omen of
19 Lady
20 007's introduction
23 Dustin's role in "Midnight Cowboy"
24 Sand holders at the beach
25 Slugger's stat
28 Mag. workers
29 Hip-hop doc?
31 Part of an ellipsis
32 Prominent part of a dachshund
33 Easy as ___
34 Except
35 Birthday dessert
36 Embroidered sampler phrase
40 Guns, as a motor
41 Cravat
42 Almost forever
43 Byron's "before"
44 "My gal" of song
45 Branch
46 Commercial suffix with Gator
49 Each
50 Map book
52 County on the Thames
54 Repeatedly
57 Soup eater's sound
59 Kitchen or bath
60 Aroma
61 Hearing-related
62 College digs
63 Traveled
64 Tableau
65 Airport screening org.
66 Snake's sound

DOWN

1 Man of La Mancha
2 Transfer to a mainframe, maybe
3 Contaminates
4 Alphabetically first pop group with a #1 hit
5 ___ l'oeil
6 Tragic woman in Greek drama
7 Maximally
8 Nasty
9 Nightmare
10 Britney Spears's "___ Slave 4 U"
11 Mr. Turkey
13 Jar tops
15 Ashes, e.g.
21 "Panic Room" actress Foster
22 Ink soaker-upper
26 Make a 35-Across
27 Anger
30 Say again just for the record, say
33 Afternoons, for short
34 Queen who might create quite a buzz?
35 Pro's opposite
36 Roll-call call
37 Orchestral intro
38 Weatherman Scott
39 "The Simpsons" dad
40 Agent, in brief
44 Just a taste
45 Noted family of financiers and philanthropists
46 Parenthetical comments
47 Fiends
48 Puts forth, as effort
51 In progress
53 Put away
55 Gulf land
56 Gwyneth Paltrow title role
57 Carrier to Stockholm
58 Capt. Jean-___ Picard of the U.S.S. Enterprise

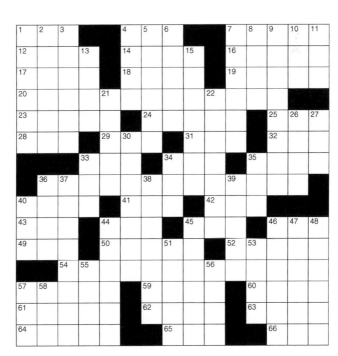

by Andrea Carla Michaels

146

ACROSS

1 Tempest
6 Cub Scout group
9 Singer Turner and others
14 Chili con ___
15 N.Y.C.'s Park or Lexington
16 "Dying / Is ___, like anything else": Sylvia Plath
17 E. M. Forster novel
20 Brooks of comedy
21 Old punch line?
22 Disreputable
23 Mia of women's soccer
24 To ___ (perfectly)
25 Car parker
32 One of the Astaires
33 Dictionary unit
34 Australian hopper, for short
35 Manner
36 Property encumbrances
38 "Cómo ___ usted?"
39 Hosp. scan
40 Cost of a cab
41 C-3PO, for one
42 Entities cited in the Penitential Rite
46 Tipplers
47 The Vatican's home
48 "La Nausée" novelist
51 "Star Wars" guru
52 Opposite of 'neath
55 What conspiracy theorists look for (as hinted at by 17-, 25- and 42-Across)
58 Colorado ski town
59 Dined
60 Spanish hero played by Charlton Heston
61 Louts
62 "Two clubs," e.g., in bridge
63 Cuts down on calories

DOWN

1 E-mail offer of $17,000,000.00, e.g.
2 Reel-to-reel ___
3 Spoken
4 I.C.U. helpers
5 Communiqué
6 Explorer Vasco ___
7 Even once
8 Ping-Pong table divider
9 Last part
10 Wanting
11 Zilch
12 Phoenix's home: Abbr.
13 Order to Fido
18 Peak
19 Some blenders
23 Robust
24 Lots
25 Letter after beta
26 Decorate
27 Excavate again
28 11- or 12-year-old
29 Crime sometimes done for the insurance
30 Untagged, in a game
31 Creatures said to cause warts
36 Remained
37 Gershwin and others
38 Cleveland's lake
40 Old gold coins
41 Requiring repair
43 Rolle who starred in "Good Times"
44 Spoke so as to put people to sleep
45 Ice cream drink
48 Dagger wound
49 "I see," facetiously
50 "___ Man," Emilio Estevez movie
51 Dubious sighting in the Himalayas
52 A single time
53 Blue-pencil
54 X-ray units
56 Small amount, as of hair cream
57 Inventor Whitney

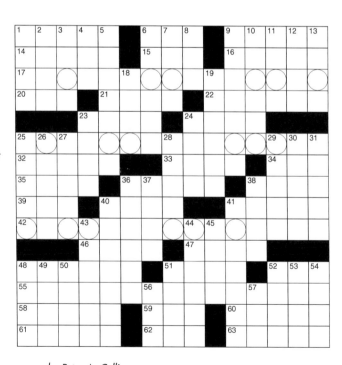

by Peter A. Collins

ACROSS

1 Digging tool
6 ___ McAn shoes
10 Felt remorse
14 Israel's Sharon
15 Lira's replacement
16 "Don't Tread ___"
(old flag warning)
17 Planter without hired
hands
19 Game-stopping
call
20 "Zip-___-Doo-Dah"
21 "I didn't know
that!"
22 Nervous giggle
24 Fabrics for towels,
robes, etc.
26 Sukiyaki side dish
27 Auto mechanic
32 Nests, for birds
35 Fall site in Genesis
36 Eco-friendly org.
37 ___ Brothers,
who sang "Rag
Mop"
38 Fur tycoon John
Jacob
40 Trickle out
41 A Bobbsey twin
42 Leave off
43 Storied engineer
Casey
44 Any member of
Nirvana or Pearl
Jam
48 Java dispensers
49 Take back
53 Popular drink mix
56 Extra-wide, on a
shoebox
57 Fitzgerald who
knew how to scat
58 Eurasia's ___
Mountains
59 Smear campaigner
62 Race that once
had a four-minute
barrier
63 Give off
64 Knight's mount

65 Borscht vegetable
66 D.C. nine, for short
67 Pig voiced by Mel
Blanc

DOWN

1 Begin's co-Nobelist
2 Family of lions
3 Broadcaster
4 Cleanses
5 Keebler baker,
in ads
6 Humanitarian
Mother ___
7 Actor Cronyn
8 Smelter input
9 Edgar Bergen
dummy ___ Snerd
10 Way past ripe
11 Condo or apartment
12 Noted plus-size
model
13 ___ Xing (sign)

18 "The Morning
Watch" writer James
23 Clickable screen
symbol
25 E-file receiver
26 Change the décor of
28 Brief tussle
29 Like an eagle's vision
30 Blunted sword
31 Big fat mouths
32 Nail to the wall
33 Epps of TV's
"House"
34 Chalkboard writing
at a cafe
38 Emphatic words of
agreement
39 Knighted ones
40 Bay of Naples tourist
city
42 Hideous sort
43 Namath, for most of
his career

45 Small seed
46 Blue jay toppers
47 It runs from stem to
stern
50 "Ragged Dick" writer
Horatio
51 One iron, in old golf
lingo
52 Late, on a report
card
53 Under the effects of
Novocain
54 Lake named after an
Indian tribe
55 Red-tag event
56 Trim, as text
60 Actress Thurman
61 AOL, e.g.: Abbr.

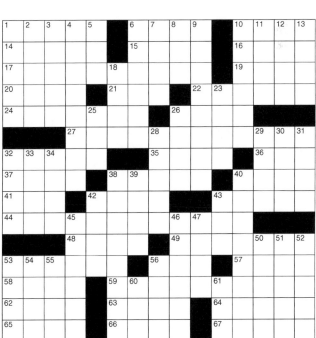

by Fred Piscop

148

ACROSS

1 More eccentric
6 "Moby-Dick" captain
10 Reaction to a knee-slapper
14 Old pal
15 Food that may come in small cubes
16 Giant-screen film venue
17 Sign for a person in therapy?
20 ___, due, tre . . .
21 Abominable Snowman
22 Turtle's covering
23 Like college aptitude tests, for many students
26 Highway
28 Compete in a slalom
29 Moist
31 Lawyer: Abbr.
35 Together
38 "Well, then . . ."
40 By way of
41 Sign for a recovering alcoholic?
43 Annoy
44 Completely cover
46 "Hmmm . . ."
48 Japanese drink
49 Numbered hwys.
51 Faux ___
52 Perlman of "Cheers"
54 Comedian's gimmick
58 Candidate Stevenson of '52 and '56
61 Level
63 Rhetorical question, possibly
64 Sign for a gangster?
68 Fork prong
69 Washington daily
70 ___ Ste. Marie, Mich.
71 Went fast

72 Aussie jumpers
73 ___ Rose Lee

DOWN

1 Happen
2 Pilotless aircraft
3 Sign for a jury selector?
4 Suffix with differ
5 Seedy loaf
6 Eventgoer
7 Party thrower
8 Uphold
9 Prickly seed cover
10 Religious time
11 French girlfriend
12 Room connector
13 Skating jump
18 Science guy Bill
19 Cool ___ cucumber
24 Letters before an alias
25 Twists to be worked out

27 Eye-catching designs
30 Enough
32 Sign for a sunbather?
33 Went fast
34 Oxen connector
35 Currier and ___
36 Companion of the Pinta and Santa Maria
37 Plowmaker John
39 Pretty maiden of Greek myth
42 Mousse and mud pie
45 Exposed to oxygen
47 Consume
50 Skin art
53 Go quickly
55 ___-Magnon
56 They're stirred in the fire
57 Meower

58 Many urban homes: Abbr.
59 Annoyance from a faucet
60 "The ___ Ranger"
62 In that case
65 E.M.T.'s skill
66 "No ___" (Chinese menu notation)
67 It's pitched with a pitchfork

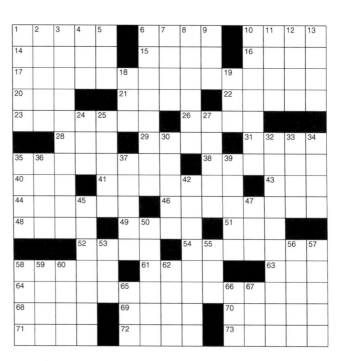

by Kevin G. Der

ACROSS

1 Like some committees
6 Designer Lauren
11 Lunch counter sandwich, for short
14 How most mail goes nowadays
15 Accustom to hardship
16 Whopper
17 Sinuous Mideast entertainer
19 Multivolume Brit. reference
20 Ballpark fig.
21 WWW addresses
22 Beaded counter
24 Basic course for a future M.D.
25 The "A" in DNA
26 Chance, at cards
31 Compass part
33 David Sedaris's comic sister
34 Springsteen's "Born in the ___"
35 Golfer Palmer, familiarly
36 Gives the green light
37 Pesto ingredient
39 Comic Caesar
40 New Year's ___
41 Yield
42 One way to fall in love
46 Goatee site
47 Blockheads
48 Dietetic
51 Novelist Ambler
52 "Without further ___ . . ."
55 ___ carte
56 Host of a Friars Club event
59 Chess pieces
60 ___ forth (et cetera)
61 Vibes

62 Word that may precede the beginning of 17-, 26-, 42- or 56-Across
63 Most common craps roll
64 Yahoo! or AOL offering

DOWN

1 French cleric
2 Colors, as Easter eggs
3 Sentry's command
4 Mideast export
5 Throw in the towel
6 Theater district
7 Raggedy ___ (dolls)
8 Film director Jean-___ Godard
9 Tediously didactic
10 Jazz's Hancock or Mann
11 Voting group
12 Stead
13 Senators Kennedy and Stevens
18 Explorer Sir Francis
23 Append
24 BMW competitor
25 Places to get quick money, quickly
26 ___ hand (help)
27 Fraud
28 Stratagems
29 Z ___ zebra
30 Poet Whitman
31 Poet Ogden
32 Shallowest of the Great Lakes
36 Pizzeria fixture
37 Muscle mag photos
38 Cure-___ (panaceas)
40 Satan, with "the"
41 Adjust one's sights
43 Roman 700

44 Tara plantation family
45 Dr. Seuss's "___ Hears a Who"
48 Genie's home
49 Butter alternative
50 Privation
51 To be, in old Rome
52 Gillette ___ Plus
53 Prefix with god
54 Said aloud
57 Really or truly, e.g.: Abbr.
58 Wal-Mart founder Walton

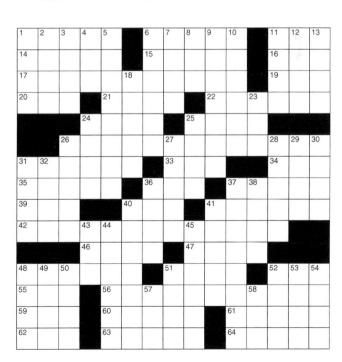

by Richard Chisholm

150

ACROSS

1 Cousins of mandolins
6 Marx with a manifesto
10 Not shallow
14 "Faust" or "Don Giovanni"
15 Hodgepodge
16 Neutral tone
17 Simple pleasure
20 Doctors' bags
21 Often-stained piece of attire
22 Manipulate
23 Drip from a pipe, e.g.
24 Leftover bit
28 Old Iran
30 Preordain
32 Daily allowance
35 Unruly head of hair
36 1978 Rolling Stones hit
40 Caribbean, e.g.
41 Worker in a stable
42 Humor that's often lost in an e-mail
45 Proverb
49 ___ B. Anthony dollar
50 Two of a kind
52 Word with neither
53 Four-alarm fire
56 Where 6-Down is
57 Sex appeal
61 Aria singer
62 ___ quilt (modern memorial)
63 Kind of pole
64 Plow pullers
65 Gait between walk and canter
66 Tickle

DOWN

1 Put in jail
2 Revolt
3 Be on the verge of falling
4 Periods in history
5 Day of the wk. . . . or an exam usually taken on that day
6 Seoul's home
7 Smart ___
8 Basketball coach Pitino
9 Stolen money
10 Flaw
11 Modern prefix with tourism
12 Blow it
13 Postpone, with "off"
18 Digs up
19 "Little ___ Sunshine"
23 Untruths
25 Coating of frost
26 In the near future
27 Get-up-and-go
29 Where you might get into hot water
30 Credit card bills, e.g.
31 Photographic film coating
33 Inevitable destruction
34 No ___, ands or buts
36 Boyfriend
37 Distinctive features of Mr. Spock
38 Backside
39 Empty, as a well
40 Radiator sound
43 Alligatorlike reptile
44 "The King and I" woman
46 Where originally found
47 Bump and thump
48 British weight
50 Home of many Velázquez paintings
51 Uneasy feeling
54 Kansaslike
55 Arab chieftain
56 ___ smasher
57 Hurly-burly
58 Veto
59 "If ___ told you once . . ."
60 When the pilot is due in, for short

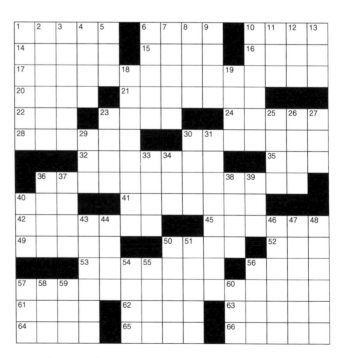

by Eric Fischer

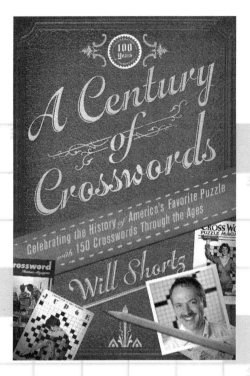
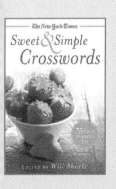   

ANSWERS

1

A	N	D	E	S	■	S	N	I	D	E	■	S	A	L	E
H	I	R	E	E	■	N	O	R	S	E	■	E	M	I	T
O	V	E	R	T	H	E	H	I	L	L	■	L	A	S	H
Y	E	A	■	S	A	R	I	S	■	■	E	F	I	L	E
■	A	R	O	U	N	D	T	H	E	C	O	R	N	E	R
■	■	U	P	S	■	■	L	A	N	E	■	■	■	■	■
A	S	K	T	O	■	S	P	L	I	T	■	L	A	R	A
B	E	Y	O	N	D	T	H	E	H	O	R	I	Z	O	N
C	A	L	F	■	E	R	I	T	U	■	E	A	T	E	N
■	■	S	I	N	O	■	■	L	M	N	■	■	■	■	■
U	N	D	E	R	T	H	E	C	O	U	N	T	E	R	■
L	I	R	A	S	■	D	O	U	L	A	■	M	E	A	■
T	K	O	S	■	S	I	G	H	T	U	N	S	E	E	N
R	E	P	O	■	A	D	E	A	R	■	T	O	R	S	O
A	S	S	N	■	C	A	R	N	E	■	S	T	Y	E	S

2

W	O	E	S	■	W	A	V	E	■	A	F	T	E	R
O	P	E	C	■	E	X	I	T	■	T	R	A	D	E
L	A	N	A	■	A	L	S	O	■	T	U	L	I	P
F	L	Y	L	I	K	E	A	N	E	A	G	L	E	■
■	■	A	C	E	S	■	T	R	A	■	■	■	■	■
D	A	R	W	I	N	■	S	H	H	■	L	A	B	S
I	S	A	A	C	■	S	P	A	I	N	■	D	E	L
S	I	N	G	L	I	K	E	A	C	A	N	A	R	Y
C	A	T	■	E	R	I	C	S	■	R	E	P	E	L
S	N	O	B	■	I	N	K	■	K	N	O	T	T	Y
■	■	U	S	S	■	S	L	I	P	■	■	■	■	■
■	W	A	T	C	H	L	I	K	E	A	H	A	W	K
Q	A	T	A	R	■	U	T	E	P	■	Y	E	A	R
E	C	O	N	O	■	N	E	W	T	■	T	O	R	I
D	O	Z	E	D	■	A	M	S	O	■	E	N	D	S

3

J	A	S	M	I	N	E	■	O	M	N	I	B	U	S
E	M	P	E	R	O	R	■	L	A	N	T	A	N	A
W	O	R	D	S	W	O	R	D	S	W	O	R	D	S
S	K	Y	S	■	D	U	E	T	■	R	E	E	S	
■			S	N	E	E	R	E	D	■	D	R	Y	
S	H	A	S	T	A	■		R	I	P	■			
P	I	C	K	Y	P	I	C	K	Y	P	I	C	K	Y
A	L	A	I	■	G	N	U	■		L	O	L	A	
M	O	N	E	Y	M	O	N	E	Y	M	O	N	E	Y
■		R	O	I	■			E	S	T	E	E	S	
F	A	D	■	W	R	I	T	T	E	N	■			
A	F	R	O	■	A	S	E	A	■		E	P	E	E
C	L	A	N	G	C	L	A	N	G	C	L	A	N	G
T	A	C	T	I	L	E	■	G	O	O	S	I	N	G
S	T	O	O	G	E	S	■	O	N	E	A	D	A	Y

4

M	A	U	L	■	T	E	R	P	■	M	I	R	T	H
A	R	N	E	■	A	T	I	E	■	I	D	E	A	S
L	O	I	N	■	B	O	N	O	■	N	O	N	E	T
T	O	O	T	H	A	N	D	N	A	I	L	■		
A	M	N	I	O	S	■	S	Y	N	C	■	F	A	A
■		L	O	C	H	■		O	A	T	E	R	S	
W	E	S	■	F	O	O	T	I	N	M	O	U	T	H
I	T	L	L	■	L	A	G	■		E	D	I	E	
C	H	E	E	K	B	Y	J	O	W	L	■	S	E	N
C	A	E	S	A	R	■	R	A	I	D	■			
A	N	T	■	R	A	I	N	■	D	R	I	L	L	S
■		H	A	N	D	O	V	E	R	F	I	S	T	
A	U	D	I	O	■	A	C	I	D	■	F	E	A	R
B	R	I	N	K	■	H	A	D	I	■	E	T	T	A
E	L	A	T	E	■	O	L	A	N	■	R	O	S	Y

5

E	G	G	S		S	N	U	B	S		S	P	C	A
L	E	A	P		E	E	R	I	E		E	L	E	C
M	E	G	A		A	S	S	E	T		T	I	L	E
			O	N	E	S	T	A	R	H	O	T	E	L	S
C	U	R		M	O	L				A	L	S	O	
O	L	D	L	I	N	E	S	T	A	T	E		
S	N	E	E	R			P	A	D	S		B	I	S
T	A	R	T		B	I	R	D	S		H	A	S	P
A	S	S		A	L	O	E			T	I	T	L	E
		I	T	U	N	E	S	T	O	P	T	E	N
	F	A	R	M			O	A	F		L	S	D
B	O	N	E	S	T	R	U	C	T	U	R	E	
E	R	I	N		H	E	N	C	E		Y	A	R	N
N	A	M	E		E	N	T	E	R		A	X	L	E
D	Y	E	S		M	O	O	R	S		N	E	S	T

6

B	A	H	A		E	R	A	S	E		S	G	T	S
E	B	O	N		L	O	R	N	A		T	O	R	O
G	O	H	A	L	F	S	I	E	S		A	H	E	M
U	V	U	L	A		A	D	E	E		R	A	K	E
N	O	M	O	R	E		Z	L	O	T	Y		
		G	A	L	A	X	Y		K	I	W	I	S
O	R	G	Y		I	R	E		C	A	N	I	N	E
N	E	O		G	O	C	R	A	Z	Y		R	N	A
T	A	B	L	E	T		O	L	E		B	E	S	T
O	D	E	O	N		E	X	A	C	T	A		
	L	A	T	E	R			H	E	D	G	E	S
G	O	L	F		D	R	A	G		R	H	I	N	O
A	S	Y	E		G	O	C	O	M	M	A	N	D	O
S	L	U	R		A	R	T	O	O		I	S	E	E
P	O	P	S		R	S	V	P	S		R	U	D	Y

7

```
C E L L O ■ A M F M ■ M E M O
A R I E L ■ B O O P ■ I R A N
B R E A D D O U G H ■ S O N Y
S S N ■ B I A S ■ R A D I O
■ G A R R Y T R U D E A U
F L O A T E D ■ O V I D ■
A U D I ■ A D E N ■ I R A
W A I T I N G F O R G O D O T
N U N ■ T A R T ■ S E A M
■ E S A U ■ C A E S A R S
M A R L O N B R A N D O ■
E B O O K ■ O R E G ■ A P O
L I S P R E A R W I N D O W
O D I E U G L I ■ E R A S E
N E E D ■ M O D E ■ R A M E N
```

8

```
E T H A N ■ B O M B S ■ T W O
T I A R A ■ A R I A L ■ E O N
C E N T S ■ S A L M O N R O E
E R G ■ M I M E ■ V O I D S
T R A F F I C A R T E R Y ■
C A R E L L ■ I N M A T E
■ M A D A M S P E A K E R
I F S ■ R O I ■ I D S
R U L E S O F O R D E R ■
K R O G E R ■ O N E I L L
■ P R E S I D E N T S D A Y
S W E E P ■ N E A T ■ U R N
L U S T A F T E R ■ O W N E D
O S U ■ S L E P T M O N D O
E S P ■ T O R S O ■ S W O O N
```

9

```
P I P P I ■ A S O F ■ A D Z E
E N R O N ■ L O W E ■ T O A D
S T A N D S T A L L ■ E G G S
T R I G ■ A O K ■ I D I G ■
L A S ■ K I S S A N D T E L L
E Y E L I D ■ L E E ■ R O E
■ E N H A L O ■ F E L T
■ H A N D I N T H E T I L L ■
R E N T ■ G R A V E L ■
A M A ■ I R R ■ I A M S A M
H I G H W A Y T O L L ■ U Z I
■ R O O M ■ I C E ■ E T A S
A R A B ■ J E T H R O T U L L
L I M B ■ E L L E ■ P A R E E
P O S Y ■ T I E R ■ S T E A D
```

10

```
S A T C H ■ O V E R T ■ D A B
A R R A Y ■ D A R E R ■ E D U
B E A R D E D L A D Y ■ N I N
E S P R E S S O ■ R O A M E D
R O S Y ■ S O R T I N G O U T
■ M O O N ■ A V E R T ■
W A K E N ■ E X E ■ O H O K
O B I ■ T H E W I R E ■ E L O
K E N T ■ A X E ■ Y A R D S
■ G I M L I ■ I B E T ■
N I C K O F T I M E ■ I L S A
E G O I S M ■ H E R E S I E S
R I B ■ H I D E A N D S E E K
D V R ■ E L I A S ■ G U N I T
S E A ■ R E T R Y ■ Y E S N O
```

11

```
A C H  ▓  T O N G S  ▓  O F F E R
R N A  ▓  O N I O N  ▓  R A I S A
N O V  ▓  M O L D E D G L A S S
A T E A T  ▓ ▓  S E E  ▓  S T O P
Z E A L O T S  ▓  Z A N E  ▓ ▓
▓  H A M M E R E D S T E E L
C H E  ▓  S A G O  ▓ ▓  A T A R I
L O A N  ▓  N A S A L  ▓  O S L O
A P R O N  ▓ ▓  I C O N  ▓  Y E N
P E T R I F I E D W O O D  ▓
▓ ▓  T A L C  ▓  C E N S O R S
S U C H  ▓  O E D  ▓  U S E U P
C R U S H E D R O C K  ▓  S N L
A G R E E  ▓  U N D U E  ▓  I I I
R E L A X  ▓  P O E T S  ▓  T N T
```

12

```
G R E E K  ▓  H D T V  ▓  M A Z E
M I A M I  ▓  Y O R E  ▓  O R A L
T O T E M  ▓  P O O R  ▓  O T I S
▓  R O B E R T D E N I R O
▓  S P I N E  ▓  U N R E E L
M A R L O N B R A N D O  ▓
E L O  ▓  S E R U M  ▓  S C H W A
A V O N  ▓  T U N I S  ▓  K A H N
L O F A T  ▓  N I N A S  ▓  N I T
▓  V I T O C O R L E O N E
S T R I V E  ▓ ▓  A E R I E  ▓
T H E G O D F A T H E R  ▓
U R S A  ▓  I O N E  ▓  V A U L T
M E E T  ▓  U R N S  ▓  E N S U E
P E T E  ▓  M E A T  ▓  S T A G E
```

13

E	L	K	■	F	E	D	■		M	O	V	I	N	G
V	A	N	I	L	L	A	■		R	E	C	I	T	A	L
E	C	O	N	O	M	Y	■		A	R	T	D	E	C	O
N	E	W	E	R	A	■	Y	W	C	A	■	M	R	S
■	I	V	A	N	H	O	E	■	V	A	S	E	S	■
I	N	T	E	L	■	D	U	R	B	I	N	■		
L	I	A	R	■	I	T	S	■	R	A	I	L	E	D
E	L	L	■	H	A	V	A	N	A	N	■	O	L	E
S	E	L	D	O	M	■	I	O	N	■	C	O	S	A
■	■	D	O	S	I	D	O	■	D	A	K	A	R	■
G	A	P	E	D	■	N	I	R	V	A	N	A	■	
A	P	E	■	W	H	A	T	■	I	T	A	L	I	A
L	A	T	V	I	A	N	■	A	T	E	D	I	R	T
A	R	R	A	N	G	E	■	C	A	R	A	V	A	N
S	T	I	N	K	S	■	■	E	L	S	■	E	N	O

14

A	P	A	R	T	■	D	E	B	S	■		S	I	S
P	R	I	E	S	■	A	L	A	I	■	L	I	M	P
P	O	R	C	H	S	W	I	N	G	■	E	X	P	O
S	P	Y	R	I	N	G	■	■	M	A	T	T	E	R
■	■	U	R	L	■	S	M	A	S	H	H	I	T	■
P	L	A	I	T	■	D	U	O	■	P	E	G	■	
L	I	N	T	■	T	U	B	U	L	E	■	R	O	B
A	M	Y	■	B	U	L	L	R	U	N	■	A	B	A
Y	A	O	■	O	G	L	I	N	G	■	I	D	O	L
■	L	A	Y	■	E	M	S	■	K	N	E	E	L	
M	U	D	S	L	I	D	E	■	M	I	D	■	■	
A	N	T	H	E	M	■	E	A	S	Y	W	I	N	
I	L	I	E	■	P	I	A	N	O	S	C	O	R	E
D	I	M	S	■	L	O	R	D	■	M	A	R	K	S
S	T	E	■	Y	U	K	S	■	E	R	N	S	T	

15

C	A	S	K	■	S	H	R	E	D	■	B	E	S	S
A	M	O	O	■	P	E	E	V	E	■	E	L	H	I
S	O	U	R	G	R	A	P	E	S	■	D	I	R	E
A	S	P	■	E	I	R	E	■	A	B	Z	U	G	
■	S	A	L	T	Y	L	A	N	G	U	A	G	E	
C	A	P	S	I	Z	E	■	M	O	O	G	■		
A	V	O	I	D	■	W	I	N	G	S	P	A	N	
R	I	O	■	B	S	I	D	E	■	O	R	E		
S	A	N	S	K	R	I	T	■	D	O	L	L	S	
■	I	N	E	Z	■	T	S	E	L	I	O	T		
B	I	T	T	E	R	E	N	E	M	I	E	S	■	
O	N	I	C	E	■	I	R	I	S	■	H	I	C	
I	N	T	O	■	S	W	E	E	T	T	O	O	T	H
S	E	A	M	W	E	L	S	H	■	P	U	R	E	
E	R	N	S	E	S	S	A	Y	■	S	T	Y	X	

16

■	M	E	T	■	A	S	S	■	N	I	E	C	E	S
M	A	N	E	■	B	O	A	■	O	O	L	A	L	A
O	R	G	S	■	S	T	U	D	M	U	F	F	I	N
A	G	A	T	E	■	D	E	A	■	E	E	K		
B	I	G	E	N	C	H	I	L	A	D	A	■		
■	N	E	E	D	L	E	■	M	A	T	Z	O	H	
J	A	M	S	■	E	L	A	L	■	W	E	A	R	Y
O	L	E	■	G	O	O	D	E	G	G	■	S	A	P
H	I	N	D	U	■	T	O	G	A	■	P	I	N	E
N	A	T	U	R	E	■	U	R	G	I	N	G	■	
■	H	U	M	A	N	P	R	E	T	Z	E	L		
A	S	H	■	P	R	E	■	L	E	E	R	Y		
S	W	E	E	T	I	E	P	I	E	■	O	B	I	E
P	A	R	L	O	R	■	A	D	D	U	R	N	S	
S	T	R	I	P	E	L	O	T	■	S	A	D	■	

17

Puzzle 17:

P	A	S	T	D	U	E		P	I	T	A	P	A	T
H	Y	P	H	E	N	S		I	N	A	R	A	G	E
D	E	F	I	C	I	T		M	E	N	T	I	O	N
			N	O	T		P	A	R	K	I	N	G	
J	E	R	K		E	A	R		T	I	S			
E	S	A	I			F	O	R		N	T	E	S	T
S	K	I	N		I	R	V	I	N	G		Q	U	E
T	I	N	G		D	I	O	D	E		F	U	M	E
E	M	O		L	O	C	K	E	T		L	A	M	P
R	O	N	D	O		A	I	R		A	T	O	E	
		C	O	D		N	S	C		N	E	N	E	
	P	E	A	K	I	N	G		A	C	K			
B	U	R	R	I	T	O		S	I	L	I	C	O	N
A	L	I	E	N	T	O		I	R	O	N	O	R	E
D	E	C	A	G	O	N		R	O	Y	G	B	I	V

S	T	E	W		B	E	T	T	E		T	O	D	O
N	O	T	E		O	N	R	E	D		I	G	O	R
O	R	A	L		B	R	I	D	G	E	C	L	U	B
B	I	L	L	Y	B	O	B		E	N	T	E	R	S
		R	A	I	N		B	O	N	A				
C	A	V	E	R	N		B	L	U	E	C	R	A	B
A	P	I	A	N		B	A	I	T		O	N	O	
R	A	N	D	S		E	N	S		P	L	A	I	N
I	C	Y			P	A	D	S		R	I	N	S	E
B	E	L	L	Y	R	U	B		S	A	S	S	E	D
		I	V	E	S		D	E	N	T				
A	P	P	L	E	S		B	R	A	K	E	J	O	B
B	R	U	I	S	E	D	R	I	B		N	A	P	A
L	I	R	E		N	A	I	V	E		U	K	E	S
E	X	E	S		T	W	E	E	D		P	E	C	K

19

S	C	O	O	B		P	O	O	H		D	R	E	W
W	A	N	D	A		A	N	N	O		I	O	T	A
I	C	I	E	R		P	E	S	O		A	L	T	S
G	H	O	S	T	F	A	C	E	K	I	L	L	A	H
S	E	N	S	E	I		E	T	U	D	E			
				A	R	L	E	N	S	P	E	C	T	E	R
B	R	A			E	N	T			A	T	R	I	A
R	U	G	R	A	T	S		K	I	S	S	E	R	S
O	T	H	E	R			C	I	V			Y	E	P
S	H	A	D	O	W	B	O	X	I	N	G			
			S	N	E	A	D		E	A	R	T	H	A
D	I	S	T	I	L	L	E	D	S	P	I	R	I	T
O	K	L	A		O	L	I	O		P	L	A	N	S
P	E	A	T		S	E	N	T		E	L	I	D	E
E	A	V	E		T	R	E	E		D	E	L	I	A

20

D	E	B	T		S	I	M	P		Z	A	P	S
V	A	L	I	D		U	S	E	R		E	U	R	O
D	R	O	N	E		C	A	S	E		A	R	I	A
	W	A	T	C	H	T	H	E	C	L	O	C	K
A	D	O		E	A	T		E	M	U		R	E	S
C	O	V	E	R	T	H	E	S	P	R	E	A	D
T	R	E	X		S	A	L		T	E	L		
S	A	R	A	N		T	O	T		S	L	U	G	S
		M	O	E		P	A	L		E	N	Y	A
	W	A	S	H	T	H	E	L	A	U	N	D	R	Y
S	A	D		I	C	U		L	I	L		E	O	S
T	U	R	N	T	H	E	C	O	R	N	E	R	
A	S	I	A		E	V	E	N		A	N	W	A	R
R	A	F	T		R	O	L	E		S	T	A	N	D
R	U	T	S		S	S	T	S			S	Y	N	S

21

S	T	I	R	■	S	T	A	Y	■	G	O	V	T
C	A	N	A	■	P	H	O	T	O	■	R	H	E	A
O	H	B	Y	T	H	E	W	A	Y	■	A	C	T	S
T	O	O	B	A	D	■	E	R	O	■	N	O	O	K
T	E	X	A	S	■	S	L	I	M	J	I	M	■
■	■	N	E	S	T	■	A	U	T	E	U	R
D	U	O	S	■	H	U	L	A	■	D	E	N	N	Y
A	S	H	■	O	H	M	Y	G	O	D	■	O	D	E
Z	E	B	R	A	■	P	E	R	P	■	T	W	O	S
E	R	R	O	R	S	■	E	T	C	H	■
■	O	N	S	T	A	G	E	■	L	E	G	A	L
L	U	T	Z	■	R	C	A	■	M	O	H	A	V	E
E	C	H	O	■	O	H	F	O	R	G	E	T	I	T
G	L	E	N	■	L	O	F	A	T	■	L	O	L	A
S	A	R	I	■	L	O	S	T	■	P	R	A	T

22

E	N	T	■	P	A	I	N	E	■	R	A	P	I	D
X	E	R	■	A	M	M	A	N	■	O	P	E	R	A
U	B	I	■	C	O	A	S	T	■	C	I	T	E	D
R	U	B	B	E	R	C	H	I	C	K	E	N	■
B	L	O	O	D	■	■	T	A	S	■	A	L	A
A	A	R	P	■	B	A	B	Y	B	O	O	M	E	R
N	E	O	■	S	I	N	O	■	L	O	E	W	E
■	■	B	U	G	G	Y	W	H	I	P	■
C	H	E	A	P	■	E	Y	E	D	■	B	U	T
B	U	M	P	E	R	C	R	O	P	■	S	O	P	H
S	N	O	■	R	A	H	■	W	R	O	T	E
■	T	O	N	G	U	E	T	W	I	S	T	E	R
A	M	I	N	O	■	B	R	U	I	N	■	I	M	O
L	E	O	I	V	■	B	I	B	L	E	■	E	P	A
F	A	N	T	A	■	Y	E	A	T	S	■	S	O	D

23

C	R	A	W		P	R	A	G	U	E		P	C	B
X	E	N	A		H	U	M	A	N	E		A	A	A
V	E	N	U	S	D	E	M	I	L	O		G	P	S
I	D	E	S	T			O	T	O		S	A	R	I
		A	I	R			C	L	I	N	I	C		
S	A	T	U	R	N	R	O	C	K	E	T			
I	C	Y			S	E	T	H		N	A	D	I	R
N	E	P	A	L		L	A	O		T	R	I	N	I
G	R	E	C	O		I	R	I	S		E	G	O	
		M	E	R	C	U	R	Y	C	O	M	E	T	
A	M	O	E	B	A			L	A	X				
B	A	S	S		V	I	A		E	I	G	H	T	
A	R	C		M	A	R	S	C	A	N	D	I	E	S
T	I	A		A	G	A	T	E	S		E	Z	R	A
E	A	R		D	E	N	I	E	S		S	A	A	R

24

G	A	B	S		O	G	R	E	S	S		F	A	D
R	E	A	M		A	P	A	C	H	E		I	R	E
U	R	G	E		F	A	L	L	E	N	I	D	O	L
F	I	E	L	D		P	A	R		M	G	M	T	
F	E	L	L	O	W	S	H	I	P		P	E	A	S
		Y	E	O	W		R	A	B	A	T			
A	D	O		R	A	W		E	L	I	S	E		
F	I	L	L	I	N	T	H	E	B	L	A	N	K	S
L	E	D	I	N		O	V	O		G	A	P		
	Y	O	K	E	D		I	N	E	Z				
A	M	E	N		F	O	L	L	O	W	S	U	I	T
B	A	L	E		F	L	A		E	A	T	M	E	
F	U	L	L	N	E	L	S	O	N		Z	A	H	N
A	R	E		O	C	A	S	E	Y		S	H	O	D
B	A	R		S	T	R	O	D	E		A	N	T	S

25

Z	E	S	T		G	U	T			K	I	S	S	U	P	S
I	N	C	H		U	N	H			O	C	E	A	N	I	A
O	T	O	E		E	S	O			L	E	T	I	T	B	E
N	O	W	H	E	R	E	M	A	N		N	O	B	S		
			U	N	R	E	A	L			E	A	T			
	G	O	L	D	E	N	S	L	U	M	B	E	R	S		
F	O	L	K				W	A	I	L			I	L	L	
A	N	I		M	I	C	H	E	L	L	E		C	A	Y	
N	O	V		I	T	O	O				G	E	N	E		
	W	E	C	A	N	W	O	R	K	I	T	O	U	T		
		O	S	O		K	A	N	S	A	S					
C	O	H	N			R	E	V	O	L	U	T	I	O	N	
H	E	Y	J	U	D	E		I	T	E		A	N	D	Y	
U	N	P	O	S	E	D		N	U	T		L	C	D	S	
B	O	O	B	O	O	S		G	P	S		E	A	S	E	

26

M	U	I	R		S	C	U	B	A			A	M	F	M
A	N	N	O		M	I	T	E	R			R	I	D	E
L	A	V	A		E	V	E	R	T			L	S	A	T
T	W	I	N	K	L	I	N	G	E	Y	E	S			
E	A	T		I	L	L	S			A	S	Y	E	T	
D	R	E	A	M	Y		I	M	A	C		O	S	U	
S	E	E	S			F	L	A	S	H	B	U	L	B	
		I	M	S	O		Z	E	T	A					
J	I	F	F	Y	L	U	B	E			G	E	A	R	
A	D	A		T	O	R	I		S	E	S	A	M	E	
B	O	T	C	H		G	E	E	S		R	N	S		
	I	N	S	T	A	N	T	C	O	F	F	E	E		
L	O	G	O		O	M	A	H	A		I	L	S	A	
B	R	U	T		R	O	M	A	N		N	A	T	L	
S	K	E	E		T	R	E	N	T		S	P	Y	S	

27

E	X	I	T		A	S	W	A	N		N	A	P	E
A	M	O	S		M	E	A	R	A		O	X	E	N
T	A	T	A		O	L	D	E	R		H	I	N	D
	S	A	R	T	R	E	S	A	R	R	E	S	T	
			H	E	C				A	O	L			
	P	R	O	U	S	T	S	S	T	U	P	O	R	
C	H	A	R	D		I	S	E	E		R	A	P	
O	I	N	K		H	A	Z	E	S		E	A	V	E
B	A	G		W	I	P	E			A	L	T	E	R
	L	E	S	A	G	E	S	E	A	G	L	E	S	
		A	S	H			N	B	A					
	R	A	C	I	N	E	S	C	A	R	N	I	E	
J	E	F	F		O	R	E	O	S		A	N	T	I
E	A	R	L		T	R	A	D	E		I	R	A	Q
T	R	O	Y		E	S	S	E	S		L	E	S	S

28

T	O	P	A	Z		H	A	N	G		A	G	E	E
O	K	A	P	I		A	L	O	E		D	U	N	G
L	A	W	S	T	U	D	E	N	T		D	E	N	Y
D	Y	N	E		R	O	C		S	E	T	S	U	P
			B	A	N	K	D	E	P	O	S	I	T	
D	O	T	E	L	L			O	V	A				
A	P	O	L	O		S	A	M	E		T	A	R	P
N	E	W	S	C	O	M	M	E	N	T	A	T	O	R
A	N	N	E		U	E	Y	S		A	R	O	M	A
			S	T	L			F	L	O	P	P	Y	
R	E	C	O	R	D	L	A	B	E	L				
A	V	A	T	A	R		H	U	T		C	R	O	P
V	E	N	T		I	C	E	M	A	C	H	I	N	E
E	R	T	E		N	E	A	P		O	A	T	E	R
S	T	I	R		K	E	D	S		B	R	E	A	K

29

M	E	C	C	A	■	B	A	G	S	■	A	J	A	R
A	U	R	A	S	■	E	X	I	T	■	S	O	M	E
T	R	O	P	H	Y	W	I	F	E	■	S	H	I	N
H	O	P	S	■	E	A	S	T	■	A	A	N	D	E
■	■	■	U	S	S	R	■	■	E	R	I	C	■	■
■	G	O	L	D	M	E	D	A	L	F	L	O	U	R
L	A	N	E	S	■	■	W	O	K	S	■	U	N	A
A	M	Y	S	■	A	D	E	L	E	■	T	G	I	F
M	A	O	■	T	R	E	E	■	■	P	R	A	T	T
B	L	U	E	R	I	B	B	O	N	J	U	R	Y	■
■	■	R	A	I	D	■	■	N	O	S	E	■	■	■
L	E	T	G	O	■	O	R	E	O	■	L	A	R	A
I	D	O	L	■	C	R	O	W	N	R	O	Y	A	L
A	G	E	E	■	N	C	A	A	■	E	V	E	N	T
M	E	S	S	■	N	A	R	Y	■	P	E	S	T	O

30

A	P	S	E	■	H	A	S	T	E	■	A	W	E	D
L	I	T	E	■	E	R	N	I	E	■	C	O	V	E
O	X	Y	G	E	N	T	A	N	K	■	C	R	E	W
H	A	L	■	A	S	I	F	■	V	E	R	N	E	■
A	R	E	A	S	■	S	U	C	H	A	P	I	T	Y
■	■	■	C	E	R	T	■	H	U	N	T	S	■	■
S	O	R	T	I	E	■	D	A	B	■	■	O	V	A
T	H	E	I	N	V	I	S	I	B	L	E	M	A	N
P	O	D	■	■	A	L	L	■	L	A	T	E	L	Y
■	■	P	A	L	M	S	■	S	E	C	T	■	■	■
F	E	L	L	A	P	A	R	T	■	K	E	A	T	S
S	C	A	L	P	■	■	A	O	N	E	■	B	O	A
T	O	N	E	■	H	I	N	D	U	D	E	I	T	Y
O	L	E	G	■	A	S	I	G	N	■	O	D	E	S
P	E	T	E	■	T	O	N	Y	S	■	N	E	M	O

31

M	I	C	A	■	P	E	R	C	H	■	S	L	O	G
A	N	A	S	■	O	L	I	O	S	■	A	E	R	O
D	A	R	K	K	N	I	G	H	T	■	G	N	A	T
■	P	O	S	E	I	D	O	N	■	M	A	T	C	H
P	A	L	■	N	E	E	R	■	M	A	N	I	L	A
U	N	I	■	T	D	S	■	T	A	N	■	L	E	M
N	I	N	E	■	■	M	A	R	I	O	■	■	■	■
■	C	A	P	E	D	C	R	U	S	A	D	E	R	■
■	■	■	A	L	E	R	T	■	■	E	V	E	N	■
B	I	S	■	S	L	Y	■	D	I	S	■	I	T	O
A	C	T	I	I	I	■	L	U	S	T	■	L	U	G
T	E	A	S	E	■	F	A	L	L	O	V	E	R	■
M	A	I	N	■	B	R	U	C	E	W	A	Y	N	E
A	G	R	O	■	B	E	R	E	T	■	V	E	E	S
N	E	S	T	■	S	T	A	T	S	■	A	D	D	S

32

M	E	S	S	■	A	C	T	I	■	■	C	A	S	A
A	N	T	E	■	C	O	O	N	■	G	A	L	E	N
C	R	A	P	S	H	O	O	T	■	E	L	L	E	N
H	O	T	T	I	E	■	F	E	A	T	■	A	T	E
O	N	S	E	T	■	B	A	L	L	O	T	B	O	X
■	■	■	T	E	L	L	S	■	A	V	E	O	■	■
A	S	S	■	■	S	I	T	S	■	E	N	A	C	T
B	A	N	K	R	U	N	■	C	O	R	N	R	O	W
S	W	I	N	E	■	I	C	E	S	■	■	D	N	A
■	■	F	E	D	S	■	A	N	S	E	L	■	■	■
L	I	F	E	C	Y	C	L	E	■	R	O	A	S	T
E	N	S	■	E	S	S	O	■	S	I	N	N	E	R
A	T	O	L	L	■	P	R	I	C	E	D	I	V	E
C	R	U	E	L	■	A	I	D	A	■	O	M	E	N
H	A	T	E	■	N	E	O	N	■	N	E	R	D	

33

S	C	A	T	■	D	E	B	I	T	■	P	H	E	W
P	E	E	R	■	I	N	U	R	E	■	H	O	R	A
A	L	I	I	■	O	C	E	A	N	L	I	N	E	R
S	L	O	P	■	N	O	N	■	■	E	L	E	C	T
M	O	U	L	I	N	R	O	U	G	E	■	S	T	Y
■	■	■	E	P	E	E	■	P	E	S	O	■	■	■
T	H	E	T	A	■	■	C	O	L	■	N	I	C	E
S	O	L	I	D	F	O	U	N	D	A	T	I	O	N
A	T	O	M	■	A	P	E	■	■	R	H	I	N	O
■	■	■	E	A	S	E	■	W	A	G	E	■	■	■
T	S	P	■	C	O	C	O	A	P	O	W	D	E	R
A	T	O	L	L	■	■	V	I	A	■	H	I	Y	A
M	A	K	E	U	P	T	E	S	T	■	O	N	I	T
E	V	E	N	■	E	A	R	T	H	■	L	E	N	T
R	E	D	S	■	G	U	T	S	Y	■	E	D	G	Y

34

P	L	A	Z	A	■	S	P	U	R	■	E	R	O	S
R	E	D	I	D	■	U	O	M	O	■	L	O	O	K
O	V	A	T	E	■	P	U	P	U	■	L	A	Z	Y
B	E	G	I	N	N	E	R	S	G	U	I	D	E	■
E	R	E	■	A	A	R	■	H	M	O	S	■	■	■
■	■	■	D	U	M	B	Q	U	E	S	T	I	O	N
S	O	I	R	E	E	■	U	K	R	■	■	G	T	O
I	N	N	E	R	■	D	E	E	■	C	A	N	O	E
L	T	S	■	■	B	Y	E	■	T	A	S	S	E	L
T	O	U	G	H	A	S	N	A	I	L	S	■	■	■
■	■	R	O	A	R	■	■	S	N	L	■	A	C	T
■	L	A	D	Y	N	A	N	C	Y	A	S	T	O	R
C	U	B	E	■	O	H	I	O	■	C	U	R	V	Y
U	C	L	A	■	W	O	N	T	■	A	M	I	E	S
E	K	E	D	■	L	Y	E	S	■	B	O	A	S	T

35

S	P	A	M		A	C	M	E		S	C	H	M	O
T	O	G	A		B	A	I	L		A	R	E	A	R
A	L	E	C		O	R	M	E		L	A	M	P	S
P	E	N	E	L	O	P	E	C	R	U	Z			
L	A	D		I	K	E		T	O	T	E	B	A	G
E	X	A	C	T		T	W	I	C	E		A	L	A
		A	H	A		O	O	O		C	L	A	M	
S	H	A	K	E	D	O	W	N	C	R	U	I	S	E
K	O	B	E		A	R	E		O	E	R			
A	P	E		E	G	A	D	S		L	E	A	R	Y
T	I	T	A	N	I	C		I	I	I		L	E	A
			G	R	O	U	N	D	S	C	R	E	W	S
M	A	R	G	O		L	O	N	E		A	X	I	S
A	V	A	I	L		A	V	E	R		M	E	R	E
J	E	W	E	L		R	A	Y	E		P	I	E	R

36

N	E	S	T	S		B	O	S	S		E	G	A	D
O	N	T	A	P		A	L	T	O		N	O	D	E
A	D	E	L	A		Y	E	A	S		S	L	O	T
H	O	T	C	R	O	S	S	B	U	N		D	R	E
		S	R	O		S	E	E	D	I	E	R		
N	E	B		O	N	U	S		M	A	I	L		
A	R	E		W	A	R	M	W	E	L	C	O	M	E
R	O	D	E		A	I	R		E	C	O	N		
C	O	O	L	M	I	L	L	I	O	N		K	A	Y
	F	L	A	N		E	T	T	E		S	T	A	
C	A	N	A	S	T	A		T	W	A				
A	M	A		C	O	L	D	C	O	M	F	O	R	T
R	U	I	N		N	O	R	A		A	I	M	E	E
O	S	L	O		E	N	O	S		T	R	A	N	S
B	E	S	T		S	E	P	T		H	E	R	D	S

37

S	T	R	A	T	A	■	Z	A	P	■	C	L	I	P
T	H	E	S	I	S	■	I	M	A	■	A	O	N	E
R	E	D	I	N	K	■	P	B	S	■	R	I	C	E
A	M	O	D	E	S	T	P	R	O	P	O	S	A	L
F	R	E	E	■	■	W	O	O	■	A	L	L	■	■
E	S	S	■	I	D	O	■	S	A	Y	■	A	S	H
■	■	S	S	R	■	A	I	R	L	A	N	E	S	■
P	R	I	O	R	E	N	G	A	G	E	M	E	N	T
M	O	N	T	A	G	U	E	■	U	S	A	■	■	■
S	E	A	■	E	S	T	■	W	E	S	■	P	J	S
■	■	S	O	L	■	C	O	W	■	■	A	L	A	I
A	M	E	R	I	C	A	N	W	E	D	D	I	N	G
H	O	N	E	■	U	S	E	■	D	O	M	A	I	N
A	L	S	O	■	L	E	N	■	E	V	I	N	C	E
B	E	E	S	■	L	S	D	■	N	E	T	T	E	D

38

C	L	A	S	P	■	I	C	O	N	■	F	L	A	B
H	A	I	T	I	■	R	O	M	A	■	L	U	L	L
I	D	T	A	G	■	A	M	A	T	■	U	R	G	E
■	■	■	L	S	D	■	P	H	I	L	■	C	A	N
S	E	D	A	T	E	■	L	A	V	I	S	H	E	D
T	R	I	C	Y	C	L	E	■	E	M	T	■	■	■
A	N	A	T	■	A	U	T	O	■	B	A	L	D	S
M	I	N	I	■	F	I	E	L	D	■	L	O	R	N
P	E	A	T	S	■	S	C	A	R	■	A	R	O	O
■	■	E	A	R	■	O	V	E	R	G	R	O	W	■
N	U	T	S	H	E	L	L	■	G	A	M	E	L	Y
E	N	E	■	L	U	A	U	■	S	R	I	■	■	■
A	L	A	N	■	B	U	M	P	■	E	T	T	A	S
R	I	S	E	■	E	R	N	E	■	S	E	W	E	R
S	T	E	T	■	N	A	S	A	■	T	S	A	R	S

39

L	A	T	H	■	U	C	L	A	■	S	T	A	I	D
E	C	H	O	■	M	R	E	D	■	W	A	L	D	O
A	L	A	S	■	B	E	A	M	■	E	N	T	E	R
P	U	R	P	L	E	P	R	O	S	E	■	O	A	K
■	■	■	E	R	E	■	N	A	P	S	■	■	■	■
I	P	A	N	A	■	S	H	I	V	■	M	A	S	S
D	I	N	E	R	O	■	I	S	O	■	E	D	N	A
L	A	V	E	N	D	E	R	H	I	L	L	M	O	B
E	N	I	D	■	E	V	E	■	R	E	T	I	R	E
S	O	L	E	■	S	A	S	S	■	A	S	T	E	R
■	■	■	D	I	S	C	■	T	A	S	■	■	■	■
A	H	A	■	M	A	U	V	E	D	E	C	A	D	E
M	A	N	I	A	■	A	E	R	O	■	H	U	R	L
A	L	O	N	G	■	T	I	E	R	■	E	R	A	S
D	O	N	N	E	■	E	L	O	N	■	W	A	G	E

40

B	O	R	E	S	■	L	A	M	A	■	C	H	A	P
E	L	I	T	E	■	O	W	E	D	■	R	O	S	E
A	G	O	R	A	■	M	O	O	D	■	O	M	I	T
M	A	T	E	R	I	A	L	W	I	T	N	E	S	S
■	■	■	■	E	R	N	S	■	T	H	Y	■	■	■
P	A	R	A	D	E	■	■	L	I	O	N	E	S	S
A	M	O	S	■	■	S	W	O	O	N	■	A	P	E
S	I	G	H	T	S	E	E	I	N	G	T	R	I	P
T	E	E	■	H	A	T	E	S	■	■	A	T	R	A
E	S	T	E	E	M	S	■	■	R	A	C	H	E	L
■	■	■	R	I	O	■	A	M	E	N	■	■	■	■
O	B	S	E	R	V	A	T	I	O	N	D	E	C	K
T	A	L	C	■	A	L	A	N	■	A	R	L	E	N
T	R	O	T	■	R	O	L	E	■	L	I	S	L	E
O	N	E	S	■	S	E	E	D	■	S	P	A	T	E

41

O	D	D	S	■	S	P	O	K	E	S	■	B	A	R
L	I	E	U	■	E	L	A	I	N	E	■	E	M	U
G	E	M	M	Y	C	A	R	T	E	R	■	F	E	B
A	D	O	■	E	A	T	■	■	■	G	L	O	B	E
■	■	■	W	A	N	O	L	D	R	E	A	G	A	N
O	L	D	E	S	T	■	A	W	A	I	T	■	■	■
V	A	U	L	T	■	D	Y	E	R	■	H	A	L	E
A	C	O	L	Y	T	E	■	L	E	V	E	L	E	R
L	E	S	S	■	S	L	O	T	■	A	R	D	O	R
■	■	I	R	A	T	E	■	C	L	E	A	N	S	■
J	E	S	T	E	R	A	R	T	H	U	R	■	■	■
A	X	L	E	S	■	■	H	U	E	■	E	R	A	■
V	I	E	■	H	A	I	R	Y	T	R	U	M	A	N
A	L	P	■	I	N	C	O	M	E	■	S	I	G	N
N	E	T	■	P	A	Y	E	E	S	■	A	R	E	A

42

E	L	M	S	■	A	G	R	E	E	■	M	I	L	K
C	I	A	O	■	P	R	O	M	S	■	A	V	O	W
H	O	C	U	S	P	O	C	U	S	■	T	O	G	A
O	N	E	■	T	E	A	K	■	■	S	I	R	E	N
■	■	■	H	E	N	N	Y	P	E	N	N	Y	■	■
D	E	M	A	N	D	■	■	A	D	O	S	■	■	■
A	G	E	S	■	■	M	A	N	G	O	■	S	P	A
D	O	T	H	E	H	O	K	E	Y	P	O	K	E	Y
E	S	E	■	B	A	N	A	L	■	■	N	Y	S	E
■	■	■	B	O	R	E	■	■	I	S	L	E	T	S
■	■	H	A	N	K	Y	P	A	N	K	Y	■	■	■
S	T	O	R	Y	■	■	A	N	T	I	■	A	O	K
P	A	G	E	■	H	O	D	G	E	P	O	D	G	E
A	R	A	L	■	M	A	R	I	N	■	V	A	L	E
M	A	N	Y	■	S	K	E	E	T	■	A	M	E	N

43

E	U	R	O		E	M	I	T		A	L	I	A	S
S	T	A	N		P	O	R	E		B	A	D	G	E
C	A	K	E	W	A	L	K	S		S	W	E	E	T
	H	E	R	O		A	S	T	O		C	A	S	H
		U	R	L	S		E	T	A	L				
	C	A	N	D	Y	S	T	R	I	P	E	R	S	
A	L	S		E	E	R		S	T	R	A	I	T	
D	I	T	C	H		S	U	P		S	K	I	L	L
S	M	I	L	E	S		C	A	P		T	A	C	
	B	R	O	W	N	I	E	P	O	I	N	T	S	
		I	S	O	N		A	L	T	O				
A	C	T	S		B	A	R	B		C	F	O	S	
T	O	O	T	H		P	I	E	C	H	A	R	T	S
V	I	D	E	O		E	G	A	D		I	S	E	E
S	N	O	R	E		T	A	R	S		R	O	M	A

44

U	S	D	A		P	L	O	P		A	S	C	A	P
L	E	E	R		C	A	V	S		S	C	A	L	E
T	O	M	B	O	S	L	E	Y		P	O	K	E	S
R	U	M	O	R		A	R	C	H	I	T	E	C	T
A	L	E	R	T			H	A	R	T				
			H	A	L	F		W	E	B	C	A	M	
R	O	N	H	O	W	A	R	D		R	A	M	B	O
A	S	E	A		E	N	E	R	O		I	D	B	E
F	L	A	P	S		E	R	I	N	M	O	R	A	N
T	O	P	P	L	E		E	P	E	E				
		Y	O	U	R			C	A	N	A	L		
D	E	A	D	W	R	O	N	G		C	R	A	N	E
A	D	L	A	I		M	I	L	W	A	U	K	E	E
B	A	B	Y	S		P	L	E	A		B	E	N	D
S	M	A	S	H		S	E	E	D		A	D	D	S

45

L	O	W	S	■	W	A	S	P	S	■	A	M	P	S
O	A	H	U	■	A	L	L	I	N	■	D	O	L	E
I	T	O	L	D	Y	O	U	S	O	■	A	L	E	X
S	H	A	K	E	S	P	E	A	R	E	P	L	A	Y
■	■	■	S	C	I	■	■	N	E	S	T	■	■	■
A	S	H	■	A	D	A	M	■	■	S	A	L	S	A
T	H	E	I	D	E	S	O	F	MARCH	■	B	E	L	L
W	O	R	S	E	■	O	V	I	■	B	L	O	O	P
A	V	O	N	■	MARCH	F	I	F	T	E	E	N	T	H
R	E	N	T	S	■	■	N	E	E	D	■	A	H	A
■	■	■	S	T	A	G	■	■	E	E	K	■	■	■
F	A	M	O	U	S	L	A	S	T	W	O	R	D	S
I	B	A	R	■	S	O	O	T	H	S	A	Y	E	R
J	E	E	R	■	A	R	N	I	E	■	L	E	F	T
I	T	S	Y	■	D	Y	E	R	S	■	A	S	T	A

46

L	I	L	I	■	E	W	E	R	■	D	W	A	R	F
E	D	E	N	■	V	I	C	E	■	O	N	C	U	E
G	O	N	E	W	I	T	H	T	H	E	W	I	N	D
O	L	D	P	A	L	■	O	R	E	S	■	D	T	S
■	■	■	T	I	T	O	■	O	A	T	S	■	■	■
B	A	M	■	T	W	A	S	■	T	I	M	B	E	R
A	L	O	E	■	I	S	E	E	■	M	O	O	L	A
S	I	N	G	I	N	I	N	T	H	E	R	A	I	N
E	V	E	R	T	■	S	O	H	O	■	E	T	T	A
D	E	T	E	S	T	■	R	O	T	H	■	S	E	T
■	■	■	T	A	I	L	■	S	W	A	P	■	■	■
A	O	L	■	D	E	E	M	■	A	G	E	N	D	A
T	H	E	P	E	R	F	E	C	T	S	T	O	R	M
T	I	A	R	A	■	T	A	P	E	■	T	R	E	E
Y	O	D	E	L	■	S	L	U	R	■	Y	A	W	N

47

M	A	C	S	█	H	O	U	R	█	H	A	Z	E	L
U	G	L	Y	█	E	S	S	E	█	A	V	E	R	Y
N	O	O	N	█	A	H	E	M	█	M	O	U	S	E
C	R	U	C	I	V	E	R	B	A	L	I	S	T	█
H	A	D	█	T	E	A	█	R	U	E	D	█	█	█
█	█	█	B	E	N	█	M	A	R	T	█	J	A	B
A	X	I	O	M	█	B	O	N	A	█	C	O	L	A
C	R	O	S	S	W	O	R	D	E	D	I	T	O	R
H	A	W	N	█	H	O	S	T	█	I	N	S	E	T
E	Y	E	█	P	E	K	E	█	U	T	E	█	█	█
█	█	█	F	I	L	M	█	T	N	T	█	D	I	S
█	E	N	I	G	M	A	T	O	L	O	G	I	S	T
G	L	E	N	S	█	K	A	T	E	█	R	O	L	E
U	B	O	A	T	█	E	X	E	S	█	I	D	E	A
M	A	N	L	Y	█	R	I	M	S	█	D	E	S	K

48

J	A	M	S	█	M	A	Y	O	R	█	S	E	L	F
O	B	O	E	█	A	R	E	W	E	█	T	R	I	O
T	E	N	C	O	M	M	A	N	D	M	E	N	T	S
S	T	O	O	L	I	E	█	█	D	A	V	I	E	S
█	█	█	N	E	E	D	E	D	█	R	E	E	S	E
E	G	A	D	S	█	█	X	E	D	I	N	█	█	█
C	L	U	E	█	P	A	P	U	A	N	█	M	B	A
H	U	N	D	R	E	D	A	C	R	E	W	O	O	D
O	T	T	█	U	S	E	N	E	T	█	H	A	Z	E
█	█	█	G	L	O	P	S	█	█	H	I	T	O	N
F	A	I	R	E	█	T	E	A	M	U	P	█	█	█
A	C	C	O	R	D	█	█	G	A	L	L	O	P	S
T	H	O	U	S	A	N	D	I	S	L	A	N	D	S
E	O	N	S	█	F	E	I	N	T	█	S	C	A	T
D	O	S	E	█	T	O	N	G	S	█	H	E	S	S

49

P	A	S	T	E	L	■	T	B	A	R	■	A	L	T
E	L	O	I	S	E	■	I	A	G	O	■	L	E	A
C	O	U	N	T	R	Y	C	L	U	B	■	B	A	N
S	T	L	■	E	N	O	■	D	E	E	P	E	N	D
■	■	M	O	S	E	Y	S	■	■	A	R	T	E	■
M	C	A	N	■	R	O	C	K	B	O	T	T	O	M
P	U	T	T	S	■	H	O	Y	L	E	■	■	■	■
H	E	E	H	A	W	S	■	P	E	E	R	S	A	T
■	■	E	M	A	I	L	■	S	N	A	C	K	■	■
R	A	P	S	E	S	S	I	O	N	■	A	L	T	O
O	V	A	L	■	■	P	R	O	W	L	S	■	■	■
L	I	L	Y	P	A	D	■	I	T	O	■	A	E	R
L	A	M	■	S	W	I	N	G	B	R	I	D	G	E
E	T	E	■	S	A	S	E	■	A	S	S	I	G	N
R	E	D	■	T	Y	K	E	■	D	E	S	P	O	T

50

L	O	B	O	■	N	A	D	I	A	■	I	M	P	S
A	L	U	M	■	U	S	E	R	S	■	N	A	R	C
M	E	R	E	■	D	I	N	E	S	■	B	R	I	E
B	O	R	N	A	G	A	I	N	■	S	E	D	A	N
■	■	S	K	I	■	M	E	A	L	T	I	M	E	■
B	T	U	■	I	N	C	■	S	O	W	■	■	■	■
L	I	V	I	N	G	O	N	T	H	E	E	D	G	E
E	D	E	N	■	M	E	R	■	■	E	I	R	E	■
D	E	A	D	A	S	A	D	O	O	R	N	A	I	L
■	■	I	W	O	■	■	N	Y	E	■	L	P	S	■
R	E	V	E	R	S	E	S	■	S	P	A	■	■	■
E	D	I	F	Y	■	T	H	A	T	S	L	I	F	E
U	G	L	I	■	O	H	A	R	E	■	A	L	E	X
S	E	L	L	■	L	E	V	E	R	■	M	I	L	E
E	D	A	M	■	D	R	E	S	S	■	O	A	T	S

51

F	A	R	O	■	A	R	R	O	W	■	O	P	U	S
O	L	A	F	■	U	H	H	U	H	■	M	E	T	A
W	A	I	F	■	G	O	O	S	E	■	S	T	U	B
L	I	L	Y	M	U	N	S	T	E	R	■	U	R	L
■	■	■	E	A	S	E	■	■	D	I	A	N	N	E
D	E	P	A	R	T	■	B	I	L	O	X	I	■	■
O	Z	A	R	K	■	J	I	B	E	■	E	A	T	S
U	R	N	■	S	L	A	K	E	R	S	■	P	O	T
P	A	S	T	■	A	P	E	X	■	H	A	I	T	I
■	■	Y	A	W	N	E	R	■	D	O	D	G	E	R
H	E	Y	D	A	Y	■	■	B	E	A	D	■	■	■
E	L	O	■	D	A	I	S	Y	C	L	O	V	E	R
M	I	K	E	■	R	H	I	N	O	■	N	O	P	E
A	Z	U	R	■	D	O	N	O	R	■	T	I	E	D
N	A	M	E	■	S	P	E	W	S	■	O	D	E	S

52

S	W	A	M	■	R	A	S	H	■	D	A	I	S	Y
O	H	N	O	■	E	S	T	A	■	O	L	D	I	E
N	E	A	T	■	E	S	A	U	■	A	G	E	N	T
G	E	T	T	O	F	I	R	S	T	B	A	S	E	■
■	■	■	O	N	E	S	■	■	O	L	E	■	■	■
E	S	S	■	T	R	I	R	E	M	E	■	F	I	T
L	O	T	T	O	■	■	A	L	E	■	H	I	D	E
B	A	L	L	P	A	R	K	F	I	G	U	R	E	S
O	P	E	C	■	S	U	E	■	■	C	H	E	A	T
W	Y	O	■	T	H	E	R	M	A	L	■	S	L	Y
■	■	■	S	H	E	■	■	U	T	E	S	■	■	■
■	O	U	T	I	N	L	E	F	T	F	I	E	L	D
R	U	N	O	N	■	S	A	F	E	■	X	I	I	I
O	R	I	N	G	■	A	S	I	S	■	T	R	E	E
E	S	T	E	S	■	T	E	N	T	■	Y	E	N	S

53

A	P	T		C	H	I	L	I		G	O	R	E	N
D	A	Y		L	U	R	I	D		A	N	I	S	E
H	U	P	M	O	B	I	L	E		Z	A	P	P	A
O	L	E	I	N		S	Y	S	T	E	M			
C	A	S	S	I	S			A	B	A	S	E	D	
			O	N	E	L	U	M	P	O	R	T	W	O
M	A	D		G	R	E	T	A		S	C	R	E	W
A	L	I	E		B	A	T	O	N		H	A	R	E
S	P	A	Y	S		P	E	R	I	L		Y	S	L
T	H	R	E	E	S	T	R	I	K	E	S			
S	A	Y	S	N	O			E	V	E	N	E	D	
			L	O	W	E	R	S		I	R	A	Q	I
O	U	T	E	R		P	E	T	I	T	F	O	U	R
K	N	I	F	E		I	N	A	N	E		M	A	T
S	A	L	T	S		C	O	R	D	S		I	L	S

54

J	E	T	S		I	M	A		A	R	E	T	O	O
U	P	R	O	O	T	E	D		B	A	S	I	N	S
T	H	U	R	G	O	O	D		A	Z	T	E	C	S
			B	R	O	W	N	V	B	O	A	R	D	
S	P	R	E	E				E	A	R				
H	U	I	T		A	N	N	E		E	E	L	E	D
O	L	D		A	S	E	A		O	D	D	I	T	Y
P	L	E	S	S	Y	V	F	E	R	G	U	S	O	N
P	I	R	A	T	E		T	R	E	E		T	I	A
E	N	S	O	R		E	A	R	L		T	E	L	S
			O	P	T				B	I	N	E	T	
	O	F	E	D	U	C	A	T	I	O	N			
P	A	R	L	O	R		M	A	R	S	H	A	L	L
A	T	E	A	M	S		P	R	E	S	A	G	E	S
C	H	E	N	E	Y		S	T	S		T	O	D	D

55

D	I	R	E	■	T	R	A	M	P	■	C	A	S	A
I	D	O	L	■	R	E	C	U	R	■	A	V	O	N
R	E	D	S	K	Y	A	T	M	O	R	N	I	N	G
T	S	E	■	H	I	P	S	■	■	A	V	A	I	L
■	■	■	B	A	N	S	■	F	I	N	A	N	C	E
S	P	R	A	N	G	■	S	O	A	K	S	■	■	■
I	R	A	N	■	■	K	I	N	T	E	■	T	W	O
D	O	G	D	A	Y	A	F	T	E	R	N	O	O	N
E	W	E	■	R	E	N	T	S	■	■	O	G	R	E
■	■	■	S	N	A	G	S	■	D	R	E	A	M	S
T	E	M	P	E	R	A	■	H	E	A	L	■	■	■
A	L	O	E	S	■	■	S	O	L	I	■	A	C	E
B	L	U	E	S	I	N	T	H	E	N	I	G	H	T
L	E	N	D	■	B	E	A	U	T	■	R	E	I	N
E	N	D	S	■	N	O	T	M	E	■	E	D	N	A

56

M	O	L	L	■	D	E	J	A	■	P	O	S	I	T
E	D	I	E	■	E	R	O	S	■	A	L	I	C	E
S	O	S	O	■	V	E	N	I	■	N	I	L	E	S
A	R	T	I	F	I	C	I	A	L	T	O	O	T	H
■	■	■	V	A	S	T	■	■	I	R	S	■	■	■
L	A	C	■	T	E	S	T	I	F	Y	■	G	T	O
A	R	U	B	A	■	■	A	R	E	■	W	R	A	P
P	O	P	U	L	A	R	C	A	R	D	G	A	M	E
E	M	I	T	■	R	F	K	■	■	U	N	D	E	R
L	A	D	■	R	E	D	S	T	A	R	■	E	R	A
■	■	■	T	E	N	■	■	A	G	E	S	■	■	■
H	I	G	H	W	A	Y	O	V	E	R	P	A	S	S
A	G	O	R	A	■	A	M	E	N	■	R	U	L	E
T	O	N	E	R	■	P	O	R	T	■	A	R	E	A
S	T	E	E	D	■	S	O	N	S	■	Y	A	W	N

57

L	O	Y	A	■	C	A	P	S	■	K	I	S	S
I	R	E	N	E	■	A	S	H	E	■	A	C	M	E
D	E	L	T	A	■	M	E	A	N	■	T	O	O	T
S	O	L	I	D	R	E	A	S	O	N	I	N	G	■
■	■	■	P	E	R	■	E	R	I	E	■	■	■	■
L	I	Q	U	I	D	A	S	S	E	T	■	S	A	Y
U	S	U	R	P	S	■	H	I	S	■	Y	A	L	E
C	A	I	N	E	■	F	I	N	■	H	O	W	L	S
C	A	T	S	■	H	I	P	■	H	O	G	T	I	E
I	C	E	■	G	A	S	S	T	A	T	I	O	N	S
■	■	P	O	S	H	■	I	M	P	■	■	■	■	■
■	W	H	A	T	S	T	H	E	M	A	T	T	E	R
J	A	I	L	■	L	A	I	R	■	N	A	I	V	E
I	D	L	E	■	E	I	R	E	■	T	U	N	E	S
M	E	T	S	■	S	L	E	D	■	S	T	A	R	T

58

S	A	U	L	■	T	H	I	N	■	C	H	A	N	T
W	I	N	E	■	R	O	S	E	■	O	I	L	E	R
A	R	E	A	■	A	L	E	E	■	I	N	L	A	Y
R	O	A	D	S	I	D	E	D	I	N	E	R	■	■
M	U	S	S	E	L	S	■	C	A	S	I	N	O	■
S	T	Y	■	M	E	T	■	M	E	G	■	G	E	N
■	■	F	I	R	E	S	I	D	E	C	H	A	T	■
A	L	S	O	■	A	H	S	■	O	T	T	O	■	■
R	I	N	G	S	I	D	E	S	E	A	T	■	■	■
T	E	A	■	P	R	Y	■	T	N	N	■	P	B	S
Y	U	P	P	I	E	■	H	A	N	G	O	U	T	■
■	B	E	D	S	I	D	E	M	A	N	N	E	R	■
C	R	E	T	E	■	L	O	C	O	■	A	C	N	E
O	N	A	I	R	■	S	O	U	R	■	S	H	O	W
W	A	N	T	S	■	A	M	T	S	■	H	O	S	S

59

T	G	I	F	■	B	R	E	W	S	■	A	S	A	N
A	R	L	O	■	M	A	R	I	A	■	L	E	G	O
P	I	L	L	O	W	T	A	L	K	■	L	O	R	I
S	P	O	I	L	S	■	■	M	I	S	C	U	E	S
■	G	O	D	■	S	E	A	■	A	L	L	E	Y	■
A	S	I	S	■	P	I	N	■	A	T	E	■	■	■
B	I	C	■	S	O	F	A	■	D	E	A	C	O	N
B	L	A	N	K	E	T	C	O	V	E	R	A	G	E
A	L	L	O	Y	S	■	T	W	I	N	■	M	R	S
■	■	F	L	Y	■	E	E	L	■	D	E	E	T	■
L	A	U	R	A	■	A	D	D	■	S	U	R	■	■
E	X	H	I	B	I	T	■	■	S	A	L	A	D	A
D	I	A	L	■	S	H	E	E	T	M	U	S	I	C
G	A	U	L	■	L	O	R	N	A	■	T	H	E	M
E	L	L	S	■	E	L	E	C	T	■	H	Y	D	E

60

G	R	I	D	■	D	A	T	E	■	S	T	A	L	E
A	E	R	O	■	O	M	A	R	■	T	I	M	E	X
B	L	O	C	■	R	A	V	I	■	R	E	E	V	E
S	Y	N	T	H	E	T	I	C	F	A	B	R	I	C
■	■	■	R	A	M	■	■	O	N	A	■	■	■	■
A	R	T	I	F	I	C	I	A	L	G	R	A	S	S
M	O	U	N	T	■	A	N	N	I	E	■	L	E	E
A	R	T	E	■	O	P	T	I	C	■	M	E	N	D
T	E	T	■	B	U	R	R	O	■	L	O	U	S	E
I	M	I	T	A	T	I	O	N	B	U	T	T	E	R
■	■	■	A	R	R	■	■	A	S	H	■	■	■	■
C	O	U	N	T	E	R	F	E	I	T	B	I	L	L
H	O	R	D	E	■	E	A	R	L	■	A	L	O	E
U	N	S	E	R	■	E	R	I	E	■	L	I	N	T
M	A	A	M	S	■	L	E	N	D	■	L	A	G	S

61

W	A	V	E		F	A	R	M		M	A	R	K	S
A	U	E	R		A	R	E	A		I	N	A	L	L
X	X	X	R	A	T	I	N	G		R	A	D	I	O
			A	R	C		E	N	G	A	G	I	N	G
S	C	O	T	I	A		W	A	R	C	R	I	E	S
P	A	P	I	S	T	S		I	L	A				
O	N	I	C	E		A	A	A	M	E	M	B	E	R
R	A	N			B	B	B			R	N	A		
E	L	E	V	E	N	E	E	E		A	M	A	S	S
		A	X	E		T	A	P	E	S	U	P		
S	T	E	N	C	I	L	S		R	I	N	S	E	S
P	E	N	D	U	L	U	M		A	N	D			
A	N	D	Y	S		G	E	O	R	G	E	I	I	I
S	T	O	K	E		E	L	L	A		R	O	A	N
M	O	R	E	S		S	T	E	T		S	U	N	K

62

T	A	S	T	E		S	W	A	M	P		T	I	L
A	N	T	E	S		P	A	N	E	L		O	N	E
B	Y	Y	E	S	T	E	R	D	A	Y		U	T	E
			E	R	A	S		W	A	T	E	R		
S	P	O	O	N	E	R		P	R	O	U	D	L	Y
H	E	N	L	E	Y		C	H	O	O	S	E		
R	A	T	E	S		R	O	A	L	D		S	U	N
E	C	H	O		P	U	R	S	E		T	U	N	E
W	E	E		M	E	L	E	E		B	R	I	D	E
		D	O	O	L	E	Y		L	O	O	T	E	D
A	M	O	U	N	T	S		F	I	N	D	E	R	S
B	O	U	T	S		A	L	O	E					
O	R	B		T	H	I	S	I	N	S	T	A	N	T
M	E	L		E	E	R	I	E		U	R	I	A	H
B	Y	E		R	E	E	F	S		P	A	R	T	Y

63

B	A	S	H		C	A	B	S		A	D	H	O	C
E	L	I	A		O	R	E	O		D	R	A	W	S
D	E	L	I		F	R	E	D		D	O	N	N	A
S	E	L	L	S	F	O	R	A	S	O	N	G		
			S	L	E	W			U	N	E	A	S	Y
	A	R	T	I	E		A	P	E	S		R	O	I
S	W	O	O	N		A	R	I	D		S	O	U	P
C	H	A	N	G	E	S	O	N	E	S	T	U	N	E
R	I	D	E		L	A	S	T		W	A	N	D	S
A	R	T		D	U	P	E		W	A	R	D	S	
P	L	O	W	E	D		P	E	R	T				
	F	A	C	E	S	T	H	E	M	U	S	I	C	
C	R	A	V	E		H	O	O	D		R	U	S	H
H	E	M	E	N		A	N	N	E		N	I	L	E
E	X	E	R	T		D	Y	E	D		S	T	E	W

64

R	O	C	K		I	N	L	E	T		A	B	L	E
U	G	L	I		B	O	O	T	H		S	L	U	G
B	R	O	N	Z	E	S	T	A	R		T	U	N	A
Y	E	T		E	R	E		L	I	P	R	E	A	D
		M	L	I				L	E	A	R			
P	A	G	O	D	A	S		S	L	A	Y	I	N	G
I	L	O	N	A		M	I	T	E	R		B	O	L
P	O	L	K		F	A	D	E	D		A	B	O	U
E	N	D		A	A	R	O	N		S	H	O	N	E
D	E	M	E	R	I	T		O	C	T	A	N	E	S
	E	M	I	R				O	R	B				
R	E	D	C	A	P	S		D	R	U		P	S	I
A	L	A	E		L	O	V	I	N	G	C	U	P	S
M	I	L	E		A	D	O	R	E		O	P	A	L
P	A	S	S		Y	A	W	E	D		Z	A	N	E

S	T	O	R	E	■	E	S	A	U	■	S	O	A	R
T	R	A	I	L	■	C	H	I	N	■	Y	U	L	E
O	U	T	O	F	D	O	O	R	S	■	R	T	E	S
W	E	S	T	■	O	N	R	Y	E	■	I	O	T	A
■	■	■	E	P	C	O	T	■	N	O	N	F	A	T
P	O	O	D	L	E	■	L	E	T	S	G	O	■	■
E	M	U	■	E	N	C	Y	C	■	M	E	R	C	I
R	A	T	■	A	T	A	■	R	I	O	■	D	A	D
T	R	O	T	S	■	P	O	U	T	S	■	E	R	E
■	■	F	E	E	D	E	R	■	S	I	E	R	R	A
I	M	P	E	D	E	■	B	L	E	S	S	■	■	■
T	A	R	P	■	S	T	I	L	L	■	P	A	C	S
E	R	I	E	■	O	U	T	O	F	S	I	G	H	T
M	I	N	E	■	T	R	E	S	■	E	E	R	I	E
S	O	T	S	■	O	K	R	A	■	A	D	A	P	T

W	A	L	K	S	■	A	B	E	L	■	N	A	T	S
I	N	E	R	T	■	C	L	I	O	■	I	N	I	T
S	T	E	A	L	■	C	A	N	O	P	E	N	E	R
P	I	C	K	U	P	T	H	E	P	A	C	E	■	■
■	S	H	A	K	E	S	■	■	■	L	E	M	O	N
■	■	■	T	E	N	■	B	A	W	L	■	E	R	E
E	S	S	O	■	S	E	R	G	E	I	■	A	B	S
P	U	T	A	F	I	R	E	U	N	D	E	R	I	T
S	I	R	■	R	O	D	E	N	T	■	V	A	T	S
O	T	O	■	O	N	E	D	■	A	L	I	■	■	■
M	E	N	D	S	■	■	■	A	P	O	L	L	O	■
■	■	G	E	T	T	H	E	L	E	A	D	O	U	T
C	U	B	B	Y	H	O	L	E	■	■	T	O	R	T	E
S	P	O	T	■	O	M	A	R	■	■	H	E	A	R	S
I	N	X	S	■	R	E	N	T	■	■	E	R	N	E	S

T	A	R	O	█	A	S	T	A	█	B	A	B	A	S
O	D	O	R	█	D	A	I	S	█	A	M	I	G	O
N	A	S	A	█	O	M	N	I	█	Y	O	D	E	L
S	M	A	L	L	P	O	T	A	T	O	E	S	█	█
█	█	█	A	T	A	█	█	H	U	B	█	█	█	█
A	W	A	R	D	S	█	T	O	E	█	A	S	S	T
C	O	N	E	D	█	M	A	N	I	A	█	H	I	E
T	R	I	V	I	A	L	P	U	R	S	U	I	T	S
O	R	S	█	E	R	I	E	S	█	S	P	R	A	T
R	Y	E	S	█	G	I	S	█	R	I	S	E	R	S
█	█	█	T	O	O	█	█	A	E	S	█	█	█	█
█	█	P	E	T	T	Y	O	F	F	I	C	E	R	S
A	D	U	L	T	█	A	N	T	E	█	A	V	O	W
T	U	L	L	E	█	L	E	E	R	█	L	I	M	A
M	O	L	A	R	█	E	R	R	S	█	F	L	A	T

B	E	E	C	H	█	S	A	L	T	█	I	S	A	K
A	D	L	A	I	█	O	R	E	O	█	A	C	R	E
Y	U	M	M	Y	Y	U	M	M	Y	█	G	R	A	D
█	█	P	A	A	R	█	█	S	C	R	U	B	S	█
A	C	T	S	█	N	O	D	S	█	H	E	M	S	█
T	H	A	I	█	K	N	E	E	D	E	E	P	█	█
R	U	S	T	S	█	█	S	T	Y	E	█	T	I	A
I	N	T	E	A	R	S	█	H	E	R	O	I	N	E
A	G	E	█	H	A	H	A	█	S	N	O	U	T	█
█	█	S	T	A	G	E	M	O	M	█	T	U	R	N
█	A	G	A	R	█	A	S	I	A	█	A	S	E	A
A	O	R	T	A	S	█	█	L	A	I	R	█	█	█
G	L	E	E	█	M	M	M	M	M	M	G	O	O	D
R	E	A	R	█	O	B	O	E	█	P	E	D	R	O
A	R	T	S	█	G	A	I	N	█	S	T	E	E	R

H	A	U	L	■	I	R	I	S	H	■	C	H	I	A
A	S	T	A	■	T	A	B	O	O	■	L	O	O	N
S	T	I	C	K	S	H	I	F	T	■	U	P	T	O
N	I	C	E	L	Y	■	■	A	R	A	B	I	A	N
T	R	A	D	E	■	A	C	R	O	S	S	■	■	■
■	■	■	■	E	C	R	U	■	D	I	O	N	N	E
L	I	M	B	■	H	O	E	S	■	A	D	I	O	S
A	R	I	A	■	O	S	C	A	R	■	A	T	I	T
R	A	N	T	S	■	E	A	S	T	■	S	E	R	E
A	N	I	M	A	L	■	R	H	E	A	■	■	■	■
■	■	■	O	N	E	I	D	A	■	C	R	E	M	E
S	O	Y	B	E	A	N	■	■	S	N	A	R	E	S
A	L	A	I	■	P	A	D	D	L	E	B	O	A	T
G	I	R	L	■	E	N	T	R	E	■	I	D	L	E
A	N	N	E	■	R	E	S	E	W	■	N	E	S	S

S	T	E	P	S	O	N	■	T	H	E	L	O	O	P
T	A	X	R	A	T	E	■	N	I	C	E	O	N	E
E	X	P	E	C	T	A	N	T	M	O	T	H	E	R
R	I	L	E	■	E	T	E	■	■	S	L	O	T	■
I	W	O	N	■	R	O	W	D	Y	■	L	A	V	E
L	A	D	E	■	■	B	O	A	■	I	L	E	S	■
E	Y	E	D	■	B	R	O	N	X	■	P	A	R	T
■	■	■	■	L	E	R	O	I	■	■	■	■	■	■
P	A	T	H	■	A	U	N	T	S	■	L	E	A	R
A	S	E	A	■	I	N	B	■	■	A	X	L	E	■
T	I	N	S	■	R	E	A	D	S	■	L	I	D	O
E	S	T	D	■	■	B	A	P	■	A	G	E	R	■
L	A	B	O	R	D	A	Y	W	E	E	K	E	N	D
L	I	E	N	O	R	S	■	E	N	T	E	N	T	E
A	D	D	E	D	U	P	■	S	T	A	R	T	E	R

71

P	L	O	P	■		N	C	O	■	A	P	P	L	E
R	I	P	A	■	K	O	O	L	■	G	L	E	A	M
E	S	A	U	■	L	E	A	D	■	R	E	L	I	T
P	A	L	L	M	A	L	L	■	Z	E	A	L	■	■
■	■	V	A	T	S	■	■	L	E	E	■	G	T	O
R	A	P	I	D	S	■	A	N	D	I	R	O	N	■
E	M	I	■	A	C	T	O	R	■	R	A	M	S	■
P	O	L	L	T	H	E	A	U	D	I	E	N	C	E
E	E	L	S	■	■	S	T	E	A	D	■	T	A	T
A	B	O	U	N	D	S	■	B	E	A	S	T	S	■
L	A	W	■	A	A	A	■	T	B	A	R	■	■	■
■	■	T	R	I	M	■	P	U	L	L	O	V	E	R
A	V	A	I	L	■	N	U	D	E	■	M	A	Y	O
W	I	L	D	E	■	I	Z	O	D	■	A	M	E	X
L	A	K	E	R	■	T	O	R	■	S	P	R	Y	■

72

S	A	I	L	■	E	L	E	V	■	L	O	G	A	N
M	U	L	E	■	L	O	B	E	■	I	V	A	N	A
E	L	L	A	■	D	E	A	N	■	V	A	L	E	T
L	A	I	D	D	O	W	N	T	H	E	L	A	W	■
T	I	N	■	E	R	E	■	I	A	N	■	■	■	■
S	T	I	G	M	A	■	O	L	D	■	W	E	A	K
■	■	E	U	D	O	R	A	■	H	O	R	D	E	■
P	O	W	E	R	O	F	A	T	T	O	R	N	E	Y
A	N	I	S	E	■	F	L	E	E	T	S	■	■	■
N	O	N	E	■	C	C	S	■	A	T	E	A	S	E
■	■	■	A	P	E	■	D	R	U	■	M	T	A	■
■	C	O	P	S	A	N	D	R	O	B	B	E	R	S
L	O	P	E	S	■	T	O	E	S	■	A	L	I	T
O	C	A	L	A	■	E	D	G	E	■	R	I	P	E
S	A	L	T	Y	■	R	O	S	S	■	B	A	E	R

S	T	E	M	■	S	T	A	B	■	C	E	D	A	R
S	O	U	R	■	H	E	R	O	■	A	L	I	V	E
T	E	R	M	■	E	R	G	O	■	N	A	K	E	D
■	S	O	O	N	E	R	O	R	L	A	T	E	R	■
■	■	M	O	N	O	■	■	O	R	E	■	■	■	■
R	A	M	■	V	A	R	S	I	T	Y	■	G	P	A
A	T	O	N	E	■	■	A	N	T	■	F	R	A	N
D	O	U	B	L	E	O	R	N	O	T	H	I	N	G
I	L	S	A	■	P	O	D	■	■	O	A	T	E	R
O	L	E	■	A	C	H	I	E	S	T	■	S	L	Y
■	■	G	T	O	■	■	N	E	E	D	■	■	■	■
■	F	E	A	S	T	O	R	F	A	M	I	N	E	■
A	L	E	U	T	■	P	O	O	L	■	T	O	B	E
L	O	N	G	U	■	E	L	L	E	■	S	N	A	G
K	E	Y	E	D	■	R	E	D	D	■	Y	O	Y	O

S	W	E	P	T	■	A	J	A	R	■	S	I	P	S
P	A	T	I	O	■	N	O	P	E	■	T	N	U	T
A	D	A	G	E	■	E	K	E	D	■	R	A	R	A
■	■	■	S	H	O	W	E	R	S	H	O	W	E	R
S	K	I	T	O	W	■	■	■	A	V	E	R	T	■
M	O	B	I	L	E	M	O	B	I	L	E	■	■	■
E	A	S	E	D	■	I	M	O	F	F	■	C	P	R
A	L	E	S	■	P	A	N	T	S	■	S	H	O	O
R	A	N	■	C	O	M	I	C	■	C	O	A	S	T
■	■	P	O	L	I	S	H	P	O	L	I	S	H	■
C	L	E	A	N	■	■	■	E	N	U	R	E	S	■
A	U	G	U	S	T	A	U	G	U	S	T	■	■	■
R	A	Y	S	■	E	X	P	O	■	O	I	L	E	D
D	U	P	E	■	A	L	T	O	■	L	O	T	T	O
S	S	T	S	■	L	E	O	N	■	E	N	R	O	N

D	I	S	C	■	S	M	A	S	H	■	A	S	P	S
U	T	A	H	■	E	S	T	E	E	■	S	P	A	M
C	O	M	E	O	N	D	O	W	N	■	S	I	N	E
■	■	A	M	O	O	N	■	P	L	U	N	G	E	■
B	U	T	T	E	R	S	■	C	A	I	R	O	■	■
A	T	H	E	N	S	■	B	A	R	T	E	R	E	D
D	O	E	R	■	N	O	R	T	H	■	S	S	E	
E	P	A	■	G	O	O	D	B	Y	E	■	O	P	S
G	I	N	■	O	B	O	E	S	■	A	L	I	A	
G	A	S	M	A	S	K	S	■	M	A	R	V	E	L
■	W	I	P	E	S	■	F	O	R	R	E	S	T	
C	R	E	M	E	S	■	E	A	T	M	E	■	■	
H	E	R	O	■	S	U	R	V	E	Y	S	A	Y	S
I	B	I	S	■	E	A	S	E	L	■	T	R	A	Y
N	A	S	A	■	D	R	E	S	S	■	S	K	Y	S

O	N	R	Y	E	■	S	A	R	A	N	■	D	A	B
B	A	C	O	N	■	E	L	O	P	E	■	I	G	O
S	H	A	K	E	S	P	E	A	R	E	■	L	A	W
■	■	■	E	M	O	T	E	D	■	S	M	A	Z	E
D	U	B	L	I	N	■	■	S	C	O	O	P	E	R
O	S	U	■	E	Y	E	S	■	A	N	N	I	■	
G	U	L	F	S	■	A	T	M	S	■	I	D	E	A
M	A	L	L	■	F	R	U	I	T	■	C	A	R	T
A	L	F	A	■	O	L	D	S	■	N	A	T	A	L
■	■	I	N	C	A	■	Y	O	G	A	■	E	S	A
B	I	G	G	A	M	E	■	■	A	S	I	D	E	S
O	T	H	E	R	■	V	A	U	L	T	S	■	■	
R	A	T	■	H	A	I	R	R	A	I	S	I	N	G
O	L	E	■	O	R	L	O	N	■	E	U	R	O	S
N	O	R	■	P	E	S	O	S	■	R	E	A	T	A

T	A	T	A	■	O	N	U	S	■	P	R	A	D	O
O	B	I	T	■	F	E	S	T	■	R	E	S	I	N
M	E	E	T	S	F	A	C	E	T	O	F	A	C	E
S	T	R	I	P	■	G	R	A	F	■	P	E	A	■
■	■	L	A	N	E	■	E	M	I	L	■	■	■	■
■	S	T	A	N	D	S	T	O	E	T	O	T	O	E
A	L	I	■	K	A	T	E	■	S	N	A	R	L	■
L	E	A	N	■	K	E	E	P	S	■	G	R	A	M
P	E	R	O	N	■	N	E	A	L	■	D	T	S	■
S	T	A	R	E	S	E	Y	E	T	O	E	Y	E	■
■	■	A	M	I	N	■	R	E	G	S	■	■	■	■
A	B	E	■	E	G	G	S	■	A	C	H	O	O	
W	A	L	K	S	H	A	N	D	I	N	H	A	N	D
A	D	L	A	I	■	G	O	O	D	■	E	L	I	E
Y	E	A	T	S	■	E	W	E	S	■	W	E	T	S

P	R	I	M	■	G	E	R	M	■	T	O	A	S	T
O	O	N	A	■	E	L	I	A	■	O	L	L	I	E
O	M	A	N	■	T	A	L	C	■	P	E	S	O	S
L	E	T	I	T	A	L	L	H	A	N	G	O	U	T
■	■	R	A	N	G	■	O	N	O	■	P	X	S	■
A	S	A	■	T	R	E	S	■	S	T	P	■	■	■
R	U	N	S	■	I	D	L	Y	■	C	O	N	G	A
K	I	C	K	U	P	Y	O	U	R	H	E	E	L	S
S	T	E	I	N	■	S	E	M	I	■	T	A	U	T
■	■	N	C	O	■	S	A	P	S	■	T	E	A	■
S	C	H	■	U	P	S	■	C	O	I	F	■	■	■
P	A	I	N	T	T	H	E	T	O	W	N	R	E	D
I	D	T	A	G	■	O	D	O	R	■	T	E	A	R
T	E	M	P	E	■	R	E	A	D	■	R	A	V	E
S	T	E	A	M	■	E	N	D	S	■	O	K	E	D

79

L	Y	N	X		P	S	S	T		S	T	A	R	E
B	E	A	M		E	C	H	O		E	A	S	E	L
S	A	N	E		R	O	A	M		A	R	I	E	L
	H	A	N	D	O	N	H	A	N	D	O	F	F	S
			O	N	E		H	O	O	T				
D	E	C	A	Y	S		H	A	I	G		T	A	P
A	L	A	M	O		S	E	W	S		L	O	G	O
T	A	K	E	U	P	T	A	K	E	D	O	W	N	S
U	T	E	S		O	A	R	S		I	V	I	E	S
M	E	D		S	P	I	T		T	S	E	T	S	E
		S	T	I	R		T	A	C					
W	O	R	K	I	N	W	O	R	K	O	U	T	S	
A	L	I	E	N		A	L	E	E		C	O	O	L
S	L	E	E	T		Y	E	A	R		L	U	R	E
P	A	N	T	S		S	O	T	S		A	R	E	A

80

I	C	E	S		B	A	L	M		S	W	O	R	E
D	I	S	H		E	S	A	U		M	A	Y	O	R
E	N	T	R		A	C	D	C		O	G	L	E	R
A	C	E	I	N	T	H	E	H	O	L	E			
L	O	R	N	A			O	R	D		A	S	A	
		K	I	N	G	O	F	B	E	A	S	T	S	
I	F	S		L	A	I	R		R	O	S	E	S	
R	O	O	F		M	A	D	A	M		L	E	N	A
A	C	R	E	S		E	D	A	M		T	O	Y	
Q	U	E	E	N	F	O	R	A	D	A	Y			
I	S	R		E	T	A			Y	E	A	S	T	
		J	A	C	K	B	E	N	I	M	B	L	E	
N	O	V	A	K		L	A	M	E		E	B	A	N
O	X	I	D	E		E	L	M	S		N	E	T	S
D	O	Z	E	R		Y	E	A	S		I	S	E	E

A	C	C	T	■	C	A	R	N	E	■	E	D	I	T
H	O	O	K	■	E	L	I	A	S	■	N	Y	S	E
S	O	L	O	F	L	I	G	H	T	■	A	N	O	N
O	L	D	■	L	E	S	S	■	R	O	M	A	N	S
■	■	H	A	R	T	■	S	A	L	E	M	■	■	■
W	A	T	E	R	Y	■	P	A	N	E	L	I	S	T
A	G	R	E	E	■	T	A	N	G	O	■	C	H	A
S	A	I	L	■	S	I	R	E	E	■	A	D	I	N
T	I	O	■	O	U	T	E	R	■	D	R	U	N	K
E	N	S	E	M	B	L	E	■	D	E	C	O	Y	S
■	■	O	L	I	V	E	■	P	O	L	O	■	■	■
D	O	N	A	T	E	■	A	I	N	T	■	A	H	A
A	H	A	T	■	R	A	J	Q	U	A	R	T	E	T
R	I	T	E	■	T	R	O	U	T	■	B	O	A	T
T	O	A	D	■	S	T	Y	E	S	■	I	N	D	Y

T	I	F	F	S	■	S	T	U	D	■	B	A	R	A
A	D	U	L	T	■	P	O	S	E	■	E	T	A	L
M	A	R	I	O	■	E	R	M	A	■	E	L	H	I
■	■	G	L	A	C	I	A	L	S	T	A	R	E	■
M	U	S	H	E	R	■	I	T	T	■	S	A	N	■
A	T	I	T	■	R	A	I	L	■	O	A	T	H	■
R	A	S	P	■	A	I	D	■	G	M	C	■	■	■
C	H	I	L	L	Y	R	E	C	E	P	T	I	O	N
■	■	A	U	S	■	A	P	T	■	Y	O	G	A	■
■	C	O	N	S	■	S	L	A	M	■	O	N	L	Y
S	O	N	■	T	O	P	■	■	A	M	U	S	E	S
C	O	L	D	S	H	O	U	L	D	E	R	■	■	■
O	K	I	E	■	M	U	S	E	■	T	A	P	E	D
F	I	N	E	■	A	S	E	A	■	A	G	I	L	E
F	E	E	D	■	N	E	R	D	■	L	E	T	I	N

83

T	Y	R	O	█	B	E	A	M	█	T	U	B	A	S
R	O	A	R	█	U	C	L	A	█	U	S	U	R	P
I	D	L	E	█	G	R	I	D	█	R	O	M	E	O
B	E	L	L	Y	B	U	T	T	O	N	█	B	A	T
E	L	Y	S	E	E	█	█	V	I	T	A	L	█	█
█	█	█	E	G	A	D	S	█	L	O	V	E	I	N
J	E	B	█	G	R	I	T	T	Y	█	E	B	A	Y
A	M	A	S	S	█	S	I	R	█	F	R	E	T	S
D	I	L	L	█	S	C	R	I	B	E	█	E	E	E
E	L	L	I	O	T	█	S	O	I	L	S	█	█	█
█	█	O	P	R	A	H	█	█	G	L	E	A	M	S
A	G	T	█	B	R	E	A	D	B	A	S	K	E	T
R	A	B	B	I	█	E	L	L	A	█	T	I	D	E
A	B	O	U	T	█	D	O	I	N	█	E	R	I	N
T	E	X	T	S	█	S	W	I	G	█	T	A	C	O

84

N	A	R	C	█	F	L	A	T	S	█	M	E	S	A
O	L	I	O	█	R	O	G	U	E	█	E	M	I	R
B	L	O	C	█	A	C	U	R	A	█	T	U	N	E
O	U	T	O	F	T	H	E	B	L	U	E	█	█	█
D	R	E	A	R	█	█	█	O	U	T	R	A	G	E
Y	E	R	█	O	R	E	S	█	P	A	M	P	A	S
█	█	S	T	O	R	E	S	█	█	A	I	N	T	█
█	W	I	T	H	N	O	W	A	R	N	I	N	G	█
R	A	T	A	█	█	S	E	G	U	E	D	█	█	█
I	N	B	R	E	D	█	R	O	T	H	█	E	A	T
B	E	E	G	E	E	S	█	█	R	A	N	G	E	█
█	█	A	L	L	O	F	A	S	U	D	D	E	N	█
W	H	I	Z	█	E	D	I	C	T	█	D	E	N	S
H	A	T	E	█	T	A	R	R	Y	█	L	A	D	E
O	D	O	R	█	E	S	S	E	X	█	E	R	A	S

85

A	M	O	R		A	V	I	D		E	J	E	C	T
R	O	L	E		D	I	N	O		V	A	L	O	R
I	T	S	D	E	J	A	V	U		E	Z	I	N	E
A	T	E	S	T		L	O	B	E		Z	A	N	Y
S	O	N	T	A	G		L	L	A	M	A			
			A	L	L	O	V	E	R	A	G	A	I	N
T	S	A	R		A	W	E		T	S	E	T	S	E
E	L	I		D	S	L		S	H	H		O	A	T
R	A	D	I	U	S		E	T	D		I	N	N	S
I	T	S	D	E	J	A	V	U	A	L	L			
			C	L	A	R	O		Y	A	L	I	E	S
M	E	G	A		W	I	L	D		V	E	R	V	E
E	X	E	R	T		O	V	E	R	A	G	A	I	N
S	P	A	D	E		S	E	E	D		A	T	A	D
H	O	R	S	E		O	D	D	S		L	E	N	S

86

S	C	H	E	M	E		T	O	D	O		I	M	P
O	L	I	V	E	R		A	M	I	D		T	A	O
M	A	K	E	S	A	S	C	E	N	E		L	I	P
E	D	E	N	S		H	O	N	G		A	L	D	A
			T	U	T	U		B	I	T	T	E	R	
A	M	C		P	U	L	L	S	A	S	T	U	N	T
H	E	A	R	S	T		E	S	T	H	E	R		
A	L	L	A		A	N	T		S	N	I	T		
		C	I	C	A	D	A		A	T	T	U	N	E
C	A	U	S	E	S	A	S	T	I	R		P	T	A
A	S	L	E	E	P		O	L	A	F				
C	H	A	D		I	N	O	N		M	O	R	S	E
K	I	T		D	R	A	W	S	A	C	R	O	W	D
L	E	O		N	I	T	E		R	A	G	T	A	G
E	R	R		A	N	O	N		C	R	E	E	P	Y

87

A	L	E	C		S	P	E	E	D		B	A	A	L
M	I	D	I		P	R	U	D	E		A	R	N	O
P	E	E	R		H	O	R	A	S		N	A	T	O
	U	N	C	L	E	T	O	M	S	C	A	B	I	N
			L	I	R	E		E	O	N				
	I	R	E	M	E	M	B	E	R	M	A	M	A	
S	N	A	R	E		L	I	T	E		O	R	E	
I	S	I	S		S	P	I	N	S		P	U	R	E
P	U	N		S	T	A	N		F	E	R	A	L	
	M	Y	C	O	U	S	I	N	V	I	N	N	Y	
			L	O	N		O	I	L	S				
A	L	L	I	N	T	H	E	F	A	M	I	L	Y	
P	A	I	N		C	A	L	E	B		O	Y	E	Z
S	T	A	G		A	R	I	E	L		N	O	T	A
O	H	M	Y		R	E	E	S	E		S	N	I	P

88

S	H	I	P		S	K	I	M		P	E	E	P	S
P	A	N	E		H	E	M	I		E	X	T	R	A
A	S	T	R	O	N	A	U	T		O	A	T	E	S
R	A	H		M	O	N	S	T	E	R	M	A	S	H
S	T	E	R	E	O		S	L	I	P				
		W	A	L	K	T	O		B	A	L	S	A	M
J	A	I	M	E		E	S	T	O		E	T	R	E
U	R	N		T	V	S	H	O	W	S		A	C	E
N	I	G	H		I	S	E	E		A	U	G	H	T
E	A	S	I	E	R		A	S	P	I	R	E		
			B	I	G	D		E	D	I	C	T	S	
P	O	T	A	T	O	C	H	I	P	S		O	O	H
I	L	I	C	H		C	O	R	P	O	R	A	T	E
N	I	C	H	E		A	H	M	E		I	C	E	D
T	O	S	I	R		B	O	A	R		O	H	M	S

P	E	S	T	■	B	U	N	K	■	A	B	B	O	T
E	L	I	E	■	A	R	E	A	■	S	O	R	T	S
N	A	T	T	U	R	N	E	R	■	T	R	I	C	K
S	P	U	R	N	S	■	■	A	M	O	R	E	■	■
I	S	A	A	C	■	N	E	T	P	R	O	F	I	T
V	E	T	■	I	L	E	N	E	S	■	W	E	R	E
E	S	E	■	V	E	A	L	■	■	B	E	R	E	T
■	■	■	N	I	T	P	I	C	K	E	R	■	■	■
S	E	O	U	L	■	■	S	H	I	N	■	V	A	R
A	L	A	I	■	A	T	T	I	R	E	■	E	N	E
N	O	T	S	O	F	A	S	T	■	A	R	R	I	D
■	■	B	A	N	T	U	■	■	A	T	E	A	S	E
E	A	R	N	S	■	N	U	T	N	H	O	N	E	Y
S	P	A	C	E	■	T	R	O	T	■	I	D	E	E
T	E	N	E	T	■	S	I	N	E	■	L	A	D	S

O	L	I	V	E	■	C	O	R	A	■	R	A	N	K
N	A	D	I	A	■	A	V	E	R	■	A	L	E	E
T	W	E	N	T	Y	S	E	V	E	N	D	O	W	N
O	N	A	■	D	O	I	N	■	■	O	N	E	T	O
■	■	■	S	I	G	N	■	S	A	N	E	■	■	■
■	T	O	P	R	I	G	H	T	C	O	R	N	E	R
D	A	V	I	T	■	■	E	Y	E	S	■	E	A	U
E	L	A	N	■	S	A	X	E	S	■	L	E	V	I
A	I	L	■	S	H	U	E	■	■	W	I	D	E	N
L	A	S	T	W	O	R	D	A	C	R	O	S	S	■
■	■	■	R	I	T	A	■	G	A	I	N	■	■	■
S	L	A	I	N	■	■	E	A	S	T	■	A	L	I
C	E	N	T	E	R	O	F	T	H	E	G	R	I	D
U	N	D	O	■	A	R	T	E	■	R	E	G	A	L
M	O	A	N	■	M	E	S	S	■	S	T	O	R	Y

```
S I R   L I D O     M O J O S
O D E   O V E N   P A T E N T
N A H   C A B C A L L O W A Y
A H A   A N T E D A T E
R O B O T S     V I A   A T M
    C R I   B R A N   A R O O
C R E D O   R U N S   I A G O
H U N A N   A B C   U R B A N
A L T I   O K I E   P A C E S
S E E N   B E N D   P R O
E R R   T E M     L E M U R S
      C A R E S F O R   N E T
G R A B C O N T R O L   T A R
T A K E I N   D E S I   R T E
O P A R T     S E E P   Y A P
```

```
S P A S     N A S T   A R M S
E A M E S   U S E R   B E A T
T R U T H   D A T A   E B R O
  A N T I S E P T I C T A N K
U N D O N E     E T A   T E E
M O S   E D U C E   L E E R S
P I E   A A A   A I M
  A N T I T R U S T F U N D
    D O E   S A O   U R I
C R E S T   H E N N A   M I T
H E S   A P E   A S S E N T
A N T I S O C I A L W O R K
S T E P   S T O P   A B A S H
T A R S   S O N S   N I T T I
E L S E   E R S E   G E O M
```

93

Q	U	A	F	F	■	W	A	T	T	■	B	L	E	W
E	L	G	A	R	■	E	L	H	I	■	R	A	V	E
D	E	E	R	E	■	A	L	U	M	■	O	P	E	N
■	■	■	M	E	R	R	Y	G	O	R	O	U	N	D
P	H	I	■	W	A	S	■	■	T	E	M	P	T	S
A	E	N	E	A	S	■	S	A	H	L	■	■	■	■
S	I	L	L	Y	P	U	T	T	Y	■	A	C	T	S
T	R	E	K	S	■	N	U	T	■	S	M	A	R	T
A	S	T	O	■	F	U	N	N	Y	M	O	N	E	Y
■	■	■	H	E	M	S	■	A	E	R	I	A	L	
A	P	P	E	A	L	■	■	I	L	L	■	S	T	E
L	A	U	G	H	I	N	G	G	U	L	L	■	■	■
E	R	M	A	■	N	O	E	L	■	O	U	T	E	R
R	E	A	D	■	E	L	M	O	■	U	T	U	R	N
T	E	S	S	■	S	O	S	O	■	T	E	T	R	A

94

J	A	P	A	N	■	J	A	W	S	■	S	A	N	G
A	L	O	N	E	■	E	R	I	E	■	E	V	I	L
C	O	N	D	O	L	E	E	Z	Z	A	R	I	C	E
K	E	Y	■	L	O	R	N	■	■	G	I	V	E	N
■	■	■	H	A	V	E	A	B	E	E	F	■	■	■
R	E	L	A	T	E	D	■	O	N	E	S	T	O	P
E	C	O	L	I	■	■	A	N	O	■	■	E	W	E
D	O	E	S	N	T	K	N	O	W	B	E	A	N	S
R	L	S	■	■	O	R	G	■	■	U	P	S	E	T
Y	E	S	O	R	N	O	■	M	R	D	E	E	D	S
■	■	■	S	A	Y	C	H	E	E	S	E	■	■	■
A	G	A	I	N	■	■	I	R	A	E	■	K	A	I
B	U	R	R	I	T	O	F	I	L	L	I	N	G	S
B	A	L	I	■	I	W	I	N	■	I	D	I	O	T
A	M	O	S	■	P	E	S	O	■	G	E	T	G	O

R	A	W	E	R		J	A	I	L	S		G	M	C
A	N	E	R	A		U	N	C	A	P		I	C	E
I	N	S	E	V	E	N	T	H	H	E	A	V	E	N
L	E	T		E	L	K			R	E	S	E	N	T
S	T	E	P		S	E	T	H		D	E	E	R	E
A	T	R	I	A		T	R	E	K		A	M	O	R
T	E	N	O	R	S		O	R	E	S		H	E	S	
		O	N	C	L	O	U	D	N	I	N	E		
	T	O	M		H	A	R	P		O	C	E	L	O	T
	A	R	E	A		W	E	E	D		S	A	L	V	O
	T	I	L	L	S		G	R	A	M		T	H	E	O
	T	E	E	P	E	E		S	A	O		A	R	R
O	N	T	O	P	O	F	T	H	E	W	O	R	L	D
O	T	T		I	N	A	W	E		E	E	R	I	E
S	S	E		A	S	T	O	R		D	R	Y	E	R

D	A	M	M	E		M	A	S	O	N		J	E	T
E	M	A	I	L		A	T	O	N	E		A	L	A
F	I	R	S	T	O	N	E	T	O	B	L	I	N	K
			D	O	R	I	A			E	L	I	E
S	E	C	O	N	D	A	M	E	N	D	M	E	N	T
A	M	A					V	E	E		R	O	O
G	I	S	M	O		I	D	E	A	L	S	
	T	H	I	R	D	M	A	N	T	H	E	M	E
		A	D	O	P	T	S		I	T	E	M	S
E	S	Q		E	R	E					T	A	U
N	E	U	T	R	A	L	L	A	N	G	U	A	G	E
T	R	I	O				I	N	A	L	L	
R	E	V	E	R	S	E	E	N	G	I	N	E	E	R
E	N	E		P	I	N	T	O		D	A	N	K	E
E	E	R		M	C	C	O	Y		E	S	S	E	X

97

P	A	R	T	■	I	T	C	H	■	U	T	E	R	O
H	O	E	R	■	N	O	D	E	■	N	E	V	E	R
I	R	M	A	■	T	O	R	N	■	I	L	I	E	D
S	T	U	C	K	O	N	O	N	E	S	E	L	F	■
H	A	S	T	Y	■	■	M	Y	D	O	G	■	■	■
■	■	S	O	M	E	■	■	O	N	R	U	S	H	■
T	S	K	■	T	A	L	O	N	■	■	A	N	T	E
S	A	I	L	O	N	A	W	I	N	D	M	I	L	L
A	L	D	A	■	■	L	E	G	E	R	■	T	O	P
R	A	S	C	A	L	■	■	H	O	A	X	■	■	■
■	■	■	E	L	I	O	T	■	■	M	E	T	E	S
■	S	T	R	E	A	K	I	N	M	A	R	B	L	E
B	O	R	A	X	■	A	B	I	E	■	X	O	U	T
I	S	I	T	I	■	Y	E	L	L	■	E	N	D	O
B	O	X	E	S	■	S	T	E	T	■	S	E	E	N

98

I	P	A	S	S	■	P	A	I	D	■	S	W	A	T
D	R	W	H	O	■	A	I	R	S	■	T	E	T	E
S	O	W	O	N	E	S	W	I	L	D	O	A	T	S
■	■	■	A	O	R	T	A	S	■	U	N	L	I	T
F	A	L	L	F	O	R	■	■	B	E	E	T	L	E
A	M	I	■	A	S	Y	L	U	M	■	■	H	A	R
S	O	F	T	G	■	■	A	R	O	S	E	■	■	■
■	S	E	W	U	P	A	V	I	C	T	O	R	Y	■
■	■	■	I	N	U	S	E	■	■	E	N	E	M	Y
A	R	G	■	■	M	A	D	C	A	P	■	N	C	O
R	U	N	S	U	P	■	■	I	D	A	H	O	A	N
I	M	A	C	S	■	Z	S	A	Z	S	A	■	■	■
S	O	W	H	A	T	E	L	S	E	I	S	N	E	W
T	R	A	M	■	A	T	O	P	■	D	O	O	N	E
A	S	T	O	■	B	A	B	Y	■	E	N	D	E	D

99

S	L	O	B		A	B	H	O	R		S	A	C	K
L	I	M	A		C	R	E	P	E		E	L	L	E
A	R	A	B		C	O	M	I	C		T	S	A	R
G	A	R	Y	C	O	O	P	E	R	S	T	O	W	N
			B	Y	R	D		U	S	O				
S	T	R	A	N	D		S	P	I	T		B	V	D
A	B	A	C	I		R	I	O	T		F	E	A	R
D	I	C	K	C	L	A	R	K	S	V	I	L	L	E
I	L	K	S		O	G	E	E		A	R	I	E	S
E	L	S		H	U	E	S		A	S	S	E	T	S
			F	A	N		A	N	E	T				
J	P	A	U	L	G	E	T	T	Y	S	B	U	R	G
E	R	R	S		E	R	A	T	O		O	S	H	A
D	E	L	E		R	I	C	A	N		R	I	O	S
I	P	O	S		S	N	O	R	E		N	A	S	H

100

V	I	A	L		S	T	A	L	E		D	A	M	E
I	N	D	O		A	R	B	O	R		I	L	E	S
A	C	A	D	E	M	I	C	C	I	R	C	L	E	S
	A	M	I	G	O			O	N	E	I	O	T	A
				G	A	P	S		N	E	W	S	Y	
A	B	A	C	I		E	I	T	H	E	R			
R	A	R	I	N		R	B	I	S		A	O	L	
E	N	G	A	G	E	M	E	N	T	R	I	N	G	S
A	G	O		D	I	R	T		U	L	T	R	A	
		P	A	T	T	I	E		S	L	E	E	T	
A	L	I	A	S		A	D	E	S					
C	A	N	Y	O	N	S		N	I	X	E	S		
T	R	A	F	F	I	C	R	O	T	A	R	I	E	S
E	R	N	O		L	A	U	D	E		A	R	L	O
D	Y	E	R		E	M	B	E	R		Y	E	L	P

101

R	I	C	K	S		U	R	G	E		T	O	D	O
U	N	H	I	P		T	O	U	T		I	P	O	D
S	K	A	T	E	D	O	N	T	H	I	N	I	C	E
		R	E	C	A	P				S	N	E	A	K	S
P	S	I			S	I	K	H		D	A	T	E	S
J	E	S	T	S		A	I	O	L	I		E	T	A
S	E	M	I	T	E		L	O	A	C	H			
	R	A	N	O	U	T	O	F	S	T	E	A	M	
		S	C	R	U	B		T	E	M	P	E	D	
C	B	S		K	O	R	A	N		D	I	E	T	S
A	L	A	R	M		F	R	O	G		R	E	L	
D	O	N	E	E	S		B	A	S	S	I			
G	O	T	I	N	T	O	H	O	T	W	A	T	E	R
E	D	E	N		L	A	U	D		A	G	I	F	T
D	Y	E	S		O	R	G	Y		G	A	F	F	E

102

O	P	R	A	H		D	I	E	S		A	C	T	S
C	L	O	N	E		R	O	T	C		C	U	R	T
C	A	P	N	C	R	U	N	C	H		O	B	I	E
U	T	E		K	E	G	S		O	N	R	A	M	P
R	E	S	O	L	E	S		G	O	O	N			
			R	E	D		H	A	N	D	S	O	M	E
S	P	E	A	R		P	E	T	E		Q	U	A	Y
W	O	R	N		S	E	D	E	R		U	S	S	R
A	G	O	G		P	E	G	S		B	A	T	H	E
N	O	S	E	D	I	V	E		T	I	S			
			C	U	K	E		F	O	G	H	O	R	N
C	H	A	R	G	E		T	O	R	O		M	O	O
L	U	L	U		L	E	M	O	N	T	W	I	S	T
A	G	E	S		E	G	A	D		R	E	T	I	E
P	O	S	H		E	O	N	S		Y	E	S	E	S

103

```
O N S E T ■ D R I P ■ A P S E
P I A N O ■ A I D A ■ L E E R
E S T O P ■ D O E S ■ M A C E
L I E C H E A T S T E A L ■ ■
■ ■ H A Y ■ ■ T E R M ■ ■ ■
S A L ■ T I K I ■ S N A C K S
A G E D ■ N A P S ■ S T R E W
R E M I N G T O N S T E E L E
I N U S E ■ E D I T ■ R A S P
S T R A W S ■ S P E W ■ M O T
■ ■ ■ S E T S ■ ■ W A S ■ ■
■ ■ S T R O N G A S S T E E L
F A T E ■ P A L L ■ H E A V E
I G O R ■ I K E A ■ E L V I S
B O W S ■ T E E S ■ R E E L S
```

104

```
A S P I C ■ A C R O ■ P H E W
R H Y M E ■ M A U I ■ L A N E
C A R B S ■ B I L L F O L D S
S H O E S H I N E B O Y ■ ■ ■
■ ■ ■ A N D ■ R A G ■ A C E
I M I T A T E S ■ S E A S O N
N A M ■ V A L L E Y G I R L
A S P E N ■ S A O ■ S O D O I
G O O D O L E B O Y ■ E N S
E N S U R E ■ S N A R L S A T
S S E ■ M E T ■ ■ D O E ■ ■
■ ■ ■ M A T E R I A L G I R L
T R E E L I N E D ■ L U S T Y
W A G E ■ D O L E ■ E M B E R
A M O K ■ E N Y A ■ D E N S E
```

105

W	A	R	P		C	R	A	T	E		E	S	P	Y
A	L	A	I		R	E	L	A	X		O	H	I	O
R	E	D	S	K	Y	A	T	M	O	R	N	I	N	G
M	E	S	T	A		R	A	S	T	A		P	G	A
			I	B	E				I	N	G			
Y	E	L	L	O	W	B	R	I	C	K	R	O	A	D
O	L	A		B	E	R	E	T		S	E	N	S	E
U	M	P	S		S	A	L	S	A		S	E	P	T
N	E	S	T	S		V	I	O	L	S		I	C	E
G	R	E	E	N	B	A	C	K	D	O	L	L	A	R
		T	A	U				A	C	E				
U	S	C		I	R	A	T	E		I	S	L	E	S
S	T	O	P	L	I	G	H	T	C	O	L	O	R	S
E	A	S	E		A	R	E	N	A		E	D	I	T
S	N	A	P		L	A	M	A	R		Y	E	N	S

106

D	A	D	A		C	R	I			S	H	E	L	L
D	I	O	R		R	O	T		S	H	E	A	V	E
T	R	E	E		E	T	S		H	O	R	R	I	D
			N	E	W	C	A	L	E	D	O	N	I	A
M	O	S	A	I	C		H	O	L	D				
A	R	I		D	U	K	E	O	F	Y	O	R	K	
R	P	M		E	T	A	L				L	E	E	K
S	H	I	R	R		I	L	E		A	D	D	T	O
H	A	L	O				U	S	A	F		O	T	O
	N	E	W	C	O	N	V	E	R	T		E	L	K
			A	R	I	A		M	E	S	S	E	S	
S	E	R	G	E	A	N	T	Y	O	R	K			
P	R	I	E	S	T		O	E	R		I	O	T	A
A	G	O	R	A	E		W	Y	E		M	U	O	N
T	O	T	E	R		N	E	D		P	R	E	Y	

107

G	O	A	L	S		S	K	I	P			C	A	W
A	L	L	I	E		A	I	D	A		C	O	L	A
W	E	L	L	A	N	Y	W	A	Y		H	O	E	S
D	I	A	L		A	S	I	S		R	A	N	C	H
S	C	H	E	R	Z	O			C	O	L			
				L	I	K	E	Y	O	U	K	N	O	W
L	I	M	B	S		F	I	R	E	S	I	D	E	
O	D	O	R		L	O	R	N	E		U	N	I	S
K	E	R	O	S	E	N	E		S	P	E	N	T	
I	M	E	A	N	C	O	M	E	O	N				
			D	U	H		I	S	O	B	A	R	S	
D	W	E	E	B		B	O	T	H		E	L	E	C
R	I	D	S		O	R	W	H	A	T	E	V	E	R
U	N	I	T		S	O	L	E		A	N	I	S	E
G	E	T			U	S	S	R		R	E	N	E	W

108

H	A	S	P	S		N	O	C	A	L		D	A	M
A	L	L	A	H		A	L	I	C	E		R	I	O
N	U	I	S	A	N	C	E	T	A	X		A	M	O
A	M	P	S		O	R	G		D	I	G	G	E	R
			P	A	T	E		S	E	C	U	R	E	S
L	U	P	O	N	E		R	A	M	O	N	A		
O	P	A	R	T		S	E	V	E	N		C	O	W
E	D	I	T		N	A	M	E	S		P	I	N	E
B	O	N		S	A	L	E	S		P	O	N	C	E
	K	I	T	K	A	T		B	U	L	G	E	D	
A	N	I	S	E	E	D		R	O	P	E			
M	A	L	T	E	D		A	I	L		S	A	N	G
W	I	L		P	E	S	T	C	O	N	T	R	O	L
A	V	E		E	Y	D	I	E		R	A	I	S	E
Y	E	R		N	E	S	T	S		A	R	D	E	N

109

W	A	R	D		R	I	F	E		F	A	R	C	E
I	L	I	E		E	A	R	N		A	B	U	Z	Z
F	U	N	F	I	L	L	E	D		C	E	S	A	R
I	M	G	A	M	E		E	T	C	E	T	E	R	A
			C	P	A		D	O	F	F				
A	C	H	E		S	A	O		C	A	S	I	N	G
B	R	O		F	E	M	M	E		C	U	R	I	O
F	A	N	T	A	S	Y	F	O	O	T	B	A	L	L
A	N	D	E	S		S	I	N	U	S		Q	E	D
B	E	A	T	T	Y		G	S	T		P	I	S	A
			F	I	S	H		V	I	A				
S	T	E	P	O	N	I	T		O	N	C	A	L	L
M	A	R	I	O		F	E	E	T	F	I	R	S	T
U	P	E	N	D		T	R	U	E		N	E	A	R
T	E	S	T	S		S	S	R	S		O	A	T	S

110

S	C	A	M		N	O	R	M		P	L	U	T	O
H	A	R	E		A	L	O	E		R	A	V	E	N
E	R	I	C		M	A	T	A		O	P	E	R	A
B	L	A	C	K	E	Y	E	D	S	U	S	A	N	
A	S	S	A	I	L		O	R	D					
			S	W	E	E	T	W	I	L	L	I	A	M
H	O	N		I	S	T	O			Y	U	C	C	A
A	L	O	T		S	A	Y	A	H		G	O	N	G
D	I	A	N	A			O	R	A	L		N	E	E
J	O	H	N	N	Y	J	U	M	P	U	P			
			G	E	O			P	I	A	N	O	S	
	Q	U	E	E	N	A	N	N	E	S	L	A	C	E
A	T	T	A	R		N	E	O	N		L	U	T	E
R	I	N	S	E		I	A	G	O		O	R	E	M
S	P	E	E	D		E	T	O	N		R	U	T	S

111

M	E	S	S		A	T	R	A		L	I	K	E	D
A	B	U	T		C	H	O	P		U	T	H	E	R
C	A	P	O		R	E	A	L		T	I	A	R	A
K	N	E	W	T	O	O	M	U	C	H		K	I	M
	R	E	D	S			S	P	E	C	I	E	S	
R	A	N		S	T	E	P		A	R	I			
U	F	O	S		I	D	E	A		A	R	G	U	E
L	O	V	E	D	C	A	T	D	A	N	C	I	N	G
E	R	A	T	O		M	E	A	N		A	N	D	A
			O	W	L		R	Y	A	N		G	O	D
C	H	U	N	N	E	L			C	E	D	E		
R	I	N		F	E	L	L	T	O	E	A	R	T	H
E	V	I	T	A		A	E	O	N		R	A	R	E
P	E	T	A	L		M	E	N	D		I	L	I	A
E	D	S	E	L		A	R	E	A		N	E	X	T

112

V	I	V	A		D	O	O	M		P	H	O	T	O
A	D	E	N		E	B	R	O		T	E	N	O	R
N	I	N	E		P	E	E	N		B	R	O	M	O
Y	O	U	W	H	O	Y	O	O	H	O	O			
A	T	E		A	S	S		L	E	A	D	C	A	R
			D	R	E		M	I	S	T		O	L	E
A	S	H	E	S		O	A	T	S		A	L	O	E
C	H	E	K	H	O	V	C	H	E	C	K	O	F	F
R	O	L	E		P	E	A	S		H	I	N	T	S
E	V	E		F	A	R	O		F	I	N			
S	E	N	I	O	R	S		L	O	N		S	S	E
			M	Y	T	H	A	I	M	A	I	T	A	I
B	A	T	H	E		O	G	L	E		B	O	R	E
O	N	A	I	R		O	R	A	N		A	L	A	I
W	A	R	P	S		T	A	C	T		R	E	N	O

113

T	E	M		M	O	L	A	R		M	A	R	C	O
U	S	E		A	B	U	S	E		U	N	H	A	T
R	C	A		B	E	L	I	E		D	O	E	R	S
B	O	N	N	E	Y	L	A	D	D		N	O	R	
O	R	I	E	L				S	U	E		S	L	O
S	T	E	E	L	E	R	S		O	R	A	T	O	R
				T	A	O	S		I	R	A	T	E	
	L	E	A	K	E	Y	F	A	W	C	E	T	T	
F	O	L	L	Y		S	I	N	K					
D	W	E	L	L	S		A	S	S	E	R	T	E	D
R	E	V		E	E	L			L	E	A	V	E	
	G	A	L		W	I	L	D	E	O	A	T	E	S
G	E	T	I	T		N	A	O	M	I		E	N	T
A	R	O	M	A		E	L	L	I	S		R	U	R
P	E	R	O	N		N	O	L	T	E		S	P	Y

114

R	O	M	P		P	E	T	E		T	A	B	O	O
E	R	I	E		A	L	E	X		R	E	R	U	N
D	I	N	E		D	I	C	T		I	R	A	T	E
C	O	O	K	E	D	T	H	E	B	O	O	K	S	
A	L	A		R	Y	E		R	I	D		E	M	S
P	E	N	T	A		S	P	I	C	E		M	A	O
			U	S	A		R	O	E		S	E	R	B
D	U	S	T	E	D	F	O	R	P	R	I	N	T	S
U	N	O	S		D	A	N		S	E	Z			
D	R	Y		H	E	L	G	A		A	E	S	O	P
S	O	S		A	N	D		V	O	L		E	R	E
	L	A	U	N	D	E	R	E	D	M	O	N	E	Y
F	L	U	N	G		R	A	N	D		P	O	G	O
R	E	C	T	O		A	G	U	E		T	R	O	T
O	D	E	O	N		L	E	E	R		S	A	N	E

115

N	O	P	A	R	■	L	E	S	T	■	I	S	I	N
O	R	A	T	E	■	E	T	T	A	■	A	T	N	O
G	O	G	O	D	A	N	C	E	R	■	N	A	T	L
■	E	N	O	L	A	■	N	O	D	■	R	A	E	
D	O	D	O	■	Y	O	Y	O	T	R	I	C	K	S
A	L	O	F	T	■	L	U	G	■	A	S	H	E	S
N	E	W	■	E	R	I	C	■	S	S	N	■		
■	N	O	N	O	N	A	N	E	T	T	E	■		
■	■	H	A	T	■	T	O	N	I	■	V	A	N	
A	G	A	I	N	■	D	A	S	■	C	H	I	V	E
C	O	C	O	C	H	A	N	E	L	■	O	L	E	O
T	E	T	■	Y	A	K	■	C	D	R	O	M	■	
U	S	S	R	■	S	O	S	O	R	E	V	I	E	W
A	T	A	D	■	I	T	O	N	■	M	E	N	S	A
L	O	S	S	■	T	A	T	E	■	O	R	D	E	R

116

C	A	S	A	■	S	T	A	C	Y	■	C	Z	A	R
O	P	E	L	■	L	A	T	H	E	■	O	I	S	E
N	E	L	L	■	A	R	T	I	S	T	S	P	A	D
I	A	M	S	A	M	S	A	M	I	A	M	■		
C	R	A	W	L	■	U	R	N	■	D	I	S	K	S
■	■	E	G	G	S	■	E	N	A	C	T	E	D	
■	A	D	L	A	I	■	B	Y	E	■	E	L	S	
■	C	A	L	L	M	E	I	S	H	M	A	E	L	■
A	T	L	■	M	N	O	■	R	E	P	L	Y	■	
G	O	A	T	E	E	D	■	B	U	M	P	■		
T	R	I	A	L	■	G	E	R	■	O	L	S	E	N
■	M	Y	N	A	M	E	I	S	E	A	R	L		
M	A	K	E	S	A	M	I	N	T	■	P	U	R	E
A	X	I	S	■	N	E	R	D	S	■	I	T	O	R
T	E	X	T	■	A	S	S	A	Y	■	E	E	L	S

117

G	E	M	■	A	M	A	S	S	■	S	P	I	R	E
O	R	E	■	R	U	P	E	E	■	A	U	R	A	L
F	I	R	S	T	S	E	E	D	■	G	N	O	M	E
O	C	C	U	L	T	■	T	A	O	■	C	N	B	C
R	A	I	S	E	■	D	O	N	T	S	H	O	O	T
■	■	I	S	P	Y	■	■	T	R	I	X	■	■	■
P	I	P	E	S	T	E	M	■	S	N	I	P	E	
C	A	L	■	■	A	R	U	B	A	■	■	D	E	L
S	N	A	R	E	■	G	O	L	D	L	E	A	F	
■	Y	U	K	S	■	■	N	E	A	L	■	■	■	
G	I	M	M	E	A	B	U	D	■	N	A	T	C	H
R	O	O	M	■	W	A	R	■	I	G	N	O	R	E
A	N	N	A	N	■	M	A	Y	F	L	O	W	E	R
S	I	E	G	E	■	B	L	A	S	E	■	E	A	T
P	A	Y	E	E	■	A	S	T	O	R	■	D	M	Z

118

M	E	N	S	A	■	P	I	T	T	■	R	E	D	O
A	T	O	L	L	■	E	C	H	O	■	A	V	E	R
T	O	N	E	D	■	C	H	U	R	C	H	I	L	L
A	N	O	D	E	■	■	A	M	E	R	■	T	H	O
■	■	G	R	E	A	T	B	R	I	T	A	I	N	
F	I	R	E	M	A	N	■	S	O	B	S	■	■	
L	O	O	■	E	S	T	A	■	■	A	S	T	A	
A	T	L	A	N	T	I	C	C	H	A	R	T	E	R
B	A	L	I	■	■	T	O	E	S	■	A	R	I	
■	N	C	A	A	■	L	A	S	A	G	N	A		
U	N	I	T	E	D	S	T	A	T	E	S	■	■	
N	O	D	■	D	E	S	I	■	S	H	E	B	A	
R	O	O	S	E	V	E	L	T	■	S	O	W	E	R
I	S	L	E	■	I	R	E	D	■	E	R	E	C	T
P	E	S	T	■	L	T	D	S	■	D	E	S	K	S

119

L	H	A	S	A	■	G	A	S	P	■	S	C	A	T
B	O	L	O	S	■	O	M	A	R	■	I	O	T	A
S	N	I	F	F	■	L	A	C	E	■	G	L	O	P
■	G	E	T	O	F	F	T	H	E	P	H	O	N	E
■	■	P	R	O	■	■	E	N	O	■	N	E	D	■
F	L	O	E	■	N	Y	E	T	■	L	A	Y	S	■
C	O	R	D	■	D	U	G	■	P	A	C	■	■	■
C	L	E	A	N	U	P	Y	O	U	R	R	O	O	M
■	■	L	E	E	■	P	O	R	■	O	K	R	A	
■	G	O	S	H	■	A	T	O	P	■	P	S	S	T
A	R	F	■	R	O	W	■	■	L	A	H	■	■	■
D	O	Y	O	U	R	H	O	M	E	W	O	R	K	■
E	C	O	N	■	L	I	M	O	■	I	B	E	A	M
P	E	R	M	■	O	L	I	O	■	L	I	S	L	E
T	R	E	E	■	N	E	T	S	■	L	A	T	E	R

120

A	M	M	O	■	P	D	A	S	■	O	C	T	E	T
R	E	A	P	■	A	R	N	O	■	F	L	O	R	A
T	A	K	E	M	Y	W	O	R	D	F	O	R	I	T
S	T	E	N	O	■	A	N	T	I	■	A	N	N	A
■	■	■	H	O	S	T	■	O	K	O	K	■	■	■
P	A	G	O	D	A	S	■	F	E	B	■	A	F	T
A	C	L	U	■	R	O	T	■	■	I	N	T	E	R
T	R	U	S	T	I	N	W	H	A	T	I	S	A	Y
S	I	T	E	S	■	■	O	A	R	■	N	E	T	S
Y	D	S	■	P	E	A	■	M	I	D	E	A	S	T
■	■	■	U	S	S	R	■	S	A	I	L	■	■	■
G	W	E	N	■	P	A	P	A	■	M	I	D	A	S
Y	O	U	C	A	N	B	E	L	I	E	V	E	M	E
M	O	R	A	L	■	I	R	A	Q	■	E	M	I	T
S	L	O	P	E	■	C	U	D	S	■	S	O	D	S

121

S	T	E	M	■	U	R	I	S	■	J	A	F	A	R
L	A	V	A	■	P	E	C	K	■	A	T	E	I	N
A	L	A	I	■	T	R	E	E	■	G	R	A	D	S
P	E	N	T	H	O	U	S	E	S	U	I	T	E	■
■	■	R	A	I	N	■	■	H	A	S	H	■	■	■
O	D	D	E	S	T	■	B	E	E	R	K	E	G	S
F	R	I	D	A	■	F	O	L	D	■	■	R	O	I
F	I	R	S	T	C	L	A	S	S	C	A	B	I	N
T	E	T	■	■	H	A	T	E	■	A	T	O	N	E
O	D	Y	S	S	E	Y	S	■	I	D	T	A	G	S
■	■	T	O	E	S	■	■	I	N	R	E	■	■	■
■	F	R	O	N	T	R	O	W	C	E	N	T	E	R
S	L	I	T	S	■	A	B	O	O	■	D	E	L	I
C	A	C	H	E	■	M	I	N	D	■	E	X	E	C
I	N	K	E	D	■	P	E	T	E	■	E	T	C	H

122

M	I	C	E	■	M	A	I	M	S	■	R	A	J	A
A	S	E	A	■	A	R	D	E	N	■	E	V	E	R
R	E	N	T	■	N	E	E	D	L	E	W	O	R	K
X	E	S	■	K	I	T	E	D	■	T	A	N	K	S
■	■	O	P	R	A	H	■	L	A	H	R	■	■	■
H	U	R	R	I	C	A	N	E	L	A	M	P	■	■
E	S	S	E	S	■	■	E	R	I	N	■	L	O	A
A	S	H	Y	■	T	O	A	S	T	■	P	A	I	L
T	R	I	■	S	H	U	T	■	■	S	A	Y	N	O
■	■	P	O	T	A	T	O	P	A	N	C	A	K	E
■	■	N	E	I	L	■	E	D	I	T	S	■	■	■
A	B	I	D	E	■	A	E	S	O	P	■	C	O	E
F	A	C	E	P	O	W	D	E	R	■	S	E	X	Y
A	L	E	C	■	T	R	I	T	E	■	K	N	E	E
R	I	S	K	■	B	Y	E	A	R	■	Y	E	N	S

123

J	E	F	F	■	S	P	A	T	■	P	A	W	A	T
O	P	I	E	■	H	U	G	O	■	A	S	I	D	E
G	E	N	T	L	E	B	E	N	■	R	I	N	D	S
S	E	N	I	O	R	■	R	E	D	C	R	O	S	S
■	■	D	E	P	P	■	■	W	E	E	■	■	■	■
O	P	T	■	W	A	R	M	W	E	L	C	O	M	E
C	R	O	W	S	■	F	A	I	L	■	A	N	O	N
T	I	K	I	■	L	I	S	Z	T	■	L	E	N	D
E	D	E	N	■	U	R	S	A	■	B	L	U	T	O
T	E	N	D	E	R	M	E	R	C	Y	■	P	E	W
■	■	■	C	R	I	■	D	A	N	K	■	■	■	■
L	O	C	H	N	E	S	S	■	N	O	I	D	E	A
E	L	L	I	E	■	K	I	N	D	W	O	R	D	S
G	L	O	M	S	■	I	D	O	L	■	S	E	N	T
S	A	G	E	T	■	M	E	R	E	■	K	W	A	I

124

B	A	A	■	T	E	R	M	■	W	R	E	S	T	S
E	L	L	■	A	L	E	E	■	E	A	R	T	H	A
R	E	G	■	L	A	V	E	N	D	E	R	O	I	L
G	R	A	P	E	N	U	T	S	■	■	A	N	N	E
S	T	E	R	N	■	E	S	C	■	N	N	E	■	■
■	■	I	T	S	■	■	■	H	O	T	T	U	B	■
S	P	A	S	■	N	I	S	S	A	N	■	O	N	A
P	L	U	M	T	U	C	K	E	R	E	D	O	U	T
C	O	T	■	O	B	E	Y	E	D	■	E	L	M	S
A	D	O	P	T	S	■	■	Y	E	P	■	■	■	■
■	■	P	O	E	■	A	W	E	■	M	O	R	O	N
S	T	A	T	■	■	L	I	L	A	C	T	I	M	E
P	U	R	P	L	E	P	R	O	S	E	■	P	E	I
U	N	T	I	E	S	■	E	P	E	E	■	E	G	G
R	E	S	E	T	S	■	D	E	A	D	■	N	A	H

125

B	L	I	G	H		A	R	C	H		S	T	I	R
A	I	M	E	E		M	I	C	A		T	A	D	A
M	E	E	T	M	E	I	N	S	T	L	O	U	I	S
B	O	A	S		A	D	S		P	O	P	T	O	P
A	N	N	O	Y	S		E	M	I	R	S			
		R	E	E	D		I	N	D	U	T	C	H	
S	L	E	E	P	L	E	S	S		S	P	R	A	Y
K	A	T		S	C	O	U	T			O	L	D	
I	D	T	A	G		I	N	S	E	A	T	T	L	E
S	E	E	S	R	E	D		E	S	A	I			
		A	I	M	E	D		T	R	E	M	O	R	
D	E	A	R	M	E		U	K	E		D	O	R	A
A	U	T	U	M	N	I	N	N	E	W	Y	O	R	K
U	R	A	L		D	R	N	O		E	E	R	I	E
B	O	D	E		S	K	E	W		E	D	E	N	S

126

E	A	S	E		B	O	O	N	S		T	H	A	T
B	L	O	C		R	A	D	I	O		H	O	P	S
B	A	D	H	A	I	R	D	A	Y		A	R	I	E
			O	N	E		C	A	B	I	N	E	T	
I	N	P	E	N		T	R	I		A	L	E	C	S
L	A	O	S		S	A	N	D	R	A	D	E	E	
L	I	L		D	I	A	L		I	B	N			
	L	I	V	E	F	R	E	E	O	R	D	I	E	
		O	A	S		I	L	S	A		D	A	B	
P	L	A	Y	D	O	U	G	H		T	O	R	O	
A	U	R	A	E		P	H	I		J	O	L	L	Y
T	R	I	G	R	A	M		C	O	W				
R	I	S	E		P	O	S	T	A	G	E	D	U	E
I	N	T	R		E	S	T	E	S		R	O	S	A
A	G	A	S		S	T	Y	L	E		S	T	A	R

127

A	V	E	C		S	T	R	A	W		S	Y	N	C
H	I	L	O		P	R	A	D	A		H	E	A	L
A	V	E	R		R	E	P	E	L		R	O	S	A
B	A	C	K	B	A	Y		L	E	E	W	A	Y	
			T	O	N	S		S	P	E	W			
A	D	D	I	N	G		B	I	L	L	D	A	N	A
W	I	E	L	D		O	N	U	S		S	E	M	
A	X	L	E		S	L	A	N	G		S	C	A	B
S	I	T		I	N	O	R		P	E	A	R	L	
H	E	A	D	C	O	L	D		E	L	A	P	S	E
		H	O	W	L		A	X	E	L				
V	A	C	A	N	T		S	I	D	E	B	E	T	
I	G	O	R		I	M	A	C	S		V	O	T	E
S	E	A	M		R	O	B	O	T		E	R	O	S
A	S	T	A		E	T	A	T	S		L	E	N	T

128

D	I	T	C	H		B	O	G		Q	U	I	E	T
I	T	A	L	O		A	D	O		U	L	T	R	A
G	S	U	I	T		B	O	A		E	N	T	E	R
I	M	P	O	S	T	E	R	T	U	N	A			
N	E	E		E	A	R		E	M	T		T	E	A
		M	A	T	U	R	E	P	I	N	O	T	S	
	A	G	I	T	A	T	E		N	E	W	A	T	
E	T	N	A		S	H	I	L	L		V	E	T	O
S	W	A	M	P		G	O	O	B	E	R	S		
P	A	T	I	O	M	U	N	S	T	E	R			
Y	R	S		T	A	N		E	S	T		K	I	A
		P	E	R	M	U	T	A	T	I	O	N	S	
S	U	S	A	N		A	R	I		O	M	A	N	I
A	N	T	I	C		D	I	M		R	I	L	E	D
C	O	Y	L	Y		E	S	E		S	N	A	R	E

129

B	A	T	H			B	A	W	L			I	N	C	A
A	L	A	I		G	E	N	R	E			D	E	A	R
S	I	L	L		M	E	D	E	A			L	A	N	K
H	E	L	L	O	S	T	R	A	N	G	E	R			
	N	Y	E	T			E	T	T	A			B	A	Y
			L	O	O	K	W	H	O	S	H	E	R	E	
S	T	S			R	E	S			P	O	E	M	S	
H	A	N	D	G	U	N		N	O	S	I	R	E	E	
A	B	O	I	L			R	A	W			S	D	S	
H	O	W	V	E	Y	O	U	B	E	E	N				
S	O	P		N	O	U	N			O	O	P	S		
		L	O	N	G	T	I	M	E	N	O	S	E	E	
C	M	O	N		U	L	N	A	S		D	E	A	L	
H	O	W	L		R	A	T	S	O		L	U	L	L	
I	T	S	Y		T	W	O	S			E	D	Y	S	

130

M	A	C	S		O	R	K	I	N		K	U	R	D
I	T	U	P		S	O	A	M	I		I	R	O	N
N	E	L	L		H	I	T	O	N		E	S	T	A
C	A	P	I	T	A	L	O	F	J	A	V	A		
E	R	A	T	O			F	A	Q		M	A	G	
			M	I	C	E		U	S	A	I	R		
A	R	S		B	R	O	A	D	W	A	Y	J	O	E
S	H	A	G		A	T	R	I	A		R	O	L	E
C	O	M	P	A	N	Y	P	E	R	K		R	I	D
A	D	M	A	N			S	U	M	O				
P	A	Y		T	A	S			C	H	A	K	A	
		S	T	I	C	K	I	N	T	H	E	M	U	D
Z	O	O	S		C	E	D	A	R		M	I	D	I
I	L	S	A		T	I	L	D	E		A	T	O	M
P	E	A	R		S	N	E	A	K		N	Y	S	E

131

S	P	A	R	■	W	O	O	D	S	■	P	R	E	K
L	E	G	O	■	A	B	B	I	E	■	R	O	T	E
A	R	E	A	■	D	E	I	S	M	■	A	O	N	E
B	U	D	D	H	I	S	T	H	O	L	Y	M	A	N
■	■	■	S	A	N	E	■	■	L	E	S	■	■	■
S	A	W	I	N	G	■	M	A	I	D	■	C	A	W
P	R	I	D	E	■	B	A	R	N	■	M	O	P	E
A	N	D	E	S	P	A	C	K	A	N	I	M	A	L
M	I	E	S	■	O	D	E	S	■	E	N	A	C	T
S	E	N	■	A	R	E	S	■	D	A	I	S	E	S
■	■	■	A	L	T	■	■	D	O	T	S	■	■	■
B	L	A	Z	E	I	N	B	R	O	O	K	L	Y	N
E	A	S	T	■	C	A	R	O	M	■	I	I	I	I
N	I	T	E	■	O	P	I	N	E	■	R	E	N	T
E	R	I	C	■	S	A	T	E	D	■	T	U	G	S

132

C	R	A	G	■	S	C	U	B	A	■	B	A	A	S
R	O	N	A	■	E	A	S	E	L	■	L	U	L	L
I	B	I	S	■	W	R	E	S	T	■	O	R	L	Y
B	O	M	B	O	N	B	R	O	A	D	W	A	Y	■
S	T	E	A	M	■	■	S	T	R	O	P	■	■	■
■	■	■	G	A	W	K	■	■	S	T	I	F	L	E
E	A	R	■	N	A	A	C	P	■	■	P	L	A	Y
S	W	A	Y	I	N	T	H	E	B	R	E	E	Z	E
S	E	G	O	■	■	T	I	A	R	A	■	W	E	D
O	D	E	S	S	A	■	■	T	A	B	S	■	■	■
■	■	■	E	U	R	O	S	■	■	B	O	A	T	S
■	C	O	M	E	D	I	A	N	W	I	L	S	O	N
S	A	K	I	■	E	L	S	I	E	■	V	I	N	E
A	L	I	T	■	N	E	S	T	S	■	E	D	G	E
G	L	E	E	■	T	R	Y	S	T	■	S	E	A	R

133

C	L	A	N		S	C	A	R	F		E	N	D	S
Y	A	L	E		L	O	W	E	R		V	I	E	W
S	T	O	W		I	N	A	N	E		I	N	C	A
T	H	E	T	I	M	E	Y	O	U	E	N	J	O	Y
			O	N	L	Y			D	E	C	A	Y	S
E	V	E	N	L	Y		P	A	I	N	E			
M	E	N	S	A		A	U	R	A		S	A	S	S
I	N	C		W	A	S	T	I	N	G		M	A	O
L	I	E	U		R	E	I	D		E	P	O	X	Y
		P	E	C	A	N		S	L	A	K	E	S	
M	O	O	L	A	H		S	T	I	R				
I	S	N	O	T	W	A	S	T	E	D	T	I	M	E
N	A	S	A		A	W	A	R	E		I	D	O	L
E	K	E	D		Y	O	K	E	L		N	E	S	S
R	A	T	S		S	L	E	W	S		G	A	T	E

134

S	T	U	D		G	E	N	A		A	G	N	E	W
H	Y	P	O		O	L	A	V		L	E	A	S	H
O	P	E	N		S	O	M	E		B	E	T	S	Y
P	E	N	E	L	O	P	E	C	R	U	Z			
S	A	N	T	A	F	E		E	M	E	R	I	L	
		H	U	T		T	I	L		R	O	T	O	
I	D	T	A	G		M	O	T	I	F		S	S	R
S	O	U	T	H	S	E	A	S	C	R	U	I	S	E
L	O	G		S	H	A	D	Y		O	N	E	O	N
A	N	A	T		A	N	Y		O	L	D			
M	E	T	E	O	R		T	R	I	E	S	T	E	
		C	L	E	A	N	U	P	C	R	E	W	S	
M	O	T	H	S		R	O	S	H		A	L	I	T
A	N	N	I	E		A	N	K	A		G	E	N	E
E	A	T	E	N		B	O	S	N		E	S	S	E

135

C	B	S	■	■	V	O	I	C	E	■	C	O	M	P
A	U	T	O	■	I	N	C	A	S	■	O	M	A	R
S	N	A	P	■	P	U	E	R	T	O	R	I	C	O
A	C	T	R	E	S	S	■	H	A	U	N	T	E	D
S	H	E	A	R	■	S	O	T	S	■	■	■	■	■
■	T	H	E	M	U	P	P	E	T	S	H	O	W	■
M	E	R	■	C	A	P	E	■	■	T	E	M	A	■
E	L	E	C	T	R	I	C	C	O	M	P	A	N	Y
O	L	E	O	■	■	T	O	T	O	■	V	I	S	■
W	E	S	T	S	I	D	E	S	T	O	R	Y	■	■
■	■	■	■	E	M	E	R	■	■	S	A	L	S	A
L	A	S	C	A	L	A	■	T	H	E	R	I	T	Z
R	I	T	A	M	O	R	E	N	O	■	I	N	A	T
O	D	E	S	■	S	I	N	U	S	■	N	E	V	E
N	A	P	S	■	T	E	S	T	S	■	■	S	E	C

136

M	A	R	C	H	■	W	E	L	D	■	S	E	R	B
O	C	A	L	A	■	I	S	E	E	■	T	R	I	O
C	H	R	I	S	T	M	A	S	W	R	E	A	T	H
K	E	E	P	■	O	P	U	S	■	E	N	T	E	R
■	■	■	J	A	R	S	■	O	H	N	O	■	■	■
A	N	T	O	N	Y	■	S	N	I	T	■	F	A	N
N	O	H	I	T	■	G	O	O	F	■	G	A	Z	E
K	W	A	N	Z	A	A	U	N	I	T	Y	C	U	P
L	I	N	T	■	I	N	R	E	■	O	P	E	R	A
E	N	E	■	O	R	G	S	■	V	E	S	S	E	L
■	■	■	W	I	S	P	■	T	I	D	Y	■	■	■
S	C	I	O	N	■	L	O	I	N	■	M	A	R	T
H	A	N	U	K	K	A	H	M	E	N	O	R	A	H
A	T	T	N	■	A	N	T	E	■	A	T	O	N	E
M	O	O	D	■	T	K	O	S	■	P	H	O	T	O

137

A	B	L	E	■	L	A	T	H	E	■	C	R	A	M
R	A	I	N	■	A	C	R	E	S	■	L	A	N	E
A	B	C	D	A	Y	T	I	M	E	H	O	S	T	S
B	E	E	■	N	M	E	X	■	■	O	S	H	E	A
■	M	I	A	■	M	A	R	E	■	■	■	■	■	■
■	F	I	L	M	N	O	M	I	N	A	T	I	O	N
L	A	D	L	E	■	D	O	L	E	S	■	L	B	O
E	R	L	E	■	G	E	T	I	T	■	V	O	I	D
A	G	E	■	D	O	N	E	E	■	Z	E	S	T	S
F	O	R	M	E	R	S	T	U	D	E	N	T	S	■
■	■	A	L	E	E	■	■	O	L	D	■	■	■	■
B	E	A	S	T	■	B	A	N	D	■	S	H	A	■
A	L	P	H	A	B	E	T	Q	U	A	R	T	E	T
E	L	E	E	■	A	L	E	U	T	■	E	U	R	O
R	E	D	S	■	T	I	N	A	S	■	A	D	A	M

138

C	O	R	A	■	R	A	C	K	■	S	H	I	R	E
I	H	O	P	■	E	L	L	A	■	P	U	R	E	E
V	A	S	T	■	B	O	O	B	■	E	M	A	I	L
I	R	E	■	C	O	T	T	O	N	C	A	N	D	Y
C	A	G	I	E	R	■	B	E	I	N	■	■	■	■
■	A	T	O	N	A	L	■	R	E	E	S	E	S	■
P	A	R	I	S	■	G	O	A	T	S	■	U	V	A
O	L	D	S	■	B	O	W	L	S	■	A	G	E	S
L	I	E	■	R	A	G	E	S	■	U	R	A	L	S
K	A	N	S	A	S	■	R	O	U	T	E	R	■	■
■	A	N	T	S	■	■	P	A	S	S	U	P	■	■
O	R	A	N	G	E	C	R	U	S	H	■	H	M	O
V	E	R	D	E	■	R	A	S	H	■	T	A	B	S
I	N	N	E	R	■	O	R	E	O	■	A	C	R	E
D	O	O	R	S	■	D	A	R	T	■	O	K	A	Y

139

P	U	L	S	E		W	O	L	F		T	E	A	K
A	N	I	T	A		A	L	A	I		A	R	L	O
I	D	E	A	S		L	E	S	S		X	M	A	S
D	O	U	B	T	I	N	G	T	H	O	M	A	S	
			E	D	U			E	V	A				
		I	M	N	O	T	B	U	Y	I	N	G	I	T
H	O	S	E	D			E	K	E	D		E	R	A
A	R	U	G		M	O	D	E	S		S	N	O	B
Z	Z	Z		L	O	C	O			B	U	R	N	S
Y	O	U	C	A	N	T	F	O	O	L	M	E		
		R	B	I			N	B	A					
	W	H	O	S	K	I	D	D	I	N	G	W	H	O
C	H	A	W		E	S	A	U		K	A	R	A	N
C	O	L	D		R	A	N	T		E	V	E	R	T
C	A	T	S		S	W	A	Y		T	E	N	T	O

140

A	P	S	E		K	A	Y	O		S	Q	U	A	T
S	H	A	M		O	N	U	P		E	U	R	O	S
T	O	N	I		W	I	L	E		D	A	N	K	E
R	E	D	L	E	T	T	E	R	D	A	Y			
A	B	A		B	O	A		A	U	K		W	I	Z
Y	E	L	L	O	W	S	U	B	M	A	R	I	N	E
			I	N	S		S	O	B		U	F	O	S
M	O	N	E	Y		L	U	X		E	B	E	R	T
A	G	O	G		A	E	R		C	X	I			
G	R	E	E	N	B	A	Y	P	A	C	K	E	R	S
E	E	L		A	R	P		R	T	E		G	E	E
			T	R	A	F	F	I	C	L	I	G	H	T
I	N	F	E	R		R	O	M	A		S	N	I	T
Q	U	I	T	O		O	R	A	L		T	O	R	E
S	T	R	E	W		G	A	L	L		O	G	E	E

141

R	O	T			M	A	R	C	O		A	M	O	R
E	V	E	L		D	W	E	L	L		L	A	M	A
L	A	N	E	C	L	O	S	E	D		E	D	E	N
E	L	E	N	A		L	E	A	S	E		E	G	G
E	S	T	A	T	E		W	R	O	N	G	W	A	Y
			E	L	F			D	O	N	O			
N	O	P	A	R	K	I	N	G		A	R	M	S	
B	R	A	D	S		B	I	O		I	S	S	E	T
C	A	N	I			S	T	O	P	A	H	E	A	D
		T	E	A	S			N	A	G				
N	O	O	U	T	L	E	T		D	R	Y	A	D	S
E	L	M		M	I	R	E	D		E	A	T	I	T
S	L	I	M		D	O	N	O	T	E	N	T	E	R
T	I	M	E		E	S	S	E	S		G	I	G	A
S	E	E	N		R	E	E	S	E		C	O	P	

142

G	N	A	T		P	R	A	M	S		S	L	U	M
R	E	D	O		L	A	P	A	T		T	E	N	T
R	E	D	S	N	A	P	P	E	R		O	T	I	S
	D	E	C	E	N	T		A	B	O	U	T		
D	I	N	A	R		D	R	P	E	P	P	E	R	
O	E	D		F	A	R	E	A	S	T		O	R	A
G	R	A	S		R	E	V	S		T	E	N	S	E
		T	H	E	G	I	P	P	E	R				
C	A	R	L	A		A	S	E	A		E	N	I	D
A	C	E		P	A	L	E	R	M	O		E	S	E
B	E	B	O	P	P	E	R		A	L	A	R	M	
	T	O	K	Y	O		S	A	H	A	R	A		
G	A	L	A		L	A	S	T	S	U	P	P	E	R
A	T	T	Y		L	I	T	U	P		S	A	L	E
M	E	S	S		O	M	E	N	S		E	R	I	C

143

S	S	S	■	S	T	R	A	P	■	S	C	A	L	P
P	I	C	■	P	H	I	L	S	■	E	E	R	I	E
A	D	O	■	R	E	L	E	E	■	A	L	T	E	R
M	E	T	R	O	S	E	X	U	A	L	S	■	■	■
S	A	T	O	U	T	■	A	D	S	■	■	A	P	T
■	■	■	S	T	I	R	■	O	P	E	N	B	A	R
S	U	I	T	■	N	U	B	■	■	T	I	B	I	A
U	N	D	E	R	G	R	O	U	N	D	F	I	L	M
S	P	O	R	E	■	■	G	L	O	■	T	E	S	S
H	O	L	S	T	E	R	■	T	H	A	I	■	■	■
I	T	S	■	■	B	E	E	■	A	G	E	N	D	A
■	■	S	U	B	W	A	Y	S	E	R	I	E	S	■
K	A	Y	A	K	■	A	R	E	S	O	■	E	L	I
E	L	A	T	E	■	S	T	A	L	L	■	C	A	D
G	A	M	E	S	■	H	O	S	E	D	■	E	Y	E

144

A	S	C	O	T	■	C	U	B	S	■	H	A	S	P
C	H	O	R	E	■	I	S	E	E	■	O	T	T	O
C	A	P	R	A	■	C	O	N	G	E	R	E	E	L
E	L	Y	■	C	O	E	■	T	A	B	■	A	V	A
P	L	E	T	H	O	R	A	■	■	B	A	S	I	N
T	O	D	O	■	H	O	N	D	A	■	N	E	E	D
S	W	I	S	S	■	■	T	E	M	P	T	■	■	■
■	■	T	H	I	N	G	A	M	A	J	I	G	■	■
■	■	■	I	S	A	A	C	■	S	O	R	E	S	■
B	O	M	B	■	T	Y	I	N	G	■	C	O	N	E
O	C	E	A	N	■	■	D	O	N	S	H	U	L	A
I	T	S	■	O	A	K	■	R	U	M	■	N	A	B
L	A	S	T	D	A	N	C	E	■	A	N	D	R	E
E	V	E	S	■	R	E	D	S	■	S	I	E	G	E
D	E	S	K	■	P	E	S	T	■	H	A	R	E	S

145

H	U	T	■	A	T	M	■	A	M	B	I	T
O	P	A	L	■	B	R	E	R	■	T	E	A	M	O
M	L	I	I	■	B	O	D	E	■	M	A	D	A	M
B	O	N	D	J	A	M	E	S	B	O	N	D	■	
R	A	T	S	O	■	P	A	I	L	S	■	R	B	I
E	D	S	■	D	R	E	■	D	O	T	■	E	A	R
■	■	P	I	E	■	B	U	T	■	C	A	K	E	
■	H	O	M	E	S	W	E	E	T	H	O	M	E	■
R	E	V	S	■	T	I	E	■	E	O	N	■		
E	R	E	■	S	A	L	■	A	R	M	■	A	D	E
P	E	R	■	A	T	L	A	S	■	E	S	S	E	X
■	T	I	M	E	A	F	T	E	R	T	I	M	E	
S	L	U	R	P	■	R	O	O	M	■	O	D	O	R
A	U	R	A	L	■	D	O	R	M	■	W	E	N	T
S	C	E	N	E	■	T	S	A	■	S	S	S		

146

S	T	O	R	M	■	D	E	N	■	T	I	N	A	S
C	A	R	N	E	■	A	V	E	■	A	N	A	R	T
A	P	A	S	S	A	G	E	T	O	I	N	D	I	A
M	E	L	■	S	C	A	R	■	S	L	E	A	Z	Y
■	H	A	M	M	■	A	T	E	E	■				
G	A	R	A	G	E	A	T	T	E	N	D	A	N	T
A	D	E	L	E	■	W	O	R	D	■	R	O	O	
M	O	D	E	■	L	I	E	N	S	■	E	S	T	A
M	R	I	■	F	A	R	E	■	D	R	O	I	D	
A	N	G	E	L	S	A	N	D	S	A	I	N	T	S
■	S	O	T	S	■	R	O	M	E	■				
S	A	R	T	R	E	■	Y	O	D	A	■	O	E	R
T	H	E	H	I	D	D	E	N	A	G	E	N	D	A
A	S	P	E	N	■	A	T	E	■	E	L	C	I	D
B	O	O	R	S	■	B	I	D	■	D	I	E	T	S

147

S	P	A	D	E	■	T	H	O	M	■	R	U	E	D
A	R	I	E	L	■	E	U	R	O	■	O	N	M	E
D	I	R	T	F	A	R	M	E	R	■	T	I	M	E
A	D	E	E	■	G	E	E	■	T	I	T	T	E	R
T	E	R	R	I	E	S	■	R	I	C	E	■	■	
■	■	■	G	R	E	A	S	E	M	O	N	K	E	Y
H	O	M	E	S	■	■	E	D	E	N	■	E	P	A
A	M	E	S	■	A	S	T	O	R	■	S	E	E	P
N	A	N	■	O	M	I	T	■	■	J	O	N	E	S
G	R	U	N	G	E	R	O	C	K	E	R	■	■	■
■	■	■	U	R	N	S	■	R	E	T	R	A	C	T
N	E	S	T	E	A	■	E	E	E	■	E	L	L	A
U	R	A	L	■	M	U	D	S	L	I	N	G	E	R
M	I	L	E	■	E	M	I	T	■	S	T	E	E	D
B	E	E	T	■	N	A	T	S	■	P	O	R	K	Y

148

O	D	D	E	R	■	A	H	A	B	■	H	A	H	A
C	R	O	N	Y	■	T	O	F	U	■	I	M	A	X
C	O	N	T	E	N	T	S	F	R	A	G	I	L	E
U	N	O	■	■	Y	E	T	I	■	S	H	E	L	L
R	E	T	A	K	E	N	■	R	O	A	D	■	■	
■	■	S	K	I	■	D	A	M	P	■	A	T	T	Y
I	N	T	A	N	D	E	M	■	A	N	Y	H	O	O
V	I	A	■	K	E	E	P	D	R	Y	■	I	R	K
E	N	C	A	S	E	■	L	E	T	M	E	S	E	E
S	A	K	E	■	R	T	E	S	■	P	A	S	■	
■	■	■	R	H	E	A	■	S	C	H	T	I	C	K
A	D	L	A	I	■	T	I	E	R	■	■	D	O	I
P	R	O	T	E	C	T	F	R	O	M	H	E	A	T
T	I	N	E	■	P	O	S	T	■	S	A	U	L	T
S	P	E	D	■	R	O	O	S	■	G	Y	P	S	Y

149

A	D	H	O	C		R	A	L	P	H		B	L	T
B	Y	A	I	R		I	N	U	R	E		L	I	E
B	E	L	L	Y	D	A	N	C	E	R		O	E	D
E	S	T		U	R	L	S		A	B	A	C	U	S
			A	N	A	T		A	C	I	D			
		L	U	C	K	O	F	T	H	E	D	R	A	W
N	E	E	D	L	E		A	M	Y		U	S	A	
A	R	N	I	E		O	K	S		B	A	S	I	L
S	I	D		E	V	E		R	E	L	E	N	T	
H	E	A	D	O	V	E	R	H	E	E	L	S		
		C	H	I	N		O	A	F	S				
L	O	W	C	A	L		E	R	I	C		A	D	O
A	L	A		R	O	A	S	T	M	A	S	T	E	R
M	E	N		A	N	D	S	O		K	A	R	M	A
P	O	T		S	E	V	E	N		E	M	A	I	L

150

L	U	T	E	S		K	A	R	L		D	E	E	P
O	P	E	R	A		O	L	I	O		E	C	R	U
C	R	E	A	T	U	R	E	C	O	M	F	O	R	T
K	I	T	S		N	E	C	K	T	I	E			
U	S	E		L	E	A	K		S	C	R	A	P	
P	E	R	S	I	A		D	E	S	T	I	N	E	
		P	E	R	D	I	E	M		M	O	P		
	B	E	A	S	T	O	F	B	U	R	D	E	N	
S	E	A		H	O	S	T	L	E	R				
S	A	R	C	A	S	M		S	A	Y	I	N	G	
S	U	S	A	N		P	A	I	R		N	O	R	
	I	N	F	E	R	N	O		A	S	I	A		
A	N	I	M	A	L	M	A	G	N	E	T	I	S	M
D	I	V	A		A	I	D	S		T	O	T	E	M
O	X	E	N		T	R	O	T		A	M	U	S	E

The New York Times

Crossword Puzzles

The #1 Name in Crosswords

Available at your local bookstore or online at nytimes.com/nytstore

St. Martin's Griffin